A Deeper Dimension

A Deeper Dimension

A FASCINATING BENEATH-THE-SURFACE LOOK AT LIFE AND JUDAISM THROUGH THE PARASHAH

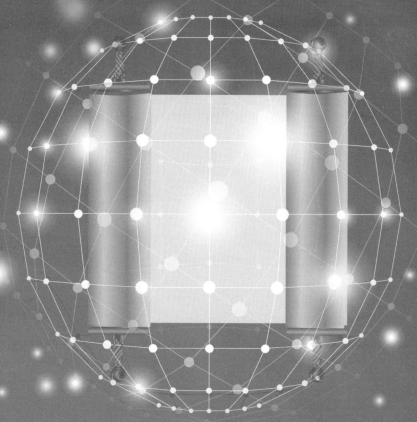

Rabbi Judah Gross

Mosaica Press, Inc.
© 2016 by Mosaica Press
Cover design by Chana Abramowitz
Designed and typeset by Brocha Mirel Strizower

All rights reserved
ISBN-10: 1-937887-94-4
ISBN-13: 978-1-937887-94-0

All rights reserved. No part of this book may be used or reproduced or transmitted in any form or by any means, electronic or mechanical, including photocopying, recording, or by any information storage and retrieval system, without written permission from the publisher.

Published and distributed by:
Mosaica Press, Inc.
www.mosaicapress.com
info@mosaicapress.com

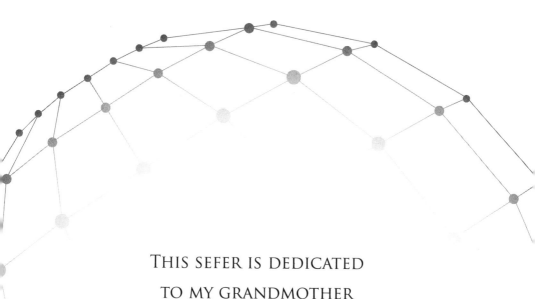

This sefer is dedicated
to my grandmother

Shirley Gross

who was nifteres on the
thirtieth of Nissan 5776.

Her commitment to learning
the parashah each week,
even as she neared the
hundredth year of her life,
was inspirational.
It is my hope that this sefer would
have come as a close second
on her night table
to the "Good Book."

מאיר אלטר הלוי הורוויץ
בן לכ"ק מרן אאמו"ר מבוסטון זצלללה"ה זיע"א
עיה"ק ירושלים תובב"א
The Bostoner Rebbe of Yerushalayim

ב"ה
ח' תמוז תשע"ו

הסכמה

לידידי הדגול ר' יהודה גרוס נ"י
שלום וברכה

Chazal tell us שבעים פנים לתורה, which means that there are seventy facets or prisms to the Torah, emphasizing that the light emanating from the Torah is eternal. Chassidic Sefarim emphasize that Moshe Rabbeinu received at Sinai both that which he transmitted to Klal Yisroel, as well as all Torah Chiddushim that would be revealed in the future. The Sfas Emes adds that each Shavuos, Klal Yisroel receives this new portion of Torah to be revealed to the world according to the degree that one prepares himself. This Sefer is your worthy contribution to the eternity of Torah.

I find it inspiring that since the age of 17 you have been meticulously jotting down questions and ideas that you felt needed further clarification. It is heartwarming to see that with Siyata D'Shmaya many of your observations and conclusions have been confirmed by earlier sources, and that the questions you pose are full of opportunities for others to expand on what you have begun.

I find your eloquent beneath-the-surface look at life and Judaism through the Parsha truly '**A Deeper Dimension**'. Your original answers should encourage others who will iy"H study your Sefer to emulate your example, and pursue all the 'hidden' lessons that the Torah has to teach.

May Hashem grant that your Sefer find favor in the eyes of the beholder and that you continue to search and find new ideas to share in future publications with your family and your children. May you merit to see generations of Torah scholars, who, like yourself will always view the reading of the Torah each year through a new prism.

Yedidcha Ha'Ne'eman

מעלות האדמו"ר מבוסטון זצ"ל 1, ת.ד. 43033, הר נוף, ירושלים 91430
Tel/Fax: 972-2-651-9688 :טל/פקס * E-mail: 6519688@gmail.com

בס"ד

From the Desk of
RABBI AHRON LOPIANSKY
Rosh HaYeshiva

Nissan 5776

זה ספר תולדות האדם

There are seforim written that are the product of a person; and then there are seforim that are somehow a statement of the very person himself. Reb Judah Gross, one of our talmidim, married to the daughter of one of the finest families in Silver Spring, the Kasdan family, has produced that very type of sefer. A very serious baal avodah, he has been recording different points on the parshios that have occurred to him, since his youth. Whenever he thought of, or came across, a vort that was meaningful to him, he would copy it. He now has decided to publish it, and share with others the ideas that have enriched his life.

At Yeshiva we have known the author as someone who is serious about life, contemplative and reflective, with a yearning for growth, and this sefer comes to no surprise for us.

May Hkb"h grant you the time and ability to keep adding to your treasure trove, and may others be motivated to emulate you.

Ahron Shraga Lopiansky

YESHIVA OF GREATER WASHINGTON – TIFERES GEDALIAH
1216 ARCOLA AVENUE, SILVER SPRING, MD 20902 ■ 301-649-7077 ■ WWW.YESHIVA.EDU

בעזהשי"ת

יום א' פ' פינחס צום הרביעי הנדחה
שנת תשכ"ן בתוך ירושלים עיר"ך לפ"ק

הנה נתבקשתי מידידי הרב יודא גראס נ"י ויזרח.
לעיין בדבריו שהוא הולך ומדפיס על פרשיות התורה,
ועיינתי בכמה מקומות וראיתי שהם בנוים על יסודות של
יראת שמים ומדות טובות.

על כן הנני מאחל לו שיזכה לחלקם ביעקב ולהפיצם
בישראל, לאותן שאינם מבינים לשון הקודש או אידיש
המדובר אלינו. ויהי נכלל בכלל מזכי הרבים.

ובזכות זה יזכה לרוות רב נחת דקדושה מכל יוצאי
חלציו ולהגדיל תורה ולהאדירה.

ויה"ר שצום הרביעי יתהפך לששון ולשמחה במהרה
בימינו אמן.

ידידן עוז

הצעיר מאיר יוסף הלוי ר"ב

בס"ד

Rabbi Don Blumberg Rosh HaKollel
Rabbi Mordechai Prager Asst. Rosh Kollel
Rabbi Avrohom Wolpin Director

הרב דן בלומברג ראש הכולל
הרב מרדכי פרגר סגן ראש כולל
ר' אברהם וואלפין מנהל

מכתב ברכה

י"ב אלול תשע"ו לפ"ק

לכבוד יקירי שאר בשרי ידיד בן ידיד צנוע ומעלי איש חי רב פעלים הרב יהודה בן ידידי הר"ר יעקב גראס שליט"א

אחדשה"ט באה"ר

ברכת השנים לך ולכל הנלווים אליך לכו"ח טובה לאלתר לחיים טובים בסשצ"ג

עיינתי בגליונות מספרך שהנך הולך ומוציא לאור עולם פרי מחשבתך ומצאתי שהוא ספר יקר מלא וגדוש בדקדוקים ישרים משמחי לב רעיונות וביאורים נחמדים ומסרים אמתיים קולעים אל המטרה ע"ס פרשיות התורה, וכבר שבחוהו מרן ורבנן. מכיר אני אותך משחר טל ילדותך, ויודע אני בך כי ממעין טהור יצאו הדברים, ובוודאי ישפיעו הדברים לטובה כדרך דברים היוצאים מן הלב, כשאיפתך מאז ועד עתה.

ואין לי אלא לברך אותך שתמשיך להתעלות בתורה ובמע"ט להגדיל תורה ולהאדירה, מתוך שלות הגוה"נ, ככל אות נפשך,

ונפש ידידו

מרדכי פרגר

Kollel Yisroel V'shimshon ❖ 646 West End Ave. New York, NY 10025 ❖ (212) 724-9848 Fax:(212) 724-5363 ❖ wskollel@wskollel.com
Kollel Yisroel V'shimshon is an institute of advanced Talmud study, with a select group of scholars-in-residence providing a full program of community Torah study opportunities on all levels.

RABBI YISROEL SCHWARTZ	ישראל שווארץ
HEAD OF THE	ראב"ד
ORTHODOX RABBINCAL COURT	בית דין צדק דקהילת היראים
B'ERETS YISROEL	בארץ ישראל
	מח"ס "אור ישראל"

בס"ד פעיה"ק ירושלים ת"ו, ט' שבט תשע"ו

מכתב ברכה

הנה בא לפני תלמידי היקר ה"ה הרב ר' יהודה גרוס שליט"א ובידו תכריך כתבים על התורה ועל המועדים ואשר את הכל עשה יפה בעט"ו ערוך ומסודר בלשון צחה וקלה בלשון המדוברת בארה"ב יע"א, כדי לזכות בזה את הרבים, ואמינא לפעלא טבא יישר ולברך על המוגמר להוציא מחברתו לאורה.

והנני לברכו שיזכה לישב באהלה של תורה רבות בשנים בבריות גופא מתוך הרחבת הדעת ויזכה להמשיך להפיץ מעיינותיו חוצה ורבים יהנו לאורה כדי להגדיל תורה ולהאדירה עדי נזכה במהרה לראות בישועתן של ישראל ובשמחתן בביאת הגואל צדק בב"א.

כ"ד הכו"ח לכבוד התורה ולומדיה
המצפה לישועה קרובה במהרה

ישראל שווארץ

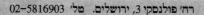

רח' פולנסקי 3, ירושלים. טל' 02-5816903

הרב דוב בערל וויין

שדרות בן מימון 15
ירושלים, עיה״ק

טל: 0515-561 (02)
פקס: 1956-567 (02)

בס״ד

9 Nissan 5776
April 17, 2016

As there are seventy facets to Torah, the commentaries and insights to the weekly portions of the Bible are limitless and timeless. My beloved student and colleague, Judah Gross, has applied himself to record his insights, especially commenting on the letters and size of the letters as they appear in our holy Torah. His comments are meaningful and valuable and anyone that will study them will gain knowledge, thought, inspiration and joy of discovery from them. His manuscript is certainly worthy of publication and dissemination and I extend in these words of mine to him my admiration and great affection.

With Torah blessings, I remain

Rabbi Berel Wein

ק"ק קול ישורון

רב אהרן קאהן

מרא דאתרא

מכתב ברכה

לידידי ר' יהודה נר"ו

בשורה טובה שמעתי ממך שאתה מוכן להדפיס חידושי תורה שלך, פירושים ועיונים מבוססים על דיוקים והערות בפרשיות התורה.

מהזמן שנכנסת להיות נמנה לאחד ממתפללי בית מדרשנו, עשית רושם עלינו בהרצינות בלימודך, ודייקנות בפרשנות המקרא.

והנני בברכה שתזכה שיפוצו מעיניך חוצה, ושתמשיך לראות הצלחה מלימודך מתוך בריאות והרחבת הדעת.

בשם הקהילה
אהרן קאהן

אהרן קאהן

540 Broadway • Passaic NJ 07055

Table of Contents

Acknowledgments 19
Introduction 23

Bereishis

Bereishis 27
Noach 41
Lech Lecha 47
Vayeira 58
Chayei Sarah 68
Toldos 77
Vayeitzei 84
Vayishlach 92
Vayeishev 99
Mikeitz 106
Vayigash 112
Vayechi 115

Shemos

Shemos 125
Va'eira 131
Bo 134
Beshalach 137
Yisro 144

Mishpatim 150

Terumah 153

Tetzaveh 157

Ki Sisa 161

Vayakhel 167

Pekudei 173

Vayikra

Vayikra 181

Tzav 184

Shemini 188

Tazria 194

Metzora 196

Acharei Mos 200

Kedoshim 203

Emor 205

Behar 208

Bechukosai 210

Bamidbar

Bamidbar 215

Nasso 221

Beha'aloscha 225

Shelach 234

Korach 240

Chukas 243

Balak 247

Pinchas 255

Matos 261

Maasei 266

Devarim

Devarim 271
Va'eschanan 276
Eikev 278
Re'eh 283
Shoftim 286
Ki Seitzei 291
Ki Savo 296
Nitzavim 297
Vayelech 300
Ha'azinu 305
Vezos Haberachah 310

Moadim

Rosh Hashanah 317
Yom Kippur 320
Succos 323
Purim 326
Pesach 332
Shavuos 339
Tisha B'av 344

About the Author 345

Acknowledgments

My first thank you is to Hashem for providing me with the *siyata di'Shmaya* for the insights contained within and for everything else You have done, do, and (should please) continue to do for me and my family.

The second thank-you goes to you, the purchaser of this *sefer*. Thanks for giving me your trust; I hope the *sefer* meets or surpasses your expectations. If not (*chas v'shalom*), you can try again with the next volume, *im yirtzeh Hashem*.

My parents, Jack and Phyllis Gross. Your unwavering support for everything I do, constant desire for *aliyah* in *ruchnius*, your open house, and all that you do for the kids is truly inspiring. Hashem should give you the health and strength to continue *ad me'ah v'esrim*.

I owe a special debt of gratitude to Rabbi Yaacov Haber and Doron Kornbluth for bringing the potential of this *sefer* to fruition. Taking a regular person like myself and turning him into an author is a noteworthy feat. I look forward to continue working together in the near future. Hashem should give both of you the wherewithal to continue in your *avodas ha-kodesh* in good health for many years to come.

Rabbi Reuven Butler — your involvement with my *sefer* was no coincidence. Had I just needed an editor, anyone could have done it. I needed a magician (my tenth-grade English teacher would certainly agree); your taking my years of notes and turning them into this beautiful *sefer* proved to be a much better trick than pulling a bunny from a hat. In addition, your tactful way of saying, "Maybe due to space constraints we should leave this one out," was such a great choice of words I almost looked forward to seeing them. Hashem should enable you to continue using your "magic" for many others.

I owe a tremendous debt of gratitude (that can never be repaid) to my *rebbi*, Rav Aryeh Rottman, *shlita*, Rosh Yeshiva Mercaz HaTorah in Talpiot. Your *vaadim* have opened my mind to Torah and *middos*, and your conduct reinforces everything you have said in your *vaadim*. By bringing in your *rebbi*, Rav Chaim Kreiswirth, zt"l, as *Moreh Derech* of the yeshiva, you taught me how a *talmid* is supposed to be *machnia* himself to his *rebbi*. It also afforded me a relationship with a *gadol hador* in Torah and *chessed*, which has changed my life forever. Hashem should *bentch* the *rebbi* with good health and much *nachas* from me and your thousands of *talmidim* all over the world.

I have a deep appreciation to Rav Yaacov Mendelson of Mercaz HaTorah. As the saying goes, "Give a man a fish, and you feed him for a day. Teach a man to fish, and you feed him for a lifetime." Your *shiurim* and *vaadim* (as recently as last week) do not just provide me (and many others) with more insight into the Gemara and life, but more importantly provide me with a *mehalech* in learning and a *mehalech* in life, both of which last a lifetime. Hashem should provide the *rebbi* with the *chochmah* and strength to continue giving *hadrachah* to all of us.

Rav Yisroel Schwartz, *shlita*, Rosh Beis Din Kehillas Yereim — our relationship started with preparing for *semichah* in *Yoreh De'ah* almost eighteen years ago but has evolved into "*orach chaim*" as well. You have been a true source of inspiration and encouragement. Hashem should bless the *rebbi* with all the *berachos* in the Torah.

Rav Michoel Maimon — your listening to many of my insights, humor, and advice have not been forgotten. Hashem should give you the energy and good cheer to continue being *mekarev kerovim*.

I would especially like to thank the Admor Mi'Kosson, *shlita*, and the Admor Mi'Boston (Har Nof), *shlita*. You have given me so much of your precious time and *eitzah*, and without it, I would not be where I am today. The infusion of the *varmkeit* of *chassidus* and the bestowal of *berachos* when needed (when aren't they needed?) are a real source of comfort. The Ribbono Shel Olam should give both of the Rebbes the *koiach* and *gezunt* to continue being *mechazek* Klal Yisrael.

Thanks to Rav Aharon Cohen, Mara D'asra Kol Yeshurun, Passaic,

New Jersey. The *rav* makes our shul into a real *makom Torah* for the *baal ha-batim* and their *mishpachos*.

A special thank you to my grandfather Jerome Turk, *amush*. Grampa, it is a big *zechus* for me to call you (almost) every *erev Shabbos* and give over my latest *chiddush*. Your desire to understand every nuance of what I say is truly inspirational. At an age when most slow down, your recent publication of books really raises the bar for all of us. Hashem should give you the health and energy to continue being productive and providing Granny with the wonderful care that you give her.

I am forever grateful to my in-laws, Yitz and Marsha Kasdan, for the Torah and *yirah* upbringing with which they provided my wife. My father-in-law, with his rigorous lawyer's schedule, always makes time for learning, giving *shiurim*, and bringing in speakers so others can benefit. My mother-in-law is always busy with being a *bobby* despite her physical distance from most of us. Hashem should grant both of you with continued *nachas* from all of us and the health to enjoy it.

Aunt Sherie, I don't think too many aunts (from the wife's side) make it into the acknowledgments section of a *sefer*; knowing you, it is not surprising — even without your title at Mosaica Press. You and Uncle Pinny have truly taken being an aunt and uncle to a deeper dimension. May Hashem give both of you *hatzlachah* and *berachah* in everything you do.

I must thank my younger — in years only — brother, Ari Gross (and his wife, my co-worker Estee). Your work on behalf of the *klal* is a sight to be seen. I am also very appreciative of your allowing us to join the Passaic-Clifton community; I'm not sure where we'd be if we didn't have your blessing. I must also thank my sister, Nechama Wisotsky, for all the things little sisters bring to the table in a family. Thank you to my brother-in-law Binyamin for agreeing to proofread the manuscript. May Hashem give both of you the health and wealth to continue in the ways of our parents and the wisdom to take my counsel when you require it.

Thanks to my brothers-in-law Chaim Kasdan, Moishe Lowinger, and Hirschel Wohl, and their spouses Fayge, Deena, and Shana for being there for us when we need you.

Thanks to my friends (I don't want to name you for fear of embarrassing myself at how few of you I have). I greatly value your indulging me of your time and patience to listen to my latest thought. Thank you for all the times you tell me how smart my *chiddush* is; I also appreciate your honesty when you tell me, "You can do better!"

Thank you R' Dani Kunstler for taking things I say seriously. If only there were more like you…

To the team at Mosaica Press, I have much gratitude to all of you who had a hand in producing this high-quality *sefer*. I wish you continued *hatzlachah* in all that you do.

I would be remiss if I didn't thank my children, Shira, Avi, Chaim, Yosef, Eli, and Chaya. You guys pay attention at the Shabbos table and really try and come up with your own original answers. May Hashem give the *nachas* that Mommy and I have from all of you to you and your families in the right time.

Rookie, my *eishes chayil*. You put up with me on a daily basis, you make sure our family has everything they need from love to nourishment, you share in the navigating and driving through the vicissitudes of life. In short, I owe all my successes to you (my failures are mine alone). Hashem should give you the strength, health, and wealth to continue all that you do and the *arichas yamim v'shanim* to reap the seeds we have planted.

Judah Gross
July 2016/ Tamuz 5776

Introduction

Baruch she-hechiyani v'kiyemani v'higiani la-zman ha-zeh. Twenty-three years ago, when I was a *bachur* in Yeshivas Mercaz HaTorah, I was having a conversation with a friend and shared with him a dream I had (while awake!) — to write a *sefer* on Chumash. Since then, I have done my best to write down any questions I had and any possible answers that came to mind. What started with a legal pad and pen has morphed into hundreds of pages of notes and *chiddushim*. What started with a very small loose-leaf morphed into several 3.5-inch floppy drives (who remembers that?), which now resides in a "cloud." What started as an ambitious project of a *bachur* has grown into a reality — of one who hopefully has acquired the *binah* of an over-forty-year-old.

The take away is this: with a little tenacity and a lot of *siyata di'Shmaya*, dreams can come true.

As you read this *sefer*, you will come across various footnotes that bring a source for an answer I mention. Please understand, my intent is not to translate or explain that *Rishon* or *Acharon*. As I learn the *parashah*, I write down all the questions that bother me, try to think of answers, and *then* look in the *mefarshim*. If I find I was *mechaven* to one of the *mefarshim*, I record the *chiddush* as such.

Over the years, several types of questions have piqued my interest. One of them is where the *pasuk* says that Moshe (or Aharon or whomever) did as Hashem said. Rashi sometimes explains that this is a praise to that person that they did not change what Hashem asked of them. The question that has bothered me is: Well, why would they change a direct request Hashem made of them; why is this such a praise? To that end, I made it a personal mission to find a *hava amina* for each time the Torah says it. I believe they are all addressed within these pages.

Another type of question that has bothered me is: What are the reasons for the big and small letters in the Torah? While *mesorah*s differ as to which letters should be different sizes, I try to address most, if not all, found in the common Chumash.

That said, my goal for this *sefer* is to inspire you, the reader, to *think* — and possibly come up with your own answers to my questions. (This is what my family does at our Shabbos table — but with offers of Slurpees, which seem to get the brain juices flowing better.) Or better yet, come up with your own questions *and* answers, and maybe even print your own *sefer* (anything less than twenty-three years is good in my book). If I have helped accomplish any of the above, I will feel I have succeeded.

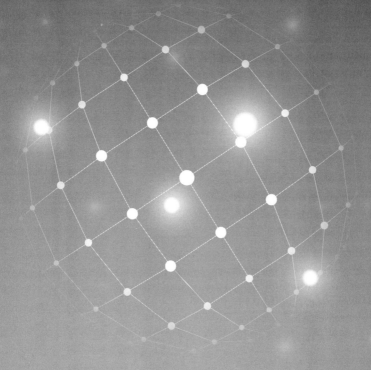

Bereishis
בְּרֵאשִׁית

BEREISHIS
בְּרֵאשִׁית

בְּרֵאשִׁית

IN THE BEGINNING... (BEREISHIS 1:1)

When written in a *Sefer Torah*, the word בְּרֵאשִׁית is written with a large letter ב. Why?

The *Baal Haturim* points out that the word בְּרֵאשִׁית contains the letters of the words בַּיִת רֹאשׁ, the primary house, which is a reference to the first Beis Hamikdash.

We may answer our question along similar lines. The letter ב is spelled ב-י-ת, which, when the *nekudos* are changed, can also be read as בַּיִת, which means "house." If we separate the letter ב from the rest of the word בְּרֵאשִׁית, we are left with בַּ(יִת) רֵאשִׁית, the first house, which is also an allusion to the first Beis Hamikdash. Additionally, the last two letters of the word בַּיִת are the *gematria* 410, representing the years the first Beis Hamikdash stood.[1]

We will now offer another approach.[2] Perhaps בַּ(יִת) רֵאשִׁית, which may also be read to mean "the home is first," teaches us that *shalom bayis*, which is of course what builds and enhances our בַּיִת, must always be first, for it is of utmost importance. In this vein, we may add that

---

1 R' Tzvi Thaler pointed this *gematria* out to me.
2 I heard this second approach from R' Moshe Don Kestenbaum.

everything begins in the home. בְּ(יִת) רֵאשִׁית, the home is first, tells us that everything seen and done in the home is what the children growing up in this environment will emulate for good, or otherwise. If a boy does not see his father learning Torah at home, he too will not learn at home. Conversely, if a girl sees her mother lighting the Shabbos candles with *kavanah* and care, she too will light with *kavanah* and care.

וַיַּרְא אֱלֹקִים אֶת הָאוֹר כִּי טוֹב וַיַּבְדֵּל אֱלֹקִים בֵּין הָאוֹר וּבֵין הַחֹשֶׁךְ:

AND HASHEM SAW THAT THE LIGHT WAS GOOD, AND HASHEM SEPARATED BETWEEN THE LIGHT AND BETWEEN THE DARKNESS. (BEREISHIS 1:4)

After the creation of light, the Torah says, "Hashem saw the light and it was good." Yet, in the other days of Creation, we are only told, "וַיַּרְא אֱלֹקִים כִּי טוֹב — Hashem saw that it was good," without mentioning the specific object created. Why was the creation of light different? Furthermore, if Hashem saw that what He made was good, why did He need to change it afterwards, by separating the light from the darkness? One would think if Hashem said that a product was good, it would no longer need to be tweaked! This question may also be asked on the creation of fish and birds described in *pesukim* 21–22, where the Torah discusses "the creation of the great sea-giants and every living being that creeps … and every winged fowl." After this creation, the Torah relates, "וַיַּרְא אֱלֹקִים כִּי טוֹב — Hashem saw that it was good." Then, "וַיְבָרֶךְ אֹתָם אֱלֹקִים לֵאמֹר פְּרוּ וּרְבוּ וּמִלְאוּ אֶת הַמַּיִם בַּיַּמִּים וְהָעוֹף יִרֶב בָּאָרֶץ — Hashem blessed them, saying, 'Be fruitful and multiply, and fill the waters of the seas, and let the fowl multiply upon the earth.'" In this *pasuk* as well, if Hashem said that the creations of this day were good — "Hashem saw that it was good" — why was the added blessing of "פְּרוּ וּרְבוּ — be fruitful and multiply" necessary?

The answer to this question is that light was the first creation that Hashem made. This placement was necessarily so, for without light, which allows us to see and differentiate, we would not have been able to appreciate any of the other parts of Creation which followed. Thus, light was both a creation within itself, as well as a "tool" through which benefit from other areas was possible.

With this in mind, we may understand that the declaration of "כִּי טוֹב — it was good" indicates the completion and perfection of the "project" Hashem was working on. The subsequent "וַיַּבְדֵּל אֱלֹקִים בֵּין הָאוֹר וּבֵין הַחֹשֶׁךְ — Hashem separated between the light and between the darkness" was not done to perfect light itself, which was already complete. This separation put the light to use in a practical way, to allow it to benefit the rest of Creation.

A similar answer may be given in explanation of the *berachah* of פְּרוּ וּרְבוּ, be fruitful and multiply, that was given to the fish and birds. Indeed, Hashem created them, completed them, and saw these creations were good. However, in order that they be fully appreciated, Hashem gave them the *berachah* of multiplying, so these species would always continue, and always be there for future generations to enjoy.

וַיַּרְא אֱלֹקִים אֶת הָאוֹר כִּי טוֹב וַיַּבְדֵּל אֱלֹקִים בֵּין הָאוֹר וּבֵין הַחֹשֶׁךְ:

AND HASHEM SAW THAT THE LIGHT WAS GOOD, AND HASHEM SEPARATED BETWEEN THE LIGHT AND BETWEEN THE DARKNESS. (BEREISHIS 1:4)

The Torah repeats "וַיַּרְא אֱלֹקִים כִּי טוֹב — Hashem saw that it was good," over and over again throughout the Six Days of Creation. Why the repetition? At the end of the chapter, we are told "וַיַּרְא אֱלֹקִים אֶת כָּל אֲשֶׁר עָשָׂה וְהִנֵּה טוֹב מְאֹד — Hashem saw everything that He made, and behold, it was very good" (1:31), which is speaking about all of Creation. Why isn't this declaration sufficient for everything created throughout the entire Six Days? Why are the words "Hashem saw that it was good" said every day?

We see from here that a person should review his actions at the end of every day, evaluate what he did during the day, and consider what their consequences will be. Hashem did not just create something, assume it was good, and if it wasn't, stay with it until somebody complained. Rather, He constantly checked His handiwork, and was satisfied that it was good.

But one should not think that our *cheshbon hanefesh* responsibility ends there. As we saw, we are told "וַיַּרְא אֱלֹקִים אֶת כָּל אֲשֶׁר עָשָׂה וְהִנֵּה טוֹב מְאֹד — Hashem saw everything that He made, and behold, it was very good." At the end of the "project," Hashem reviewed the week and saw that all that He did was very good. This is a lesson to us, as well. It is not enough to evaluate each day separately. We must also look at the big picture, and connect six work days to make a "week." After we have decided that they have been good, we, like Hashem, can then say, "I have seen all that I have made, and behold, it is very good."

וַיִּבְרָא אֱלֹקִים אֶת הָאָדָם בְּצַלְמוֹ בְּצֶלֶם אֱלֹקִים בָּרָא אֹתוֹ זָכָר וּנְקֵבָה בָּרָא אֹתָם:

AND HASHEM CREATED MAN IN HIS IMAGE; IN THE IMAGE OF HASHEM HE CREATED HIM; MALE AND FEMALE HE CREATED THEM. (BEREISHIS 1:27)

Why didn't the Torah say "וַיַּרְא אֱלֹקִים כִּי טוֹב — Hashem saw that it was good" after the creation of man, as is said after many other parts of Creation?

The Ramban explains that the Torah says "וַיֹּאמֶר ה' אֱלֹקִים לֹא טוֹב הֱיוֹת הָאָדָם לְבַדּוֹ אֶעֱשֶׂה לּוֹ עֵזֶר כְּנֶגְדּוֹ — Hashem said, 'It is not good for man to be alone, I will make him a helpmate facing him'" (2:18). This implies that when man was created, he still was not "good," for this creation still had to be "tweaked"; Chavah, Adam's wife, still had to be separated from Adam in a way that would be best for man. It was thus still too early to pronounce this creation as "good," as man was not yet complete.

Another reason why the creation of man was not immediately pronounced "טוֹב — good," lies in the basic difference between man and the myriads of Hashem's other creations. When Hashem created every other part of the world, He formed them for a purpose which they immediately began to fulfill, and, as if on auto-pilot, flawlessly continue doing so until today. The blades of grass that we see outside of our window, for example, are essentially no different than they were at Creation. Man is different. He was not created perfect, nor does he naturally continue doing what he did yesterday. On the contrary: a person is always defending his existence, by constantly trying to become better, and thereby evolving into someone who is closer to what Hashem planned at Creation. Hashem thus did not pronounce man as "good" when creating him, for the jury is still out on whether a person is indeed "good," as Hashem envisioned, and desired him to be.

אֵלֶּה תוֹלְדוֹת הַשָּׁמַיִם וְהָאָרֶץ בְּהִבָּרְאָם ...

THESE ARE THE GENERATIONS OF THE HEAVENS AND THE EARTH WHEN THEY WERE CREATED ...
(BEREISHIS 2:4)

When written in a *Sefer Torah*, the letter ה in the word בְּהִבָּרְאָם is written smaller than usual. Why?

Rashi explains that בְּהִבָּרְאָם may also be read as the two words בְּ-ה בְּרָאָם, *with the letter* ה *He [Hashem] created them*. This alludes to the Gemara (*Menachos* 29a), which tells us that Hashem created the world using the letter ה. Thus, the small ה hints to this alternative reading.

The *Midrash Tanchuma Yashan* (brought in *Torah Sheleimah*) adds insight into why the world was created specifically with the letter ה, by noting that ה is the easiest letter to pronounce. In contrast to other letters which require use of the tongue, teeth or throat, saying the ה just takes an effortless breath. Telling us that Hashem created the world using a letter ה thus tells us of the minimal effort (or lack thereof) that Hashem "used" to create the world.

Perhaps this is the message of the smaller letter ה as well. The Torah writes the "ה of creation" smaller than an ordinary ה to remind us that this ה is "smaller" than usual, that even the almost negligible breath that a person uses to pronounce the letter ה is more effort than Hashem required to create the world.

> וּמֵעֵץ הַדַּעַת טוֹב וָרָע לֹא תֹאכַל מִמֶּנּוּ ... וַיֹּאמֶר ה׳ אֱלֹקִים לֹא טוֹב הֱיוֹת הָאָדָם לְבַדּוֹ אֶעֱשֶׂה לּוֹ עֵזֶר כְּנֶגְדּוֹ:
>
> BUT OF THE TREE OF KNOWLEDGE OF GOOD AND EVIL YOU SHALL NOT EAT FROM IT ... AND HASHEM ELOKIM SAID, "IT IS NOT GOOD THAT MAN IS ALONE; I SHALL MAKE HIM A HELPMATE OPPOSITE HIM." (BEREISHIS 2:17–18)

Hashem's declaration of "It is not good that man is alone; I shall make him a helpmate opposite him," immediately follows the first prohibition, of His warning Adam that he may not eat from the *Eitz HaDaas*. Why?

As soon as Hashem made a prohibition, He immediately wanted to help Adam, by giving him the fortitude he would need to help him withstand this temptation. He thus provided him with a *helpmate* — a wife — to protect her husband, and guard him from impropriety.

> וַיֹּאמֶר ה׳ אֱלֹקִים לֹא טוֹב הֱיוֹת הָאָדָם לְבַדּוֹ אֶעֱשֶׂה לּוֹ עֵזֶר כְּנֶגְדּוֹ:
>
> HASHEM ELOKIM SAID, "IT IS NOT GOOD THAT MAN IS ALONE; I SHALL MAKE HIM A HELPMATE OPPOSITE HIM." (BEREISHIS 2:18)

Hashem anticipated Adam's need for a mate before Adam ever expressed a desire for one. This shows a kindness that we experience literally every day of our lives, that Hashem provides us with things we require, before we even know that we need them.

> וַיִּקְרָא הָאָדָם שֵׁמוֹת לְכָל הַבְּהֵמָה וּלְעוֹף הַשָּׁמַיִם וּלְכֹל חַיַּת הַשָּׂדֶה וּלְאָדָם לֹא מָצָא עֵזֶר כְּנֶגְדּוֹ:
>
> ADAM ASSIGNED NAMES TO ALL THE ANIMALS AND TO THE BIRDS OF THE SKIES, AND TO ALL THE BEASTS OF THE FIELDS, BUT ADAM, HE DID NOT FIND A HELPMATE OPPOSITE HIM. (BEREISHIS 2:20)

Hashem knew that He would create a mate for Adam. So why didn't He just create Adam and Chavah at the same time?

A person's appreciation for something that he always had is incomparable to the appreciation he feels when given something that he was lacking. For example, someone who went from rags to riches has a far greater appreciation of money than does a person who was born into wealth. In the same way, Adam would appreciate Chavah so much more, because there was a time that he had been all alone.

> וּמִפְּרִי הָעֵץ אֲשֶׁר בְּתוֹךְ הַגָּן אָמַר אֱלֹקִים לֹא תֹאכְלוּ מִמֶּנּוּ וְלֹא תִגְּעוּ בּוֹ פֶּן תְּמֻתוּן:
>
> BUT OF THE FRUIT OF THE TREE THAT IS IN THE MIDST OF THE GARDEN, HASHEM SAID, "YOU SHALL NOT EAT OF IT, AND YOU SHALL NOT TOUCH IT, LEST YOU DIE." (BEREISHIS 3:3)

Rashi points out that Hashem had only told Adam that he must not eat of the fruit of the tree. Chavah added to this prohibition, when she told the *Nachash* (the Serpent) that Hashem had also said that they must not touch the tree. Rashi adds that Chavah's episode with the *Eitz HaDaas* is a telling example of Shlomo's warning of "אַל תּוֹסְףְּ עַל דְּבָרָיו — do not add to His words," in *Mishlei* 30:6. Her adding to Hashem's command is what caused her to eventually eat from the tree's fruit, in violation of the very instruction that Hashem had told them.

The first Mishnah in *Pirkei Avos*, which says "וַעֲשׂוּ סְיָג לַתּוֹרָה — and they made a fence for the Torah," implies otherwise; "fences," that we make to protect Torah law from being violated, are a good thing and in fact very necessary. Why, then, was Chavah faulted for saying that they were not to touch the *Eitz HaDaas*? This too was a protective "fence," for if they would not even touch the tree, they surely would not eat from its fruits!

Chavah was correct in making the addition of "do not touch the tree" to prevent violation of Hashem's commandment. Her mistake, though, was that she included it as part of the halachah that she described to the *Nachash*. The difference between a preventive measure and basic halachah is that basic halachah — which is Hashem's instruction — applies to everyone in the same way. Preventive "fences," on the other hand, are personal; what is enough to keep one person away from sin is not enough for another who requires greater measures, and is beyond what is necessary for a third. As a result, it is wrong to answer with one's own level of "fences" when asked for the halachah, for these "fences" are quite possibly irrelevant to the one who is asking. When she mistakenly included the "fence" she made as part of the halachah, she gave the *Nachash* the opening to challenge her, by showing that her fence wasn't really necessary.

וַיִּקְרָא ה' אֱלֹקִים אֶל הָאָדָם ... וַיֹּאמֶר מִי הִגִּיד לְךָ כִּי עֵירֹם אָתָּה הֲמִן הָעֵץ אֲשֶׁר צִוִּיתִיךָ לְבִלְתִּי אֲכָל מִמֶּנּוּ אָכָלְתָּ:

HASHEM ELOKIM CALLED TO ADAM ... HE SAID, "WHO TOLD YOU THAT YOU ARE NAKED? HAVE YOU EATEN FROM THE TREE, ABOUT WHICH I COMMANDED YOU NOT TO EAT?" (BEREISHIS 3:9,11)

Why did Hashem first approach Adam about eating from the *Eitz HaDaas*, when in fact Chavah was the one who had initiated this *aveirah*?

In his *Sefer Darchei Mussar (Parashas Vayeira)*, Rav Yaacov Naiman asks a very similar question. The Torah tells us that Sarah laughed when she heard that she would soon bear a child at her advanced age. Hashem came to Avraham, and asked him why Sarah laughed. Why, asks Rav Naiman, did Hashem discuss Sarah's laughter with Avraham? It was Sarah who laughed; He should have asked Sarah herself! Rav Naiman explains that any void in Sarah's *emunah* could only be coming from a small deficiency in Avraham's. As her husband, Avraham was the one who set the tone in the household, and the punctiliousness and care that a man has in mitzvah observance will be subtly communicated to his wife. Had Avraham totally believed that Hashem could give them a child, he would have communicated this awareness to Sarah, who would have then lived with this *emunah* as well. The reason why Hashem came to Avraham to ask him why Sarah laughed is because Sarah's laughter was ultimately rooted in him.

This approach answers our question as well. It is true that Chavah was the first one who actually ate from the *Eitz HaDaas*. But, had Adam been stronger in his *emunah*, she never would have done this *aveirah*. Here too, Hashem first went to Adam, the ultimate source of this sin.

וַיֹּאמֶר ה' אֱלֹקִים אֶל הַנָּחָשׁ כִּי עָשִׂיתָ זֹּאת ...
וְאֵיבָה אָשִׁית בֵּינְךָ וּבֵין הָאִשָּׁה וּבֵין זַרְעֲךָ וּבֵין
זַרְעָהּ הוּא יְשׁוּפְךָ רֹאשׁ וְאַתָּה תְּשׁוּפֶנּוּ עָקֵב:

AND HASHEM ELOKIM SAID TO THE SERPENT, "BECAUSE YOU HAVE DONE THIS … I SHALL PLACE HATRED BETWEEN YOU AND BETWEEN THE WOMAN, AND BETWEEN YOUR SEED AND BETWEEN HER SEED. HE WILL CRUSH YOUR HEAD, AND YOU WILL BITE HIS HEEL."

(BEREISHIS 3:14–15)

How is the punishment that the *Nachash* (the Serpent) received of "I shall place hatred between you and between the woman ..." related to his sin?

Rashi (3:1) tells us that the reason why the *Nachash* enticed Chavah to eat from the Tree's fruit was because he desired her, after having seen Adam and Chavah living together as man and wife.

The greatest blow to someone who lusts or desires is that their advances are rejected and denied. In punishment of the *Nachash's* great desire for Chavah, Hashem arranged that there will now instead be an inborn and eternal hatred between her descendants and his.

וַיֹּאמֶר ה' אֱלֹקִים אֶל הַנָּחָשׁ כִּי עָשִׂיתָ זֹּאת אָרוּר אַתָּה מִכָּל הַבְּהֵמָה וּמִכֹּל חַיַּת הַשָּׂדֶה עַל גְּחֹנְךָ תֵלֵךְ וְעָפָר תֹּאכַל כָּל יְמֵי חַיֶּיךָ:

AND HASHEM ELOKIM SAID TO THE SERPENT, "BECAUSE YOU HAVE DONE THIS, CURSED BE YOU MORE THAN ALL THE ANIMALS AND MORE THAN ALL THE BEASTS OF THE FIELD; YOU SHALL WALK ON YOUR BELLY, AND YOU SHALL EAT DUST ALL THE DAYS OF YOUR LIFE." (BEREISHIS 3:14)

Rashi (based on the Gemara *Bechoros* 8a) explains that that the *Nachash* (the Serpent) is cursed beyond all the animals and beasts of the field by suffering a seven-year gestation period, which is longer than any other animal or beast. This punishment is in addition to the two other punishments mentioned — that he shall walk on his belly, and eat nothing but dust.

We know that the punishments that Adam and Chavah received are still very relevant. Also, the snake still crawls on his belly, and has no taste buds in his mouth allowing him to taste his food. But, a snake's pregnancy lasts nowhere near seven years!

Perhaps the answer to this question lies in examining the *trop* to this *pasuk*. An *esnachta*, indicating the *pasuk's* midpoint, lies under the word

הַשָּׂדֶה. This divides the *pasuk* into two parts; the first being אָרוּר אַתָּה מִכָּל הַבְּהֵמָה וּמִכֹּל חַיַּת הַשָּׂדֶה, and the second עַל גְּחֹנְךָ תֵלֵךְ וְעָפָר תֹּאכַל כָּל יְמֵי חַיֶּיךָ. It thus appears that כָּל יְמֵי חַיֶּיךָ, *all the days of your life*, i.e. forever, said at the *pasuk's* end, is only referring to the punishments said together with it, of עַל גְּחֹנְךָ תֵלֵךְ וְעָפָר תֹּאכַל, *you shall walk on your belly, and you shall eat dust*. The punishment of an extended pregnancy is said in the *pasuk's* first half, before the *esnachta*, where no mention is made of how long this punishment will last.

> אֶל הָאִשָּׁה אָמַר הַרְבָּה אַרְבֶּה עִצְּבוֹנֵךְ וְהֵרֹנֵךְ
> בְּעֶצֶב תֵּלְדִי בָנִים ...
>
> TO THE WOMAN HE SAID, "I SHALL SURELY
> INCREASE YOUR SORROW AND YOUR
> PREGNANCY; IN PAIN YOU SHALL BEAR
> CHILDREN." (BEREISHIS 3:16)

Rashi explains Chavah's three punishments. "עִצְּבוֹנֵךְ — your sorrow" refers to the difficulties of raising children (*tza'ar gidul banim*), "וְהֵרֹנֵךְ — your pregnancy" means the pains of pregnancy, and "בְּעֶצֶב תֵּלְדִי בָנִים — in pain you shall bear children" refers to the pains of childbirth.

The second two punishments, of difficult pregnancies and painful labor, are written in sequence, for pregnancy of course happens before childbirth. Raising the child comes next in life. Why, then, is the difficulties of raising children written *before* these other two punishments, and not after them? Why doesn't the entire *pasuk* appear in biological — chronological — order?

The reason why the difficulty of raising children (צַעַר גִּדּוּל בָּנִים) is mentioned first is because Chavah already had children. (See the Gemara *Sanhedrin* 38b, with *Tosafos*.) The troubles involved in raising them would be the first punishment that Chavah would thus encounter. Only in the future, when Chavah would bear more children, would she then experience the pain in carrying them and the difficulty in delivering them.[3]

---

3   See also *Divrei David*.

וּלְאָדָם אָמַר ... אֲרוּרָה הָאֲדָמָה בַּעֲבוּרֶךָ בְּעִצָּבוֹן תֹּאכֲלֶנָּה כֹּל יְמֵי חַיֶּיךָ:

AND TO MAN HE SAID, "... CURSED IS THE GROUND FOR YOUR SAKE; WITH TOIL SHALL YOU EAT OF IT ALL THE DAYS OF YOUR LIFE."

(BEREISHIS 3:17)

Chavah was punished with difficult labor and painful childbirth for having eaten from the *Eitz HaDaas*. Adam was punished as well, with the great difficulties of earning a living. Why, then, do some men have an easy time with *parnassah*, while labor and childbirth is difficult for every woman?

This question may be answered with a point made by the *Ohr Hachaim*, who explains that Adam tried to excuse himself before Hashem, by saying that I received the *Eitz HaDaas*'s fruit from the woman whom You gave me (3:12)! I presumed that since she was a direct gift from You, Hashem, I could assume that she was acting appropriately! Why should I have suspected Your handiwork of wrongdoing? Adam's wrongdoing was thus not treated as intentional, and it was for this reason that Adam himself was not directly cursed in punishment. Instead, his punishment was that the ground that he worked was cursed; "אֲרוּרָה הָאֲדָמָה בַּעֲבוּרֶךָ — cursed is the ground for your sake."

With this in mind, perhaps this is the reason why some men have an easier time earning a living, although every woman suffers difficult births. Unlike Adam who was not directly cursed, as the *Ohr Hachaim* explained, Chavah was, for when told "הַרְבָּה אַרְבֶּה עִצְּבוֹנֵךְ וְהֵרֹנֵךְ בְּעֶצֶב תֵּלְדִי בָנִים — I shall surely increase your sorrow and your pregnancy; in pain you shall bear children," her punishments of labor and childbirth affected her very body. Since the punishments said to Chavah are more inherent to her being than those that were said to Adam, it follows that a woman's punishments are absolute, while a man, who was not directly affected, enjoys some chance of escape.

> וְהָאָדָם יָדַע אֶת חַוָּה אִשְׁתּוֹ וַתַּהַר וַתֵּלֶד אֶת קַיִן וַתֹּאמֶר קָנִיתִי אִישׁ אֶת ה': וַתֹּסֶף לָלֶדֶת אֶת אָחִיו אֶת הָבֶל וַיְהִי הֶבֶל רֹעֵה צֹאן וְקַיִן הָיָה עֹבֵד אֲדָמָה:
>
> NOW ADAM KNEW CHAVAH HIS WIFE, AND SHE CONCEIVED AND BORE KAYIN, AND SHE SAID, "I HAVE ACQUIRED A MAN WITH HASHEM." AND SHE CONTINUED TO GIVE BIRTH, TO HIS BROTHER, TO HEVEL, AND HEVEL WAS A SHEPHERD OF FLOCKS, AND KAYIN CARED FOR THE SOIL. (BEREISHIS 4:1–2)

Why does the Torah mention Hevel's profession first, when Kayin was older? Furthermore, why wasn't Kayin's profession mentioned in *pasuk* 1, following his birth? Why does the Torah wait until Hevel has been mentioned, to discuss Kayin's profession?

Rashi explains that since the ground had been cursed, Hevel left farming and instead turned to shepherding. This shows us something important about Hevel; not only was he careful to choose a profession that was clean and honest, but he also looked for one that didn't have any bad associations. Hevel did not wish to make a living from something cursed, despite its permissibility. This is a tremendous credit to Hevel. Perhaps this is why his profession is mentioned first, despite his being younger than Kayin. Similarly, mentioning Kayin's profession in the earlier *pasuk*, when discussing his birth, would have robbed us of this profound lesson.

> וַיְהִי מִקֵּץ יָמִים וַיָּבֵא קַיִן מִפְּרִי הָאֲדָמָה מִנְחָה לַה': וְהֶבֶל הֵבִיא גַם הוּא מִבְּכֹרוֹת צֹאנוֹ וּמֵחֶלְבֵהֶן וַיִּשַׁע ה' אֶל הֶבֶל וְאֶל מִנְחָתוֹ: וְאֶל קַיִן וְאֶל מִנְחָתוֹ לֹא שָׁעָה וַיִּחַר לְקַיִן מְאֹד וַיִּפְּלוּ פָּנָיו:
>
> NOW IT CAME TO PASS AFTER A PERIOD OF DAYS, THAT KAYIN BROUGHT OF THE FRUIT

> OF THE SOIL AN OFFERING TO HASHEM. AND
> HEVEL HE TOO BROUGHT OF THE FIRSTBORN
> OF HIS FLOCKS AND OF THEIR FATTEST,
> AND HASHEM TURNED TO HEVEL AND TO
> HIS OFFERING. BUT TO KAYIN AND TO HIS
> OFFERING HE DID NOT TURN, AND IT ANGERED
> KAYIN EXCEEDINGLY, AND HIS COUNTENANCE
> FELL. (BEREISHIS 4:3–5)

When describing the *korbanos* that Kayin and Hevel offered, the Torah relates that Kayin brought a *korban*, and then tells us that Hevel brought one, as well. Next, we learn that Hashem accepted Hevel's offering, and did not accept Kayin's. Why didn't the Torah tell us what happened to Kayin's offering immediately after mentioning that Kayin brought it, and only then move on to discussing Hevel and his *korban*?

In writing the story in this way, the Torah gives credit to both Kayin and Hevel, for the contribution to *korbanos* that each one conceived. By pointing out that Hevel only brought a *korban* after Kayin did so, the Torah tells us that Kayin originated the idea of offering a *korban*. Then, we learn that Hevel's *korban* was accepted, and Kayin's was not. This tells us that Hevel advanced a *korban* to a level beyond that of Kayin, by giving Hashem a high-quality gift.

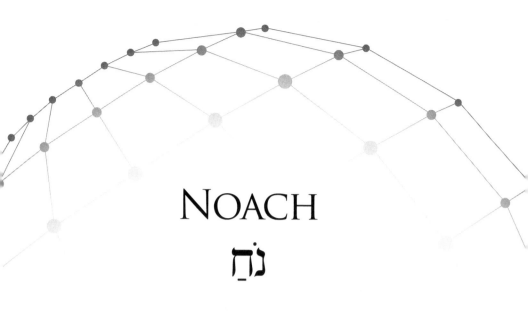

Noach
נֹחַ

אֵלֶּה תּוֹלְדֹת נֹחַ נֹחַ אִישׁ צַדִּיק תָּמִים הָיָה בְּדֹרֹתָיו אֶת הָאֱלֹקִים הִתְהַלֶּךְ נֹחַ:

THESE ARE THE GENERATIONS OF NOACH, NOACH WAS A RIGHTEOUS MAN, HE WAS PERFECT IN HIS GENERATIONS; NOACH WALKED WITH HASHEM. (BEREISHIS 6:9)

The Torah tells us that Noach was "perfect in his generation." Rashi explains that one implication of this statement is that Noach was seen as "perfect" only in relation to the generation in which he lived. Had he lived in a different generation, however, specifically, in the times of Avraham Avinu, he would not have been regarded as a great man.

Where do we find great *tzadikim* lived in the times of Avraham, who would have made Noach into a non-entity?

Perhaps the point that Rashi is comparing between the eras of Noach and Avraham, is that the sins that destroyed Noach's world were theft, robbery, and promiscuity. Against the backdrop of this world, Noach was someone who was clearly better than the rest of man; a *tzadik*. Since we don't find that the generation of Avraham was especially guilty of these crimes in the same all-encompassing way, Noach would not have especially stuck out had he lived in that era, but would have fit in as "a regular person."

Alternatively, we may understand that Noach was not being compared to the people of Avraham's generation, but to Avraham himself. Rav Schwab explains that the Torah is focusing on Noach's inability to influence others to do *teshuvah*; in the 120 years that he spent building the *Teivah*, he was unable to impact anyone (!) beyond his immediate family. In contrast, bringing others closer to Hashem was an area that Avraham excelled in. Or another related area of disparity between Noach and Avraham was each person's level of concern for the other people of his generation. When Avraham was told that Sedom and Amorah would soon be destroyed, he immediately pleaded with Hashem to spare them. Yet, we don't find that Noach asked Hashem to save his world. This lack of care that Noach felt to the people around him made it that had he lived around Avraham, he would not have been considered to be anything special.

> וַיֹּאמֶר אֱלֹקִים לְנֹחַ קֵץ כָּל בָּשָׂר בָּא לְפָנַי כִּי מָלְאָה הָאָרֶץ חָמָס מִפְּנֵיהֶם וְהִנְנִי מַשְׁחִיתָם אֶת הָאָרֶץ:
>
> AND HASHEM SAID TO NOACH, "THE END OF ALL FLESH HAS COME BEFORE ME, FOR THE EARTH HAS BECOME FULL OF ROBBERY BECAUSE OF THEM, AND BEHOLD I AM DESTROYING THEM FROM THE EARTH." (BEREISHIS 6:13)

Rashi comments that although the Generation of the *Mabul* was perverse in many ways, their sin of theft and robbery is what ultimately sealed their fate of being wiped out. This seems difficult to understand. Why is theft worse than idol worship and rampant perverse behavior?

Hashem can forgive or "look away" from any *aveirah* should He choose to do so. He can, so to speak, "forgive" the respect and honor that is due to Him, should the need arise. Thus, a world filled with idolatry and immorality didn't necessarily mean that it had to be destroyed.

When people stop respecting one another, however, no world remains, for it has simply rotted from within. [Similarly, we find that R' Akiva's students were killed only because they did not treat each other with the proper respect; see Gemara *Yevamos* 62b.] Before the *Mabul*, the social fabric that makes up the world was torn beyond repair, and it became necessary to start anew.

> עֲשֵׂה לְךָ תֵּבַת עֲצֵי גֹפֶר קִנִּים תַּעֲשֶׂה אֶת הַתֵּבָה וְכָפַרְתָּ אֹתָהּ מִבַּיִת וּמִחוּץ בַּכֹּפֶר:
>
> MAKE FOR YOURSELF AN ARK OF GOPHER WOOD; YOU SHALL MAKE THE ARK WITH COMPARTMENTS, AND YOU SHALL COVER IT BOTH INSIDE AND OUTSIDE WITH PITCH. (BEREISHIS 6:14)

Commenting on "עֲשֵׂה לְךָ תֵּבַת עֲצֵי גֹפֶר — make for yourself an ark," Rashi comments that many ways were of course available to Hashem to save Noach and his family. Why, then, did Hashem burden Noach with the tremendous job of building a *Teivah*? It was only so the people of the generation would see this unusual project, ask Noach what he was doing, and be told that Hashem would soon destroy the world. Perhaps this would encourage them to do *teshuvah*.

It seems that in telling us Hashem's reason for instructing Noach to build a *Teivah*, Rashi is answering an unspoken question on the Torah's terminology: why is the command to build the *Teivah* phrased "עֲשֵׂה לְךָ — make *for yourself*"? In answer to this question, Rashi explains that one of the reasons for the *Teivah* was to spiritually help Noach, by giving him a chance to bring other people closer to Hashem.

מִכֹּל הַבְּהֵמָה הַטְּהוֹרָה תִּקַּח לְךָ שִׁבְעָה שִׁבְעָה
אִישׁ וְאִשְׁתּוֹ וּמִן הַבְּהֵמָה אֲשֶׁר לֹא טְהֹרָה הִוא
שְׁנַיִם אִישׁ וְאִשְׁתּוֹ:
שְׁנַיִם שְׁנַיִם בָּאוּ אֶל נֹחַ אֶל הַתֵּבָה זָכָר וּנְקֵבָה
כַּאֲשֶׁר צִוָּה אֱלֹקִים אֶת נֹחַ:

OF ALL THE PURE ANIMALS YOU SHALL TAKE FOR
YOURSELF SEVEN PAIRS, A MALE AND ITS MATE,
AND OF THE ANIMALS THAT ARE NOT PURE,
TWO, A MALE AND ITS MATE.
TWO BY TWO THEY CAME TO NOACH TO THE
ARK, MALE AND FEMALE, AS HASHEM HAD
COMMANDED NOACH. (BEREISHIS 7:2,9)

Hashem commanded Noach to bring pairs of animals — "אִישׁ וְאִשְׁתּוֹ — a male and its mate" — with him into the *Teivah*. Yet, when the Torah relates that the animals actually came to Noach (*pasuk* 9), we are told that they came as "זָכָר וּנְקֵבָה — male and female." Why the different expression?

This shift in terminology may be appreciated after seeing Rashi's comments to *pasuk* 8:17, where he explains that the animals and birds were also forbidden in marital relations while in the *Teivah*. Thus, although Noach gathered sets of animals who were mates, they did not enter the *Teivah* as "אִישׁ וְאִשְׁתּוֹ — a male and its mate," rather, only as "זָכָר וּנְקֵבָה — male and female."

וַיְשַׁלַּח אֶת הָעֹרֵב וַיֵּצֵא יָצוֹא וָשׁוֹב עַד יְבֹשֶׁת
הַמַּיִם מֵעַל הָאָרֶץ:

AND HE SENT FORTH THE RAVEN, AND IT WENT
OUT, BACK AND FORTH UNTIL THE WATERS
DRIED UP OFF THE EARTH. (BEREISHIS 8:7)

Rashi explains that the raven flew back and forth around the *Teivah* instead of flying away to its mission, for it suspected Noach of having relations with its mate, who had remained in the *Teivah*.

This suspicion seems preposterous, for such a relationship is physiologically impossible. Furthermore, why was only the raven concerned of its mate's infidelity, and not the *yonah*, who Noach sent afterwards?

We may answer these questions based on the Gemara's principle of "כָּל הַפּוֹסֵל בְּמוּמוֹ פּוֹסֵל — all who invalidate others, invalidate others based on their own faults" (*Kiddushin* 70a), even when the other person is blameless. The Gemara (*Sanhedrin* 108b) tells us that three creatures had marital relations while in the *Teivah*, even though this was forbidden; the dog, the raven, and Noach's son Cham. It seems that the raven suspected others of committing the sin of which he was guilty. Furthermore, a person sees his own faults in others even when they don't make sense, to the point that he can even "see" a union between a man and a bird.

וַיִּהְיוּ בְנֵי נֹחַ הַיֹּצְאִים מִן הַתֵּבָה שֵׁם וְחָם וָיָפֶת וְחָם הוּא אֲבִי כְנָעַן:

AND THE SONS OF NOACH WHO CAME OUT OF THE TEIVAH WERE SHEM, CHAM, AND YAFES; AND CHAM, HE WAS THE FATHER OF CANAAN. (BEREISHIS 9:18)

What is this *pasuk* telling us? We already know the names of Noach's children from the beginning of the *parashah*, and we know that everyone left the *Teivah* from *pasuk* 8:18!

The Torah is not giving us a list of the people who exited the *Teivah* after the *Mabul* was over. Rather, we are being told that from now on, Noach's children were expected to be a new type of person; someone "who left the *Teivah*." When a person suffers a loss or goes through a very difficult *nisayon*, he must do more than simply survive and move on. He is expected to come out a different — a better — person.

Noach's sons were witness to the world's destruction, and were fortunate enough to be saved directly from Hashem. The Torah is telling them that they were now different from who they were before, that these three people now had the singular responsibility of repopulating the world. A double tragedy would have occurred had they lived as the same Shem, Cham, and Yafes as they had been before the *Mabul*. Not only was the world destroyed, but the people who were meant to change, grow, and build from this experience, and become "someone who left the *Teivah*" did not learn their lesson.[4]

---

4   See also *Parashas Shemini* (*Vayikra* 10:12), page 191.

LECH LECHA
לֶךְ לְךָ

וַיֹּאמֶר ה' אֶל אַבְרָם לֶךְ לְךָ מֵאַרְצְךָ וּמִמּוֹלַדְתְּךָ
וּמִבֵּית אָבִיךָ אֶל הָאָרֶץ אֲשֶׁר אַרְאֶךָּ:

AND HASHEM SAID TO AVRAM, "GO FORTH
FROM YOUR LAND AND FROM YOUR BIRTHPLACE
AND FROM YOUR FATHER'S HOUSE, TO THE LAND
THAT I WILL SHOW YOU." (BEREISHIS 12:1)

Why doesn't the Torah list the three places which Avram was told to leave chronologically, in the order that a person travels? First he leaves his father's house, then, once he is on the road for a few minutes, does he leave his birthplace, and only after much travel does he leave his land!

The answer is that in this commandment, Hashem was telling Avram to change himself, to live a life that was closer to Hashem. He was to leave his birthplace and his father's house, namely, the *hashkafos* and environment of the place where he grew up and the way of life that he was taught in his father's house. But, it is very difficult to become a *ben aliyah* with so many negative influences around, which prevent a person from change and growth. So Hashem told Avram to first leave his land. Once Avram was out of his country, he stood a better chance of ridding himself of all that he had been taught his entire life, in his birthplace and home.⁵ This idea is why *bochurim* who go to learn in a yeshiva in a different city, or in Eretz Yisrael, are often so *matzliach*. Far away from the day to day distractions of life, they are in a place that is most conducive to becoming a *ben Torah*.

> וַיֹּאמֶר ה' אֶל אַבְרָם לֶךְ לְךָ מֵאַרְצְךָ וּמִמּוֹלַדְתְּךָ וּמִבֵּית אָבִיךָ אֶל הָאָרֶץ אֲשֶׁר אַרְאֶךָּ: וְאֶעֶשְׂךָ לְגוֹי גָּדוֹל וַאֲבָרֶכְךָ וַאֲגַדְּלָה שְׁמֶךָ וֶהְיֵה בְּרָכָה:
>
> AND HASHEM SAID TO AVRAM, "GO FORTH FROM YOUR LAND AND FROM YOUR BIRTHPLACE AND FROM YOUR FATHER'S HOUSE, TO THE LAND THAT I WILL SHOW YOU. AND I WILL MAKE YOU INTO A GREAT NATION, AND I WILL BLESS YOU, AND I WILL MAKE YOUR NAME GREAT, AND YOU SHALL BE A BLESSING." (BEREISHIS 12:1–2)

The three *berachos* that Hashem gave Avram seem to correspond to the three aspects that He commanded him to leave. The first *berachah* of "וְאֶעֶשְׂךָ לְגוֹי גָּדוֹל — I will make you into a great nation," offsets the commandment of "לֶךְ לְךָ מֵאַרְצְךָ — go forth from your land." When a person leaves his country, it is very difficult to reestablish himself elsewhere, in the new place where he finds himself. For example, while our emigration to America has been quite successful for us as a whole, the Jewish people will always be a tiny minority. To address this concern, Hashem promised Avram that although he would be living in a new place, nevertheless, he will become a great nation.

Rashi explains that the second *berachah*, "וַאֲבָרֶכְךָ — I will bless you," means financial prosperity. This addresses the concern created by the command of "מִמּוֹלַדְתְּךָ — go... from your birthplace." A person in is his hometown is set up and well-connected, and has opportunities for success that he doesn't have elsewhere. All this would be

---

5 See also the *Malbim* on *Bereishis* 12:1.

lost when Avram left his place of birth, and Hashem made up for it with this *berachah*.

Lastly, the *berachah* of "וַאֲגַדְּלָה שְׁמֶךָ — I will make your name great," is in response to the need to leave "בֵּית אָבִיךָ — your father's house." The setting of home and family gives a person a sense of recognition to the people around whom he lives, for everyone knows him as part of this family, or another established group. Leaving home, especially to live in another country, requires him to start building his reputation from scratch; no one there knows, or cares, who he was at home. Hashem promised Avram that I will make your name great, and any recognition that you enjoy will be only increased.[6]

> וְאֶעֶשְׂךָ לְגוֹי גָּדוֹל וַאֲבָרֶכְךָ וַאֲגַדְּלָה שְׁמֶךָ וֶהְיֵה בְּרָכָה:
>
> AND I WILL MAKE YOU INTO A GREAT NATION, AND I WILL BLESS YOU, AND I WILL MAKE YOUR NAME GREAT, AND YOU SHALL BE A BLESSING. (BEREISHIS 12:2)

Often a person is tested with fame and fortune, and it turns out to be the biggest curse. Hashem tells Avram that this will not be the case with you: "וֶהְיֵה בְּרָכָה — it will be a blessing" from the start. This is an added blessing, that the *berachah* which I am giving you will indeed be a *berachah*.

> וַאֲבָרְכָה מְבָרְכֶיךָ וּמְקַלֶּלְךָ אָאֹר וְנִבְרְכוּ בְךָ כֹּל מִשְׁפְּחֹת הָאֲדָמָה:
>
> AND I WILL BLESS THOSE WHO BLESS YOU, AND THE ONE WHO CURSES YOU I WILL CURSE, AND ALL THE FAMILIES OF THE EARTH SHALL BE BLESSED DUE TO YOU. (BEREISHIS 12:3)

---

6   See the Malbim for a similar approach.

Hashem told Avram "וּמְקַלֶּלְךָ אָאֹר" — the one who curses you I shall curse." Why does the Torah use two different words for "curse" — קְלָלָה and אָרוּר — in the same phrase? Why not stay consistent, and say, for example, "וּמְקַלֶּלְךָ אֲקַלֵּל"?

קְלָלָה, perhaps related to "קַל — light," is a weaker form of a curse. And אָאֹר, (coming from the word אָרוּר) is a stronger form of a curse. Hashem is telling Avram that I will protect you to the degree that even when someone curses you lightly, I will curse them back heavily, in a disproportionate measure. This will certainly be a deterrent for someone who wants to harm you, knowing he will get back worse than what he will try to give.[7]

> וַאֲבָרְכָה מְבָרְכֶיךָ וּמְקַלֶּלְךָ אָאֹר וְנִבְרְכוּ בְךָ כֹּל מִשְׁפְּחֹת הָאֲדָמָה:
>
> AND I WILL BLESS THOSE WHO BLESS YOU, AND THE ONE WHO CURSES YOU I WILL CURSE, AND ALL THE FAMILIES OF THE EARTH SHALL BE BLESSED DUE TO YOU. (BEREISHIS 12:3)

What is so important about the *berachah* of "וַאֲבָרְכָה מְבָרְכֶיךָ וּמְקַלֶּלְךָ אָאֹר — I will bless those who bless you, and the one who curses you I will curse"?

Avram's life was teaching passionate idolaters about Hashem, and successfully turning these people into *ma'aminim*. Publically preaching about the stupidity of idol worship could be very dangerous, for a society who has worshipped idols for as long as they can remember will not take change sitting down. For example, we see that Nimrod had Avram thrown in the *Kivshan Ha'Eish*. To combat this "occupational hazard" that would be present wherever Avram spoke to people, Hashem fortified Avram with a *berachah* to protect him from anything that society could throw at him.

---

7   I later saw this idea in the *Kli Yakar* and in Rav Hirsch on *Bereishis* 12:3.

Lech Lecha

> וַיְהִי כַּאֲשֶׁר הִקְרִיב לָבוֹא מִצְרָיְמָה וַיֹּאמֶר אֶל שָׂרַי אִשְׁתּוֹ הִנֵּה נָא יָדַעְתִּי כִּי אִשָּׁה יְפַת מַרְאֶה אָתְּ:
>
> Now it came to pass when he drew near to come to Mitzrayim, that he said to Sarai, his wife, "Behold now I know that you are a woman of beautiful appearance."
> (Bereishis 12:11)

> וַיְהִי כְּבוֹא אַבְרָם מִצְרָיְמָה וַיִּרְאוּ הַמִּצְרִים אֶת הָאִשָּׁה כִּי יָפָה הִוא מְאֹד:
>
> And it came to pass when Avram came to Mitzrayim, that the Egyptians saw the woman, that she was very beautiful. (Bereishis 12:14)

As they were approaching Mitzrayim, Avram told Sarai that now he appreciates that she is a "אִשָּׁה יְפַת מַרְאֶה — woman of beautiful appearance." When the Egyptians saw Sarai, they saw that she was "יָפָה הִוא מְאֹד — very beautiful." Do these two phrases mean the same thing? Why the change?

Even before they traveled to Mitzrayim, Avram knew that Sarai was internally a beautiful and refined person. The only point he now realized was that her beauty was also physical. He thus told her "הִנֵּה נָא יָדַעְתִּי כִּי אִשָּׁה יְפַת מַרְאֶה אָתְּ — now I know that you are a woman of beautiful *appearance*," in addition to the inner beauty that I knew of beforehand.

When the Egyptians saw Sarai, however, they did not see anything other than her beauty on the surface. All they picked up on was that she was "יָפָה הִוא מְאֹד — very beautiful."

> וְלֹא נָשָׂא אֹתָם הָאָרֶץ לָשֶׁבֶת יַחְדָּו כִּי הָיָה רְכוּשָׁם
> רָב וְלֹא יָכְלוּ לָשֶׁבֶת יַחְדָּו:
>
> AND THE LAND COULD NOT BEAR THEM TO DWELL TOGETHER, FOR THEIR POSSESSIONS WERE MANY, AND THEY COULD NOT DWELL TOGETHER. (BEREISHIS 13:6)

Why is "וְלֹא ... לָשֶׁבֶת יַחְדָּו — they could not dwell together" said twice ("וְלֹא נָשָׂא אֹתָם הָאָרֶץ לָשֶׁבֶת יַחְדָּו — the land could not bear them to dwell together," and, "וְלֹא יָכְלוּ לָשֶׁבֶת יַחְדָּו — they could not dwell together")?

It would appear that "וְלֹא נָשָׂא אֹתָם הָאָרֶץ לָשֶׁבֶת יַחְדָּו — *the land* could not bear them to dwell together" is referring to the actual land's not being able to sustain both families. The second mention refers to the people not getting along with each other; and "וְלֹא יָכְלוּ לָשֶׁבֶת יַחְדָּו – *they* could not dwell together." Even when the land was not sufficient for both of them, perhaps they could have come up with an amicable solution. However, when two people can't live together, there is no choice other than to separate.[8]

> וַיֹּאמֶר אַבְרָם אֶל לוֹט אַל נָא תְהִי מְרִיבָה בֵּינִי
> וּבֵינֶךָ וּבֵין רֹעַי וּבֵין רֹעֶיךָ כִּי אֲנָשִׁים אַחִים אֲנָחְנוּ:
> הֲלֹא כָל הָאָרֶץ לְפָנֶיךָ הִפָּרֶד נָא מֵעָלָי אִם הַשְּׂמֹאל
> וְאֵימִנָה וְאִם הַיָּמִין וְאַשְׂמְאִילָה:
>
> AND AVRAM SAID TO LOT, "PLEASE LET THERE NOT BE A QUARREL BETWEEN ME AND BETWEEN YOU AND BETWEEN MY HERDSMEN AND BETWEEN YOUR HERDSMEN, FOR WE ARE BROTHERS. IS NOT ALL THE LAND BEFORE YOU? PLEASE SEPARATE FROM ME; IF YOU GO LEFT, I WILL GO RIGHT, AND IF YOU GO RIGHT, I WILL GO LEFT." (BEREISHIS 13:8–9)

---

8   See *Sefer Meged Yosef* and the *Malbim* on *Bereishis* 13:6.

This episode is the first place in the Torah where we see two people who are not getting along. We may learn several valuable conflict resolution tools from Avram.

Firstly, we see the tone of Avram's voice. Although they were having a disagreement, the Torah does not record Avram's statement to Lot as "וַיְדַבֵּר אַבְרָם אֶל לוֹט — Avram *spoke* to Lot," rather, as "וַיֹּאמֶר אַבְרָם אֶל לוֹט — Avram *said* to Lot," using an expression that denotes a soft tone of voice.

Aside from his manner of speaking, we may also appreciate what it is that Avram said. In saying "אַל נָא תְהִי מְרִיבָה בֵּינִי וּבֵינֶךָ — please let there not be a quarrel between me and between you," Avram puts himself first, as he is prepared to take blame. "כִּי אֲנָשִׁים אַחִים אֲנָחְנוּ – for we are brothers," adds Avram, we are above fighting with each other. Why should we be fighting? "הִפָּרֶד נָא מֵעָלָי — please separate from me"; I am the problem, and you can do whatever you think is the best way to solve it. "אִם הַשְּׂמֹאל וְאֵימִנָה וְאִם הַיָּמִין וְאַשְׂמְאִילָה — If you go left, I will go right, and if you go right, I will go left"; the choice is yours and only yours, and I will follow your direction. Nowhere in this disagreement do we find that Avram had to get his way and be "right." He was always respectful and generous, even where he didn't have to be, and was only interested in the problem being solved.

> הֲלֹא כָל הָאָרֶץ לְפָנֶיךָ הִפָּרֶד נָא מֵעָלָי אִם הַשְּׂמֹאל וְאֵימִנָה וְאִם הַיָּמִין וְאַשְׂמְאִילָה:
>
> IS NOT ALL THE LAND BEFORE YOU? PLEASE SEPARATE FROM ME; IF YOU GO LEFT, I WILL GO RIGHT, AND IF YOU GO RIGHT, I WILL GO LEFT. (BEREISHIS 13:9)

Rav Reuven Grozovsky asks why Avram felt it necessary to separate from Lot when he heard that his shepherds were grazing in other people's lands. Why didn't he just speak to Lot about the problem? Perhaps Lot would have improved his behavior, and it would not have been necessary to part ways!

Lot became wealthy through his close association with Avram. We also know that Lot learned *hachnosas orchim* from Avram. Lot lived and breathed next to the *gadol hador*. He should certainly have picked up on the lesson of the importance of not stealing, and instinctively conveyed it to his shepherds. Avram understood that Lot's refusal to apply the lessons which he had seen firsthand, that Avram muzzled his animals out of fear they would eat from other people's property, warranted a separation. The best way to teach is by example and the easiest way for a student to learn is to watch how the teacher conducts himself. Avram saw that if Lot could not pick up this lesson by example, discussing the problem with him would certainly not be productive.

וְשָׂרַי אֵשֶׁת אַבְרָם לֹא יָלְדָה לוֹ וְלָהּ שִׁפְחָה מִצְרִית וּשְׁמָהּ הָגָר: וַתֹּאמֶר שָׂרַי אֶל אַבְרָם הִנֵּה נָא עֲצָרַנִי ה' מִלֶּדֶת בֹּא נָא אֶל שִׁפְחָתִי אוּלַי אִבָּנֶה מִמֶּנָּה וַיִּשְׁמַע אַבְרָם לְקוֹל שָׂרָי: וַתִּקַּח שָׂרַי אֵשֶׁת אַבְרָם אֶת הָגָר הַמִּצְרִית שִׁפְחָתָהּ מִקֵּץ עֶשֶׂר שָׁנִים לְשֶׁבֶת אַבְרָם בְּאֶרֶץ כְּנָעַן וַתִּתֵּן אֹתָהּ לְאַבְרָם אִישָׁהּ לוֹ לְאִשָּׁה:

Now Sarai, Avram's wife, had not borne to him, and she had an Egyptian handmaid named Hagar. And Sarai said to Avram, "Behold now, Hashem has restrained me from bearing; please come to my handmaid; perhaps I will be built up from her." And Avram listened to Sarai's voice. So Sarai, Avram's wife, took Hagar the Egyptian, her handmaid, at the end of ten years of Avram's dwelling in the land of Canaan, and she gave her to Avram her husband for a wife. (Bereishis 16:1–3)

When we look closely, we see that Sarai is called "אֵשֶׁת אַבְרָם — Avram's wife" in *pesukim* 1 and 3, but not in *pasuk* 2. Why?

Sarai is of course always Avram's wife. In *pasuk* 2, however, when she tells Avram her idea of giving him Hagar as a concubine, she is essentially sacrificing the exclusiveness that she had as a wife to Avram and sharing that with Hagar. In this context, she is thus not referred to as "אֵשֶׁת אַבְרָם — Avram's wife."

וַתֹּאמֶר שָׂרַי אֶל אַבְרָם הִנֵּה נָא עֲצָרַנִי ה' מִלֶּדֶת בֹּא נָא אֶל שִׁפְחָתִי אוּלַי אִבָּנֶה מִמֶּנָּה וַיִּשְׁמַע אַבְרָם לְקוֹל שָׂרָי:

AND SARAI SAID TO AVRAM, "BEHOLD NOW, HASHEM HAS RESTRAINED ME FROM BEARING; PLEASE COME TO MY HANDMAID; PERHAPS I WILL BE BUILT UP FROM HER." (BEREISHIS 16:2)

Rashi explains that Sarai reasoned that the merit of bringing her "rival" into her home would make her deserving of a child.

Earlier in the *parashah* we learned of the *Bris Bein HaBesarim*, where "וַיּוֹצֵא אֹתוֹ הַחוּצָה — Hashem took Avram outside," and told him "הַבֶּט נָא הַשָּׁמַיְמָה וּסְפֹר הַכּוֹכָבִים אִם תּוּכַל לִסְפֹּר אֹתָם וַיֹּאמֶר לוֹ כֹּה יִהְיֶה זַרְעֶךָ — please look heavenward and count the stars, if you are able to count them... so will be your seed." Rashi explains that "going outside" meant that Hashem was taking Avram out of the natural framework of the stars; in this framework you cannot have a child. But I will change you. Avram and Sarai cannot have a child, but Avraham and Sarah will.

If Hashem had promised Avram and Sarai children, after He would change their names to Avraham and Sarah, why did Sarai feel the need to bring her rival into her home by having Avram marry Hagar?

Sarai knew Hashem would fulfill His promise. But she did not know which merits, *yesurim*, or *nisyonos* it would take for her and Avram to reach this step, until it actually happened. So, she tried to create a merit, which would then make them worthy of Hashem's *berachah*.

Perhaps Sarai made a mistake in creating this *zechus*, for the time had not yet happened for Hashem's *berachah* to take effect. We in fact do not find that Sarai bore a child soon after asking that Avram marry Hagar; Yitzchak was not born until more than thirteen years later. [See also *Tzror Hamor*, brought in *Shaarei Aharon*, who "criticizes" Avram and Sarai for bringing Hagar into their marriage.]

וַתֹּאמֶר שָׂרַי אֶל אַבְרָם הִנֵּה נָא עֲצָרַנִי ה' מִלֶּדֶת בֹּא נָא אֶל שִׁפְחָתִי אוּלַי אִבָּנֶה מִמֶּנָּה וַיִּשְׁמַע אַבְרָם לְקוֹל שָׂרָי:

AND SARAI SAID TO AVRAM, "BEHOLD NOW, HASHEM HAS RESTRAINED ME FROM BEARING; PLEASE COME TO MY HANDMAID; PERHAPS I WILL BE BUILT UP FROM HER." (BEREISHIS 16:2)

The term that Sarai uses to express "perhaps I will then have children" is "אוּלַי אִבָּנֶה מִמֶּנָּה — perhaps I will be built up from her." Rashi explains that this teaches us that someone who has not been blessed with children is not considered "built," rather, "destroyed." What does this mean?

One reason is because someone with no children has no one to perpetuate his family name and legacy. While he may still be alive and well, the lack of eventual continuity means that on some level, he is already considered "destroyed."[9]

My wife suggested a different approach. A couple that is not blessed with children will unfortunately also suffer from having more tension in the house. [See also Rashi's comments to *Bereishis* 30:23.) Sarai's expression thus gives us added insight, in all that we must be thankful for, on the birth of a child.

---

9 I later saw this explanation in *Sefer Meged Yosef* on *Bereishis* 16:2.

> וַיָּבֹא אֶל הָגָר וַתַּהַר וַתֵּרֶא כִּי הָרָתָה וַתֵּקַל גְּבִרְתָּהּ בְּעֵינֶיהָ:
>
> AND HE CAME TO HAGAR, AND SHE CONCEIVED, AND SHE SAW THAT SHE WAS PREGNANT, AND HER MISTRESS BECAME UNIMPORTANT IN HER EYES. (BEREISHIS 16:4)

Rashi comments that Hagar's conception came from her first union with Avram. Why did Hagar merit such a speedy and almost unnatural conception?

Sarai gave Hagar to Avram with the hope that the pain she brings on herself by arranging and allowing this union would be a merit to allow her to bear a child as well. Understanding this, Hashem had *rachmanus* on Sarai and to minimize Sarai's pain allowed Hagar to conceive at the initial union.

Rabbi Gedalia Elfenbein, my *rebbi* in Yeshivas Merkaz HaTorah, had a different approach. Avram was of course not interested in marrying Hagar per se, but only acquiesced to Sarai's request because of her insistence, and because he appreciated that she was correct. Hashem thus had *rachmanus* on Avram, and enabled Hagar to conceive immediately so he would not suffer with Hagar any more than he had to.

Vayeira
וַיֵּרָא

וַיֵּרָא אֵלָיו ה' בְּאֵלֹנֵי מַמְרֵא וְהוּא יֹשֵׁב פֶּתַח הָאֹהֶל כְּחֹם הַיּוֹם:

HASHEM APPEARED TO HIM IN THE PLAINS OF MAMRE, AND HE WAS SITTING AT THE ENTRANCE OF THE TENT WHEN THE DAY WAS HOT. (BEREISHIS 18:1)

Rashi explains that Hashem "took the sun out of its sheath," that is to say, made the day incredibly hot, in order that guests should not come and trouble Avraham during the few days after his *bris milah*.

The phrase the Torah uses to describe the incredible heat is "כְּחֹם הַיּוֹם," which literally means "like the heat of the day." Shouldn't בְּחֹם הַיּוֹם, meaning "*in* the heat of the day," be the more appropriate expression?

It would seem that this is the implicit question that Rashi is coming to answer in his comment to this *pasuk*. Indeed, "בְּחֹם הַיּוֹם — in the heat of the day," is more correct. Why, then, did the Torah write "כְּחֹם הַיּוֹם — like the heat of the day"? The answer to this question, explains Rashi, is because the day's incredible heat was not something that was natural. This artificially hot weather was thus *like* a hot day.

Vayeira

וַיַּעַן אַבְרָהָם וַיֹּאמַר הִנֵּה נָא הוֹאַלְתִּי לְדַבֵּר אֶל אֲדֹנָי וְאָנֹכִי עָפָר וָאֵפֶר: אוּלַי יַחְסְרוּן חֲמִשִּׁים הַצַּדִּיקִם חֲמִשָּׁה הֲתַשְׁחִית בַּחֲמִשָּׁה אֶת כָּל הָעִיר וַיֹּאמֶר לֹא אַשְׁחִית אִם אֶמְצָא שָׁם אַרְבָּעִים וַחֲמִשָּׁה:

AND AVRAHAM ANSWERED AND SAID, "BEHOLD NOW I HAVE COMMENCED TO SPEAK TO HASHEM, ALTHOUGH I AM BUT DUST AND ASHES. PERHAPS THE FIFTY RIGHTEOUS MEN WILL BE MISSING FIVE. WILL YOU DESTROY THE ENTIRE CITY BECAUSE OF FIVE?" AND HE SAID, "I WILL NOT DESTROY IF I FIND THERE FORTY-FIVE." (BEREISHIS 18:27–28)

Before Avraham asked Hashem that He spare the five cities in the merit of forty-five *tzadikim*, he said "וְאָנֹכִי עָפָר וָאֵפֶר — although I am but dust and ashes," that this request was really beyond what he deserved. Why didn't Avraham also mention his unworthiness before asking Hashem for even larger "favors," when he asked that Hashem spare the cities in the merit of lesser amounts of *tzadikim*, such as forty *tzadikim*, thirty *tzadikim*, and so on?

Rashi explains that when Avraham asked that the five cities be spared if they would include forty-five *tzadikim*, he understood that only the presence of a *minyan* of *tzadikim* within a city could spare the city from destruction. However, he argued to Hashem, each city will now have nine, and You, Hashem — the צַדִּיקוֹ שֶׁל עוֹלָם — will join with them as the Tenth, so all five cities would be saved.

This shows that asking Hashem to spare the five cities in the merit of forty-five *tzadikim* was indeed the "largest" request that Avraham made, for only here did he ask to include Hashem as "part of the *minyan*." The subsequent requests, of sparing cities on behalf of forty *tzadikim*, then thirty *tzadikim*, and so on, did not ask to spare all five cities, but, explains Rashi (*pasuk* 29), only asked for the number of cities which would have a *minyan* of *tzadikim*; four cities for forty *tzadikim*, three cities for thirty *tzadikim*, two for twenty, and one in the merit of ten. Requesting that all five cities be spared in the merit of "only" forty-five *tzadikim* asked Hashem for a new level of kindness beyond his first request of sparing five cities in the merit of fifty *tzadikim* — ten *tzadikim* per city — which is the pattern to which Avraham returned after this request of five cites for forty-five was proven impossible. Since asking Hashem to so to speak include Himself in the *"minyan"* was a whole new level of request, Avraham introduced it by stating "although I am but dust and ashes."

וַיֵּלֶךְ ה' כַּאֲשֶׁר כִּלָּה לְדַבֵּר אֶל אַבְרָהָם וְאַבְרָהָם שָׁב לִמְקֹמוֹ:

AND HASHEM DEPARTED WHEN HE FINISHED SPEAKING TO AVRAHAM, AND AVRAHAM RETURNED TO HIS PLACE. (BEREISHIS 18:33)

Rashi explains that Hashem only, so to speak, "departed" after His conversation with Avraham had finished; the Judge waited until the "defense attorney" had finished pleading the case, and, only when it was clear that the "defense attorney" had no more arguments, did the Judge begin the execution of justice.

This shows us that Hashem has little interest in punishing, and in fact waits for the defense to rest before beginning any punishment. If this is true with the immoral cities of Sedom and Amorah, it is certainly true with His beloved Jewish people. Hashem waits for us to do *teshuvah*, and when we do, we "enable" Him to interact with us favorably.

Vayeira

וַיָּבֹאוּ שְׁנֵי הַמַּלְאָכִים סְדֹמָה בָּעֶרֶב וְלוֹט יֹשֵׁב בְּשַׁעַר סְדֹם וַיַּרְא לוֹט וַיָּקָם לִקְרָאתָם וַיִּשְׁתַּחוּ אַפַּיִם אָרְצָה:

AND THE TWO ANGELS CAME TO SEDOM IN THE EVENING, AND LOT WAS SITTING IN THE GATE OF SEDOM, AND LOT SAW AND AROSE TOWARD THEM, AND HE PROSTRATED HIMSELF ON HIS FACE TO THE GROUND. (BEREISHIS 19:1)

Rashi makes two comments to this *pasuk*. The first explains the words "וְלוֹט יֹשֵׁב בְּשַׁעַר סְדֹם — Lot was sitting in the gate of Sedom," and says that the present-tense phrase of "was sitting" tells us that only now was Lot at the gate, for he had only that day been appointed a judge in Sedom. Rashi's second comment is in explanation of "וַיַּרְא לוֹט — Lot saw them." This phrase teaches us that Lot learned from Avraham about the mitzvah of *hachnosas orchim*.

In his first comment, Rashi is telling us that we should not think that Lot was sitting at the gates of Sedom looking for guests, in the same way that Avraham was sitting at the doorway of his tent. Rather, Lot was sitting at the gate for another reason, and when he saw people whom he wished to invite, he went over to them, as he learned from Avraham.

Rashi's stating that Lot's *hachnosas orchim* was less than perfect is also implicit from his *dibur hamaschil*, the phrase in the *pasuk* that he explains that Lot learned the mitzvah of *hachnosas orchim* from Avraham. Rashi tells this to us as commentary to the phrase "וַיַּרְא לוֹט — Lot saw them" — implying that Lot's *hachnosas orchim* only began after he happened to see the potential guests in the street — and not in explanation of "וְלוֹט יֹשֵׁב בְּשַׁעַר סְדֹם — Lot was sitting in the gate of Sedom," which would mean that looking for guests is the reason why he was sitting there. This description of how Lot acted is in contrast to Avraham's *hachnosas orchim* at the beginning of the *parashah*. There,

Rashi explains that Avraham was sitting outside of his tent in order to find guests to invite, in explanation of the words "פֶּתַח הָאֹהֶל — (he was sitting) at the entrance of the tent" (18:1). Lot learned to watch for guests if they come by, but he did not learn to be proactive and sit by his tent or the gates of the city to invite guests. Although he learned the mitzvah of *hachnosas orchim* from Avraham, he did not similarly absorb Avraham's passion to do this mitzvah.

> וַיִּקְרְאוּ אֶל לוֹט וַיֹּאמְרוּ לוֹ אַיֵּה הָאֲנָשִׁים אֲשֶׁר בָּאוּ אֵלֶיךָ הַלָּיְלָה ...
>
> AND THEY CALLED TO LOT AND SAID TO HIM, "WHERE ARE THE MEN WHO CAME TO YOU TONIGHT?" (BEREISHIS 19:5)

Pasuk 1 states "וַיָּבֹאוּ שְׁנֵי הַמַּלְאָכִים סְדֹמָה בָּעֶרֶב — The two angels came to Sedom in the evening." But, in *pasuk* 5, the people of Sedom came looking for these guests, and asked Lot "אַיֵּה הָאֲנָשִׁים אֲשֶׁר בָּאוּ אֵלֶיךָ הַלָּיְלָה — 'Where are the men who came to you *tonight*?'" When did the *Malachim* come, during the evening hours, or later on at night?

It would seem that Lot first saw the *Malachim* before it got dark, in the evening. But, he waited until after nightfall to bring them home, for he tried to sneak them into his house in a way that would not arouse suspicion that he was having guests.

> הִנֵּה נָא לִי שְׁתֵּי בָנוֹת אֲשֶׁר לֹא יָדְעוּ אִישׁ אוֹצִיאָה נָּא אֶתְהֶן אֲלֵיכֶם וַעֲשׂוּ לָהֶן כַּטּוֹב בְּעֵינֵיכֶם רַק לָאֲנָשִׁים הָאֵל אַל תַּעֲשׂוּ דָבָר כִּי עַל כֵּן בָּאוּ בְּצֵל קֹרָתִי:
>
> BEHOLD NOW I HAVE TWO DAUGHTERS WHO HAVE NOT KNOWN A MAN. I WILL BRING THEM OUT TO YOU, AND DO TO THEM AS YOU SEE FIT;

> ONLY TO THESE MEN DO NOTHING, BECAUSE
> THEY HAVE COME UNDER THE SHADOW OF MY
> ROOF. (BEREISHIS 19:8)

What kind of a father would offer his daughters so freely?

The Ramban makes a point that only intensifies this question. It is perhaps easier to understand how a grub and unrefined person who grew up in the jungle without any higher values could give away his daughters to a mob. But Lot was being *moser nefesh* for *chessed*, for *hachnosas orchim*. The fact that such a refined person, while he was so involved in this mitzvah, could offer his daughters so freely, indicates his absolute lack of morals in *arayos*.

A similar question can be asked about his daughters becoming pregnant from their father. How can they have had such an idea?

It seems that the answers to these questions are interrelated. A father who is so "free" with his daughters has daughters who will be "free" with him. And, a father who does not have the basic respect for his daughters, is the same father whose daughters do not have basic respect for him.

וַיֵּצֵא לוֹט וַיְדַבֵּר אֶל חֲתָנָיו לֹקְחֵי בְנֹתָיו ... וַיְהִי כִמְצַחֵק בְּעֵינֵי חֲתָנָיו:

> SO LOT WENT FORTH AND SPOKE TO HIS SONS-
> IN-LAW, THOSE WHO TOOK HIS DAUGHTERS...
> BUT HE SEEMED LIKE A JOKER IN THE EYES OF HIS
> SONS-IN-LAW. (BEREISHIS 19:14)

Why does the Torah refer to Lot's sons-in-law as "לֹקְחֵי בְנֹתָיו — those who took his daughters"?

Perhaps Lot's sons-in-law were as lawless as the rest of the people in Sedom. Instead of them asking Lot for permission to marry his daughters, they just took them.

Another answer may be that there are two ways of looking at marrying off one's child: gaining a child or losing a child. The Torah is telling us that

Lot felt as if he lost his daughters to their spouses. This is further evidenced by their mocking him when he attempted to convince them to leave Sedom.

While we may not be able to control how our parents feel as to whether they gained or lost a child, we can inculcate in ourselves that we have gained another set of parents, and treat them as such, no matter how hard that may be. This can go a long way for our own *shalom bayis*, and it may also very well help how we are viewed by our parents.

וַתָּבֹא הַבְּכִירָה וַתִּשְׁכַּב אֶת אָבִיהָ ...

The elder daughter came and lay with her father... (Bereishis 19:33)

וַתָּקָם הַצְּעִירָה וַתִּשְׁכַּב עִמּוֹ ...

The younger daughter arose and she lay with him... (Bereishis 19:35)

The Torah uses different expressions to describe Lot's union with his elder daughter, and with his younger one. The first union is prefaced with "וַתָּבֹא הַבְּכִירָה — the elder daughter came," and is described as "וַתִּשְׁכַּב אֶת אָבִיהָ — she lay with her father." Yet, the union with the younger daughter is prefaced "וַתָּקָם הַצְּעִירָה — the younger daughter arose," and is described not as "lay with her *father*," but as "וַתִּשְׁכַּב עִמּוֹ — she lay with him." Why the difference in expression?

Rashi (*pasuk* 37) explains that the older daughter immodestly named her son Moav, meaning "from my father," and thus brazenly made no attempt to hide what she had done. The younger daughter, however, was more discreet, for she named her son Ben Ami, and the nation of Amon was eventually rewarded for her sense of modesty.

This glimpse of the difference in character between Lot's two daughters gives us insight into how each of them acted. When discussing the older daughter, the *pasuk* describes "וַתָּבֹא — she came," and "וַתִּשְׁכַּב אֶת אָבִיהָ — she lay with her father." She was not embarrassed about what she was about to do, and willingly went and lived with her father, without compunction. The younger daughter is described differently; "וַתָּקָם הַצְּעִירָה — the younger daughter arose," not because she wanted to — she did not willingly "come" — but simply because she understood that now was her turn to do what had to be done. Similarly, she did not look at this union as with her father, but simply "וַתִּשְׁכַּב עִמּוֹ — she lay with him," as she would a stranger. The difference in character between Lot's two daughters did not only play a role in the naming of their children, but even with regard to the actual union there was a real difference.

> וַה' פָּקַד אֶת שָׂרָה כַּאֲשֶׁר אָמָר וַיַּעַשׂ ה' לְשָׂרָה כַּאֲשֶׁר דִּבֵּר:

> AND HASHEM REMEMBERED SARAH AS HE HAD SAID, AND HASHEM DID TO SARAH AS HE HAD SPOKEN. (BEREISHIS 21:1)

Rashi explains that "וַה' פָּקַד אֶת שָׂרָה כַּאֲשֶׁר אָמָר — Hashem remembered Sarah as He had said," refers to Sarah's being able to conceive, and "וַיַּעַשׂ ה' לְשָׂרָה כַּאֲשֶׁר דִּבֵּר — Hashem did to Sarah as He had spoken" is that Sarah gave birth to a child. In other words, the pregnancy and birth are seen as two different promises, and two separate *berachos*, instead of being lumped together.

This shows us that bearing a child is not one *berachah*, but several. Rivkah was given children but had a very difficult pregnancy. Rachel was given children but died during childbirth. Every step of the way is its own *berachah*, and is never to be taken for granted.

> וַתֵּרֶא שָׂרָה אֶת בֶּן הָגָר הַמִּצְרִית אֲשֶׁר יָלְדָה לְאַבְרָהָם מְצַחֵק: וַתֹּאמֶר לְאַבְרָהָם גָּרֵשׁ הָאָמָה הַזֹּאת וְאֶת בְּנָהּ כִּי לֹא יִירַשׁ בֶּן הָאָמָה הַזֹּאת עִם בְּנִי עִם יִצְחָק:

> AND SARAH SAW THE SON OF HAGAR THE EGYPTIAN, WHOM SHE HAD BORNE TO AVRAHAM, FOOLING AROUND. AND SARAH SAID

> TO AVRAHAM, "DRIVE OUT THIS HANDMAID AND HER SON, FOR THE SON OF THIS HANDMAID SHALL NOT INHERIT WITH MY SON, WITH YITZCHAK." (BEREISHIS 21:9-10)

When Sarah felt that she was being disparaged by Hagar (see *pesukim* 16:5–6), she said "יִשְׁפֹּט ה' בֵּינִי וּבֵינֶיךָ — Hashem will judge between you and I," and put Hagar in her place until she decided to run away on her own. Where Sarah saw that Yishmael was a bad influence on her son Yitzchak, however, she would no longer tolerate Hagar in any way, and insisted that Avraham divorce her immediately. When it came to herself, Sarah could take her time, and tolerate Hagar until she left. But when the *ruchniyus* of her son Yitzchak was concerned, getting rid of her immediately was the only option.

> וַיַּשְׁכֵּם אַבְרָהָם בַּבֹּקֶר וַיִּקַּח לֶחֶם וְחֵמַת מַיִם וַיִּתֵּן אֶל הָגָר שָׂם עַל שִׁכְמָהּ וְאֶת הַיֶּלֶד וַיְשַׁלְּחֶהָ וַתֵּלֶךְ וַתֵּתַע בְּמִדְבַּר בְּאֵר שָׁבַע:
>
> AVRAHAM AROSE EARLY IN THE MORNING, AND HE TOOK BREAD AND A LEATHER POUCH OF WATER, AND HE GAVE THEM TO HAGAR, HE PLACED THEM ON HER SHOULDER, AND THE CHILD, AND HE SENT HER AWAY; AND SHE WENT AND WANDERED IN THE DESERT OF BERSHEVA. (BEREISHIS 21:14)

Much is said about Avraham's *zerizus* regarding *Akeidas Yitzchak*. For example, Rashi (22:3) points out that Avraham was quick to go do this mitzvah, and even saddled his own donkey, in order to be more involved in the mitzvah. Similarly, almost everything was done with great speed when serving the three *Malachim*. When describing that episode, the Torah uses the root words "רץ — run" twice, and "מהר — hurry," three times.

It is interesting that we do not find much, if any, discussion about the *zerizus* that Avraham showed when he listened to his wife and sent Hagar away. This too was a mitzvah, for Hashem had told Avraham to listen to Sarah and get rid of Hagar and Yishmael. And, just like by *Akeidas Yitzchak*, the Torah tells us "וַיַּשְׁכֵּם אַבְרָהָם בַּבֹּקֶר — Avraham arose early in the morning," by this episode, as well. We see that not only was Avraham a *zariz* when Hashem told him to do something difficult, but even when this task came from someone else (Sarah), and it was a decision with which he had initially disagreed, when Hashem told him that this was the right thing to do, he did it with total *zerizus*, as well.

Chayei Sarah
חַיֵּי שָׂרָה

וַיִּהְיוּ חַיֵּי שָׂרָה מֵאָה שָׁנָה וְעֶשְׂרִים שָׁנָה וְשֶׁבַע שָׁנִים שְׁנֵי חַיֵּי שָׂרָה:

AND THE LIFE OF SARAH WAS ONE HUNDRED YEARS AND TWENTY YEARS AND SEVEN YEARS; THESE WERE THE YEARS OF THE LIFE OF SARAH.

(BEREISHIS 23:1)

Rashi explains that the Torah says "שְׁנֵי חַיֵּי שָׂרָה — these were the years of the life of Sarah" after telling us how long she lived, to tell us that כֻּלָּן שָׁוִין לְטוֹבָה, all of the parts of her life were equally good.

How? Sarah was childless for the better part of her life, and was kidnapped twice in her elder years. She brought in Hagar to her marriage as a rival co-wife who mistreated her, and had Hagar's son Yishmael to deal with. How could Rashi say that all her years were good, if they in fact were not?

When a person lives a life of כָּל מַאן דְּעָבִיד רַחֲמָנָא לְטַב עָבִיד, everything that Hashem does is for a good purpose, he expects challenges, difficulties and tests. Difficult, yes. But, difficult doesn't mean that what's going on isn't purposeful, and good. Sarah knew she had it difficult but it did not

Chayei Sarah

change her perspective on life. Sarah had a sense of perspective. She realized that it was all good.[10]

> וַתָּמָת שָׂרָה בְּקִרְיַת אַרְבַּע הִוא חֶבְרוֹן בְּאֶרֶץ כְּנָעַן וַיָּבֹא אַבְרָהָם לִסְפֹּד לְשָׂרָה וְלִבְכֹּתָהּ:
>
> AND SARAH DIED IN KIRYAS ARBA, WHICH IS CHEVRON, IN THE LAND OF CANAAN, AND AVRAHAM CAME TO EULOGIZE SARAH AND TO CRY OVER HER. (BEREISHIS 23:2)

When written in a *Sefer Torah*, the word וְלִבְכֹּתָהּ is written with a small letter כ. Why?

In answer to this question, the *Baal Haturim* explains that Avraham did not cry much over Sarah's death, because she was very old, and had lived a full life.

In his comments to the previous *pasuk*, Rashi explains that Sarah was a בַּת ק' כְּבַת כ' לְחֵטְא, which means that when she was one hundred years old, she was only like a twenty year old regarding sin. Based on the *Baal Haturim*, perhaps we can understand that Avraham did not cry a lot because he knew that Sarah did not have any *chata'im* for which she would be judged in the *Beis Din Shel Maalah*, since she was like a בַּת כ' when she died. A *remez* to this idea can be found in our *pasuk*, for the small letter כ in the word וְלִבְכֹּתָהּ, whose *gematria* value is twenty, lies between the letters ב and ת, which together spell the word בַּת. These three letters hint to בַּת כ', which means "a twenty year old," and explain why the וְלִבְכֹּתָהּ — Avraham's crying over Sarah's death — was less than it would have been otherwise.

> וַיִּקַּח הָעֶבֶד עֲשָׂרָה גְמַלִּים מִגְּמַלֵּי אֲדֹנָיו ...
>
> AND THE SERVANT TOOK TEN CAMELS OF HIS MASTER'S CAMELS... (BEREISHIS 24:10)

---

10 I later found this idea in *Sefer Darchei Mussar*.

Why did Eliezer take so many camels with him? We do not find that he took along so many people who would have needed to ride them! Similarly, he gave Rivkah some jewelry and a "gift-contract"; these things do not take up so much space!

Perhaps he took all of these camels with him only in order to test Rivkah when he would ask her for water to drink, and for his camels as well. Imagine Rivkah's reaction at having to bring water for someone who traveled with ten camels, when he could have sufficed with one or two. If a person travels with an entourage and the entourage needs to be cared for, that's understandable. But, if a person travels alone, bringing ten camels would be excessive. Who is he to ask for help with all of them, when they are all really a luxury? This did not faze Rivkah, and she gave water to all the camels when Eliezer asked her, despite the fact they had arrived without a load.

Another answer could be that Eliezer had *bitachon* that he would be coming back with a wife for Yitzchak. In order for anything not to be delayed, he brought transportation with him for whomever and whatever he would be carrying back.

וַיִּקַּח הָעֶבֶד עֲשָׂרָה גְמַלִּים מִגְּמַלֵּי אֲדֹנָיו ...

AND THE SERVANT TOOK TEN CAMELS OF HIS MASTER'S CAMELS... (BEREISHIS 24:10)

Rashi points out that the camels that Eliezer used were called "his master's camels," because it was clear to everyone that they belonged to Avraham, who was careful about *gezel*. His camels were therefore muzzled, so they would not graze in other people's fields.

Why must the Torah tell us here that Avraham was careful about *gezel*, that he made sure that his camels were muzzled? We already know this from *Parashas Lech Lecha* (13:7), were we see that Avraham's shepherds reproached Lot's for allowing their cattle to graze in other people's fields! What new insight is being told to us now?

The Torah is telling us an important message. Since Avraham, through his shepherds, was careful to warn other people about *gezel*, it behooved Avraham to be extra-careful about this area in his own life in a public fashion, lest people accuse him of being hypocritical. The Torah's telling us that Avraham's camels were muzzled is a walking advertisement that Avraham practiced what he preached.

Another answer may be that the best lesson is the one taught by example; openly showing that Avraham's camels were careful not to eat from other people's fields was the best way to bring this idea to the public conscience.

> וְהָאִישׁ מִשְׁתָּאֵה לָהּ מַחֲרִישׁ לָדַעַת הַהִצְלִיחַ ה'
> דַּרְכּוֹ אִם לֹא: וַיְהִי כַּאֲשֶׁר כִּלּוּ הַגְּמַלִּים לִשְׁתּוֹת
> וַיִּקַּח הָאִישׁ נֶזֶם זָהָב בֶּקַע מִשְׁקָלוֹ וּשְׁנֵי צְמִידִים
> עַל יָדֶיהָ עֲשָׂרָה זָהָב מִשְׁקָלָם:
>
> AND THE MAN WAS ASTONISHED AT HER, STANDING SILENT, WAITING TO KNOW WHETHER OR NOT HASHEM HAD BROUGHT SUCCESS TO HIS. AND, IT WAS WHEN THE CAMELS HAD FINISHED DRINKING, THAT THE MAN TOOK A GOLDEN NOSE RING, WEIGHING HALF A SHEKEL, AND TWO BRACELETS FOR HER HANDS, WEIGHING TEN GOLD SHEKELS. (BEREISHIS 24:21–22)

In an act of unbelievable *chessed*, Rivkah brought water for one of Eliezer's camels after another, in an apparently clear answer to his *tefillah* asking Hashem to send him a wife for Yitzchak. Why, then did he have to wait until Rivkah finished? What was it about the camels finishing their water that "sealed the deal" for Eliezer and convinced him Rivkah was *the* one, and to only then give her jewelry?

Even after she had finished *shlepping* water for all of the camels, Rivkah waited for them to finish drinking before she ran off to tell her mother. Maybe, she reasoned, the camels will want more, or there was something else that she could do to help. She did not just draw water to do a little *chessed*, and run. A true *baal* or *baalas chessed* will continue to wait by their guest, and see if something more can be done. This was the proof that Eliezer was looking for.

The *Malbim* gives a different answer. Eliezer was still not convinced after he and his camels received water from Rivkah, because there was always the chance that Rivkah may charge him for her services. When she finished serving him and the camels and there was in fact no bill at the end, he was convinced of her *middos*, and understood that this was the woman whom Hashem had sent him for Yitzchak.

וְהַנַּעֲרָה טֹבַת מַרְאֶה מְאֹד ...

NOW, THE MAIDEN WAS OF VERY BEAUTIFUL APPEARANCE... (BEREISHIS 24:16)

הִנֵּה אָנֹכִי נִצָּב עַל עֵין הַמָּיִם וְהָיָה הָעַלְמָה הַיֹּצֵאת לִשְׁאֹב וְאָמַרְתִּי אֵלֶיהָ הַשְׁקִינִי נָא מְעַט מַיִם מִכַּדֵּךְ:

BEHOLD, I AM STANDING BY THE WATER FOUNTAIN. WHEN THE MAIDEN COMES OUT TO DRAW WATER, I WILL SAY TO HER, "PLEASE, GIVE ME A LITTLE WATER TO DRINK FROM YOUR PITCHER." (BEREISHIS 24:43)

וְאָמְרָה אֵלַי גַּם אַתָּה שְׁתֵה וְגַם לִגְמַלֶּיךָ אֶשְׁאָב הִוא הָאִשָּׁה אֲשֶׁר הֹכִיחַ ה' לְבֶן אֲדֹנִי:

AND IF SHE WILL SAY TO ME, "YOU TOO MAY DRINK, AND I WILL ALSO DRAW WATER FOR

YOUR CAMELS," SHE IS THE WOMAN WHOM
HASHEM HAS DESIGNATED FOR MY MASTER'S
SON. (BEREISHIS 24:44)

The Torah keeps changing the way that it refers to Rivkah. In *pasuk* 16 she is called a נַעֲרָה. Then, in *pasuk* 43 she is called an עַלְמָה, and finally, in *pasuk* 44, Rivkah is called an אִשָּׁה. Why?

The Etymological Dictionary of Biblical Hebrew (based on the commentaries of Rav Hirsch) explains that an עַלְמָה is an undeveloped and young girl, related to the root word עלם — hidden. A נַעֲרָה is a youthful girl. Finally, an אִשָּׁה is of course a mature woman.

Rivkah was really a נַעֲרָה, a youthful girl, as the Torah describes her when relating the story as it actually unfolded, in *pasuk* 16. The second and third *pesukim* mentioned (43 and 44) are part of Eliezer's conversation with Besuel, when he told Besuel what had happened, in order that Besuel allow Eliezer to take Rivkah home to Yitzchak. In *pasuk* 43 Eliezer told Besuel about his strategy to find a wife for Yitzchak, that he had planned to stand at the well and ask someone to give him water. Here he called Rivkah an עַלְמָה, for he wanted to downplay her obvious beauty, as if to say it was hidden from him and he didn't even notice. This was to preempt Besuel's telling him that you only want my daughter for her looks.

However, in the next *pasuk* (44), Eliezer spoke about her *chessed*, how Rivkah had said "You too may drink, and I will also draw water for your camels." Here he called her an אִשָּׁה, to emphasize her maturity and sophistication. This was to preempt Besuel's saying that Rivkah is too young to leave and get married. Eliezer was an astute *shadchan* who knew how to diffuse an issue before it even came up.

וַיֵּצֵא יִצְחָק לָשׂוּחַ בַּשָּׂדֶה לִפְנוֹת עָרֶב ...

AND YITZCHAK WENT OUT TO SPEAK IN THE
FIELD TOWARDS EVENING... (BEREISHIS 24:63)

Rashi explains that "לָשׂוּחַ — to speak," means "to *daven*."

In his *Sefer Birchas Peretz* (at the beginning of *Parashas Vayeitzei*), the Steipler explains that the word "וַיֵּצֵא — he went out," or, "he left," speaks about someone who leaves a place because something there is compelling him to go, such as Yaacov who ran away from Esav. "וַיֵּלֶךְ — he went," on the other hand, means going towards a place because of something inherently positive or desirous that is there. Why, then, does our *pasuk* not say "וַיֵּלֶךְ יִצְחָק לָשׂוּחַ בַּשָּׂדֶה — and Yitzchak *went* to speak in the field"? He was going to his destination — the field — for that was the place that he could *daven* best!

The Gemara (*Berachos* 26a) tells us that each of the Avos instituted a different *tefillah*. Yitzchak instituted *tefillas Minchah*, which is said in the afternoon — in the middle of the day — when we are inevitably in the middle of doing something else. Part of *davening Minchah* is thus its preparation, of physically taking a break from what it is that we are doing, and, even more difficult, mentally detaching ourselves from the rest of our day, and doing whatever we can to give *Minchah* proper focus. This is why it was not enough for Yitzchak to only go to a good place to *daven*. He had to "וַיֵּצֵא — go out," and leave whatever he was in the middle of, literally and figuratively, to put himself in the *davening* mindset.

וַיְסַפֵּר הָעֶבֶד לְיִצְחָק אֵת כָּל הַדְּבָרִים אֲשֶׁר עָשָׂה:

AND THE SERVANT TOLD YITZCHAK ALL THE THINGS THAT HE HAD DONE. (BEREISHIS 24:66)

Rashi explains that Eliezer told Yitzchak about the miracles that he had experienced, that he had traveled to Aram Naharaim with incredible speed, and that Rivkah had arrived where he was standing in answer to his *tefillos*.

Why is Rivkah's arrival as a result of Eliezer's *tefillos* considered miraculous? Eliezer *davened* for this to happen, and Hashem answered him! Isn't this how things are supposed to work? Where is the "miracle"?

When a person *davens* to Hashem to provide him with something that he wants or even "needs," Hashem does not have to respond, whether positively or negatively. Hashem of course knows everything about us and all that we have done, and, as a result, could just ignore our request when we don't deserve it, or, simply say "no." Understanding this makes it clear that the fact that Hashem relates to what we asked of Him is a miracle in its own right. When Eliezer told Yitzchak that Rivkah appeared as a result of his *tefillah*, he understood the literal miracle of getting such a speedy and even positive response from Hashem.

A second reason may be the following. The Gemara (*Sotah* 2a) tells us that קָשִׁין לְזַוְּוגָן כִּקְרִיעַת יַם סוּף, putting two people together to become husband and wife is as "difficult" — is as big of a miracle — as was *Krias Yam Suf*. Eliezer thus told Yitzchak, that not only did my three day journey to Aram Naharaim take only one day, which by itself was a great miracle, *but* I also found you a *shidduch*, which is an even greater miracle. Eliezer understood the difficulty of his task, and appreciated the results that Hashem helped him achieve.

וַיְסַפֵּר הָעֶבֶד לְיִצְחָק אֵת כָּל הַדְּבָרִים אֲשֶׁר עָשָׂה:

AND THE SERVANT TOLD YITZCHAK ALL THE THINGS THAT HE HAD DONE. (BEREISHIS 24:66)

Rashi explains that Eliezer told Yitzchak about the miracles that he had experienced, that he had traveled to Aram Naharaim with incredible speed, and that Rivkah had arrived where he was standing in answer to his *tefillos*.

Why did Eliezer leave out an open miracle that he had seen happen to Rivkah, that the well water rose to the top, which allowed her to draw water with ease? (See Rashi to *pasuk* 17.) Telling Yitzchak about this would make it clear that Rivkah was the wife that he was looking for!

Eliezer purposely left out this *nes*, because he knew that his job was to look for a *wife* for Yitzchak, not a *ba'alas mofes*. The fact that tremendous miracles happened to Rivkah didn't testify to the quality of her *middos*. Eliezer understood that he was to find Yitzchak a mate who would help him build a Jewish home, for which performing miracles is not one of the qualifications that are needed. The water rising wasn't one of the key events on his trip that he had to report.

We must always keep this in mind when we look for a *shidduch*, whether for ourselves or for our children. Some things, like *middos* and honesty, are important. Everything else, besides for being not important, can only become a distraction. Getting excited that a potential prospect can perform miracles only detracts our focus from the criteria that are really of value.

Toldos
תּוֹלְדוֹת

וַיְהִי יִצְחָק בֶּן אַרְבָּעִים שָׁנָה בְּקַחְתּוֹ אֶת רִבְקָה בַּת
בְּתוּאֵל הָאֲרַמִּי מִפַּדַּן אֲרָם אֲחוֹת לָבָן הָאֲרַמִּי לוֹ
לְאִשָּׁה: וַיֶּעְתַּר יִצְחָק לַה' לְנֹכַח אִשְׁתּוֹ כִּי עֲקָרָה
הִוא וַיֵּעָתֶר לוֹ ה' וַתַּהַר רִבְקָה אִשְׁתּוֹ:

AND YITZCHAK WAS FORTY YEARS OLD WHEN
HE TOOK RIVKAH THE DAUGHTER OF BESUEL
THE ARAMI OF PADAN ARAM, THE SISTER
OF LAVAN THE ARAMI, TO HIMSELF FOR A
WIFE. (BEREISHIS 25:20–21)

Why does the Torah bring Rivkah's ancestry again, after we have just learned it in *Parashas Chayei Sarah*? Why is it said here, in the context of her being unable to bear children (25:21)?

The Midrash explains that the reason why the *Imahos* were barren was to make a separation between them and their families, lest these *resha'im* claim that they have a part in building Klal Yisrael. Perhaps our *pesukim* are a source to this idea, for the Torah tells us of Rivkah's lineage and immediately after says she was barren and unable to naturally continue the line. The next *pasuk* comes to tell us that she gave birth because she was *eishes Yitzchak*.

> וַיֶּעְתַּר יִצְחָק לַה' לְנֹכַח אִשְׁתּוֹ כִּי עֲקָרָה הִוא
> וַיֵּעָתֶר לוֹ ה' וַתַּהַר רִבְקָה אִשְׁתּוֹ:
>
> AND YITZCHAK PRAYED TO HASHEM OPPOSITE
> HIS WIFE BECAUSE SHE WAS BARREN, AND
> HASHEM ACCEPTED HIS PRAYER, AND RIVKAH
> HIS WIFE CONCEIVED. (BEREISHIS 25: 21)

Rashi explains the phrase "לְנֹכַח אִשְׁתּוֹ" — opposite his wife" means "זֶה עוֹמֵד בְּזָוִית זוֹ וּמִתְפַּלֵּל וְזוֹ עוֹמֶדֶת בְּזָוִית זוֹ וּמִתְפַּלֶּלֶת," which, literally translated, means "this one stands in this corner and *davens*, and this one stands in this corner and *davens*." Why does Rashi refer to Yitzchak and Rivkah as "this one and this one," instead of saying "Yitzchak stands... and Rivkah stands..."? Additionally, why does Rashi speak of the people *davening* in present tense, of "this one *stands*... and this one *stands*"? Yitzchak and Rivkah lived a long time before Rashi did; why didn't he write "this one *stood* in this corner... and this one *stood* in this corner"?

A long time had passed and Yitzchak and Rivkah were not yet blessed with children. Their solution to this problem was to *daven* for the same thing at the same time in the same room, opposite one another. Rashi replaced "Yitzchak and Rivkah" with "this one and this one," to tell us that this solution was not limited to Yitzchak and Rivkah. It is true that Yitzchak and Rivkah are the couple whom the Torah is discussing, but this approach is just as relevant to any husband and wife team who is going through a difficult time: their solution is to *daven* opposite each other and bring a *yeshuah* together. This is also why Rashi writes in the present tense instead of the more correct past tense, for this approach in *tefillah* is just as relevant to any couple who needs help.

> וַיֹּאמֶר ה' לָהּ שְׁנֵי גוֹיִם בְּבִטְנֵךְ וּשְׁנֵי לְאֻמִּים מִמֵּעַיִךְ
> יִפָּרֵדוּ וּלְאֹם מִלְאֹם יֶאֱמָץ וְרַב יַעֲבֹד צָעִיר:
>
> AND HASHEM SAID TO HER, "TWO NATIONS ARE
> IN YOUR WOMB, AND TWO KINGDOMS WILL

SEPARATE FROM INSIDE YOU, AND ONE KINGDOM
WILL BECOME MIGHTIER THAN THE OTHER
KINGDOM, AND THE ELDER WILL SERVE THE
YOUNGER." (BEREISHIS 25:23)

Rashi notes that the words "שְׁנֵי גוֹיִם — two nations," whom Rivkah was carrying in her womb, is in fact spelled שני גיים, which means "two exalted persons." This refers to Rebbi (Rav Yehudah HaNassi) and the Roman emperor Antoninus. The Baal Haturim adds that the words שני גיים are the same *gematria* as רַבִּי יְהוּדָה וְאַנְטוֹנִס (423 and 424).

The Mizrachi explains that these two leaders are alluded to in this *pasuk*, because Antoninus came from Esav and Rebbi came from Yaacov.

It is interesting that when telling us "וְהִנֵּה תְאוֹמִים בְּבִטְנָהּ — there were twins in her womb" in the next *pasuk*, the word "תְאוֹמִים — twins," is written תוֹמִם, missing the two letters א and י. Perhaps א and י stand for אנטונינוס and יְהוּדָה (רַבִּי). This tells us that the *nevuah* of "you will bear two גוֹיִם" was not entirely fulfilled when the babies were born, for it was lacking the א and the י, and would only become completely fulfilled with Rebbi and Antoninus, many years later.

וַיִּמְלְאוּ יָמֶיהָ לָלֶדֶת וְהִנֵּה תוֹמִם בְּבִטְנָהּ:

AND HER DAYS OF CHILDBIRTH WERE
COMPLETED, AND BEHOLD, THERE WERE TWINS
IN HER WOMB. (BEREISHIS 25:24)

The phrase "וְהִנֵּה" is one of surprise. Rivkah already knew that she was having twins, for Shem had already told her in the previous *pasuk*. What new, unexpected information is the Torah telling us?

We know from how Rivkah handled Yaacov and the *bechorah*, that she had never told Yitzchak about Esav's wicked behavior. Perhaps it follows that she never told Yitzchak about the *nevuah* that she heard from Shem either, that one child would be a *talmid chacham*, and the other an idol worshipper. Thus, her having twins indeed came as a surprise to Yitzchak.

> וַיִּגְדְּלוּ הַנְּעָרִים וַיְהִי עֵשָׂו אִישׁ יֹדֵעַ צַיִד אִישׁ שָׂדֶה
> וְיַעֲקֹב אִישׁ תָּם יֹשֵׁב אֹהָלִים:
>
> AND THE YOUTHS GREW UP, AND ESAV WAS A
> MAN WHO UNDERSTOOD HUNTING, A MAN OF
> THE FIELD, WHEREAS YAACOV WAS A COMPLETE
> MAN, SITTING IN TENTS. (BEREISHIS 25:27)

When Rivkah went to ask Hashem about her pregnancy (in *pasuk* 22), Rashi tells us that she went to the *beis medrash* of Shem. Yet, when the Torah describes Yaacov as being "אִישׁ תָּם יֹשֵׁב אֹהָלִים" — a complete man, sitting in tents," Rashi explains that these "tents" in which he spent his time were "אָהֳלוֹ שֶׁל שֵׁם וְאָהֳלוֹ שֶׁל עֵבֶר" — the tent of Shem and the tent of Ever." Was Shem's yeshiva in a "בַּיִת" — house," as is implied by בֵּית מִדְרָשׁ, or in "אֹהָלִים — tents"?

When the Torah tells us that Yaacov was a person who dwelled in the tents of Shem and Ever, we are not being told that he was only in the *beis medrash*, like everyone else. Yaacov also spent time in the personal tents of Shem and Ever, being *meshamesh* his *rabei'im* as well. He thus learned from them in every area, through their *shiurim*, as well as from the personal conduct in all areas of life. [I later saw a slightly similar approach in the *Shaarei Aharon* that also understands this *pasuk* to be teaching us about Yaacov's being *meshamesh* his *rabei'im*, based on *Targum Yonason*.]

> וַיְהִי כִּי זָקֵן יִצְחָק וַתִּכְהֶיןָ עֵינָיו מֵרְאֹת וַיִּקְרָא אֶת
> עֵשָׂו בְּנוֹ הַגָּדֹל וַיֹּאמֶר אֵלָיו בְּנִי וַיֹּאמֶר אֵלָיו הִנֵּנִי:
>
> IT CAME TO PASS WHEN YITZCHAK WAS OLD,
> AND HIS EYES WERE TOO DIM TO SEE, THAT HE
> CALLED ESAV, HIS OLDER SON, AND HE SAID TO
> HIM, "MY SON," AND HE SAID TO HIM, "HERE I
> AM." (BEREISHIS 27:1)

Rashi gives three possibilities in explanation of why Yitzchak's eyes became blind. One is that they became irritated from the smoke of the *ketores* that Esav's wives burned as offerings to their idols, as was described by Rashi in his comments to the previous *pasuk* (26:35). Alternatively, the tears of the *malachim*, who wept at the *Akeidah* thinking that Yitzchak would soon be killed, fell into his eyes. Finally, a third reason offered is that Hashem blinded his eyes now, to allow Yaacov to take the *berachos*.

According to the first two explanations, that Yitzchak became blind either because of the smoke of *avodah zarah* or from the *malachim's* tears, why does the Torah only mention this now? Esav got married when he was forty, which was twenty-three years before Yitzchak gave the *berachos*. And, according to the second explanation that Yitzchak became blind from the *malachim's* tears, the *Akeidah* happened eighty-six years earlier!

Perhaps indeed, Yitzchak had become blind many, many years earlier. But the Torah has not said anything about it until now because this piece of information was simply irrelevant. It did not make a difference in how Yitzchak led his life, nor did it teach us anything. However, now that Yitzchak is about to confer a life and eternity-changing *berachah*, we now need to understand how he was misled into thinking that it should go to Esav, and how Yaacov arranged that Yitzchak would give it to him instead.

> וַתֹּאמֶר לוֹ אִמּוֹ עָלַי קִלְלָתְךָ בְּנִי אַךְ שְׁמַע בְּקֹלִי וְלֵךְ קַח לִי:

> AND HIS MOTHER SAID TO HIM, "ON ME IS YOUR CURSE, MY SON. ONLY LISTEN TO MY VOICE AND GO, TAKE THEM FOR ME." (BEREISHIS 27:13)

We know that a *tzadik's* statement will take effect, even when it's a curse and the conditions were not met. If Yitzchak would in fact curse Yaacov, how was Rivkah able to accept the curse upon herself?

Rabbi Ephraim Wachsman explains that the generation in which Mashiach comes is called the עִקְבְתָא דִמְשִׁיחָא, related to the word עָקֵב, which means "heel," because the heel is the part of the body with the least feeling, as it consists of dead and rough skin. The message is that the generation of Mashiach will be lacking feeling for the things that are important.

The first letters of the three words עָלַי קִלְלָתְךָ בְּנִי are ע-ק-ב, spelling the word עָקֵב. Rivkah understood the risk she was taking in offering that a curse should come upon her, and instructed it to come to a place on her body where she would feel it the least.

> וַיֹּאמֶר הֲכִי קָרָא שְׁמוֹ יַעֲקֹב ... הֲלֹא אָצַלְתָּ לִּי בְרָכָה: וַיַּעַן יִצְחָק וַיֹּאמֶר לְעֵשָׂו הֵן גְּבִיר שַׂמְתִּיו לָךְ ... וּלְכָה אֵפוֹא מָה אֶעֱשֶׂה בְּנִי: וַיֹּאמֶר עֵשָׂו אֶל אָבִיו הַבְרָכָה אַחַת הִוא לְךָ אָבִי בָּרֲכֵנִי גַם אָנִי אָבִי וַיִּשָּׂא עֵשָׂו קֹלוֹ וַיֵּבְךְּ: וַיַּעַן יִצְחָק אָבִיו וַיֹּאמֶר אֵלָיו הִנֵּה מִשְׁמַנֵּי הָאָרֶץ יִהְיֶה מוֹשָׁבֶךָ וּמִטַּל הַשָּׁמַיִם מֵעָל:
>
> AND HE SAID, "IS IT FOR THIS REASON THAT HE WAS NAMED YAACOV? ... HAVE YOU NOT RESERVED A BLESSING FOR ME?" AND YITZCHAK ANSWERED AND SAID TO ESAV, "BEHOLD, I MADE HIM A MASTER OVER YOU... SO FOR YOU THEN, WHAT SHALL I DO, MY SON?" AND ESAV SAID TO HIS FATHER, "HAVE YOU BUT ONE BLESSING, MY FATHER? BLESS ME TOO, MY FATHER." AND ESAV RAISED HIS VOICE AND WEPT. AND HIS FATHER YITZCHAK ANSWERED AND SAID TO HIM, "BEHOLD, YOUR DWELLING PLACE SHALL BE THE FAT PLACES OF THE EARTH AND OF THE DEW OF THE HEAVEN FROM ABOVE." (BEREISHIS 27:36–39)

Esav demanded a consolation *berachah* — "הֲלֹא אָצַלְתָּ לִּי בְּרָכָה — Have you not reserved a blessing for me?" — from Yitzchak. He was rejected. He then tried asking more politely, "הַבְרָכָה אַחַת הִוא לְךָ — 'Have you but one blessing, my father? Bless me too, my father.'" This too did not work. Finally, Esav broke down in tears. Then Yitzchak gave him a lesser *berachah*.

Very often we think that something is "owed" to us, and it is well within our rights to collect it. Yet it eludes us. Sometimes we think that if we just ask nicely, we will certainly get what we want. That too does not always work. However, when something means so much to us that we break down and cry about it, then Hashem says "My dear son! What hurts you so much?" The *shaarei dema'os* are always open.

וַתֹּאמֶר רִבְקָה אֶל יִצְחָק קַצְתִּי בְחַיַּי מִפְּנֵי בְּנוֹת חֵת ...

AND RIVKAH SAID TO YITZCHAK, "I AM DISGUSTED WITH MY LIFE BECAUSE OF THE DAUGHTERS OF CHEIS..." (BEREISHIS 27:46)

When written in a *Sefer Torah*, the word קַצְתִּי is written with a small letter ק. Why?

Yaacov was sixty-three years old when he left his parents' home, and he arrived at Lavan's house when he was seventy-seven, after learning Torah for fourteen years in *Beis Ever*. He worked for Lavan for twenty years. Yaacov then left Lavan when he was ninety-seven, and traveled for two years to return home, during which time his mother Rivkah died. Thus, it comes out that Yaacov was around one hundred years old at his mother's death. Perhaps Rivkah was alluding to this when she said "קַצְתִּי בְחַיַּי," which can be also read as "the end of my life," will be when you Yaacov are ק, one hundred years old, alluded to in the small letter ק.

VAYEITZEI
וַיֵּצֵא

> וַיִּפְגַּע בַּמָּקוֹם וַיָּלֶן שָׁם כִּי בָא הַשֶּׁמֶשׁ וַיִּקַּח מֵאַבְנֵי הַמָּקוֹם וַיָּשֶׂם מְרַאֲשֹׁתָיו וַיִּשְׁכַּב בַּמָּקוֹם הַהוּא:
>
> AND HE ARRIVED AT THE PLACE AND LODGED THERE BECAUSE THE SUN HAD SET, AND HE TOOK FROM THE STONES OF THE PLACE AND PLACED THEM AT HIS HEAD, AND HE LAY DOWN IN THAT PLACE. (BEREISHIS 28:11)

Rashi points out that our *pasuk* says "וַיִּקַּח מֵאַבְנֵי הַמָּקוֹם — he took from the *stones* of the place," implying that Yaacov put several stones by his head, yet in *pasuk* 18, the Torah tells us that when Yaacov woke up in the morning, "וַיִּקַּח אֶת הָאֶבֶן אֲשֶׁר שָׂם מְרַאֲשֹׁתָיו — he took *the stone* that he had placed at his head," implying that only one stone was there. In answer, Rashi tells us that the Gemara (*Chulin* 91b) explains that Yaacov had in fact put many stones around his head and body to protect him while he slept. However, the stones began arguing among themselves, for each one wanted the privilege of being the one upon whom Yaacov the *tzadik* would place his head. Hashem thus combined the many stones into one large stone, so he would rest his head on all of them.

In *Parashas Bereishis*, Rashi (1:16) explains that the moon complained to Hashem that it was not correct that he and the sun were the same size for, "Can two kings share one crown?" As a result, Hashem diminished the moon. Why was the moon punished for his complaints, while the stones were rewarded that each of them was given what he asked for?

The stones were rewarded because each one's motivation for wanting to be close to Yaacov's head was pure. Each wanted to be close to the *tzadik*, and thus all were given this privilege. The moon, on the other hand, did not come to Hashem motivated out of *ruchniyus*, but rather out of a desire to rule. This *middah* of selfishness was thus the reason why it was punished.

When dissension stems from *ruchniyus*, a compromise will satisfy all. In a place where it comes from *gaavah*, however, no compromise will satisfy everyone.

וַיִּשָּׂא יַעֲקֹב רַגְלָיו וַיֵּלֶךְ אַרְצָה בְנֵי קֶדֶם:

NOW YAACOV LIFTED HIS FEET AND WENT
TO THE LAND OF THE PEOPLE OF THE
EAST. (BEREISHIS 29:1)

Why does the Torah say "וַיִּשָּׂא יַעֲקֹב רַגְלָיו — Yaacov lifted his feet," instead of simply "וַיֵּלֶךְ יַעֲקֹב — Yaacov went"?

Yaacov was about to embark to *Chutz La'Aretz*, to go live with Lavan. Often, when we are forced to go somewhere where we don't want to be, our feet become heavy as cement. Yaacov's leaving Eretz Yisrael required great mental and physical strength, including picking up his heavy feet.

The *Kli Yakar* gives a different answer. Yaacov had had *kefitzas haderech* that took him to the *Beis Elokim*, where he slept for the night. But the rest of the way he would have to travel as usual. Therefore, now he had to lift his feet for the rest of the journey.

> וְעֵינֵי לֵאָה רַכּוֹת וְרָחֵל הָיְתָה יְפַת תֹּאַר וִיפַת מַרְאֶה:
>
> LEAH'S EYES WERE TENDER, AND RACHEL
> HAD BEAUTIFUL FEATURES AND A BEAUTIFUL
> COMPLEXION. (BEREISHIS 29:17)

Rashi explains that Leah's eyes were tender from constantly crying, for her entire life she had been told that she would marry Esav. Why then does the Torah tell us of this physical disfigurement right next to describing Rachel's beautiful features?

Onkelous appears to argue with Rashi, for he translates "וְעֵינֵי לֵאָה רַכּוֹת" as "וְעֵינֵי לֵאָה יָאֲיָן" — Leah's eyes were beautiful." Which were they? Were Leah's eyes blemished, or were they beautiful?

The answer is that they were both, for as we saw, Leah's tears came from her crying about having to marry Esav. Often, a wrong situation initially bothers a person, but as time goes on, he gets used to it. Leah was not like this. She never resigned herself to her fate and accepted her lot in life, but since she understood that the match was wrong, she cried as hard the thousandth time that she thought about it, as much as she did the first. Rashi and Onkelous thus do not argue, but are telling us two sides of the same coin.

We thus see that although Leah's eyes were physically blemished, they were in truth very beautiful, for they showed that she was a person who would never, no matter how long it took, compromise on the truth and on what was right. Describing Leah's eyes is a tremendous compliment to her, and we now understand why this description is said alongside the description of Rachel's physical beauty.

> וַיְהִי בַבֹּקֶר וְהִנֵּה הִוא לֵאָה וַיֹּאמֶר אֶל לָבָן מַה זֹּאת
> עָשִׂיתָ לִּי הֲלֹא בְרָחֵל עָבַדְתִּי עִמָּךְ וְלָמָּה רִמִּיתָנִי:
>
> AND IT CAME TO PASS IN THE MORNING, AND
> BEHOLD SHE WAS LEAH! SO HE SAID TO LAVAN,
> "WHAT IS THIS THAT YOU HAVE DONE TO ME?

Did I not work with you for Rachel? Why have you deceived me?" (Bereishis 29:25)

Rashi explains that only in the morning did Yaacov realize that his new wife was Leah, and not Rachel. The reason why he did not realize this on the wedding night is because he requested *simanim* from his *kallah*, heard the correct answer, and as such, thought she was Rachel. Leah knew these *simanim* because Rachel had told them to her to prevent her being shamed when Yaacov saw that he was being given a different one of Lavan's daughters. When he realized what had happened the next morning, Yaacov angrily confronted Lavan about having deceived him.

Why was Yaacov upset with Lavan, and not with Rachel? *Rachel* was the one who gave the *simanim* to Leah, and allowed the trick to work. Instead of her doing something to stop the deception, she facilitated it, by telling Leah the secret code!

Yaacov realized that Lavan was the mastermind behind this scheme. He also understood that the only reason why Rachel would have given away their secret was to prevent her sister from being embarrassed, and what she had done was correct. The only one who had acted wrongly was thus Lavan, for having arranged this situation.

וַיָּבֹא גַּם אֶל רָחֵל וַיֶּאֱהַב גַּם אֶת רָחֵל מִלֵּאָה וַיַּעֲבֹד עִמּוֹ עוֹד שֶׁבַע שָׁנִים אֲחֵרוֹת:

And he also came to Rachel, and he also loved Rachel more than Leah; and he worked with him yet another seven years.
(Bereishis 29:30)

Why does the Torah reiterate "וַיֶּאֱהַב גַּם אֶת רָחֵל מִלֵּאָה"? We already know that Yaacov desired Rachel more, for she is the one for whom he worked for seven years!

As we just learned, Yaacov understood that Rachel had given the *simanim* to Leah in order to save her sister from shame, and he was proud of what she did. When he finally married her, he thus had an extra measure of love for her. "וַיֶּאֱהַב גַּם אֶת רָחֵל מִלֵּאָה," literally translated, means "he also loved Rachel *from* Leah," that is to say, as a result of what she did for Leah.[11]

> וַתַּהַר עוֹד וַתֵּלֶד בֵּן וַתֹּאמֶר הַפַּעַם אוֹדֶה אֶת ה'
> עַל כֵּן קָרְאָה שְׁמוֹ יְהוּדָה וַתַּעֲמֹד מִלֶּדֶת:
>
> AND SHE CONCEIVED AGAIN AND BORE A SON, AND SHE SAID, "THIS TIME, I WILL THANK HASHEM!" THEREFORE, SHE NAMED HIM YEHUDAH, AND THEN SHE STOPPED BEARING CHILDREN. (BEREISHIS 29:35)

Why does the Torah tell us that Leah stopped giving birth? We would have understood that on our own, when we see that the next time that she gave birth was much later in the *parashah*.

Rashi explains that Leah named her child Yehudah in thanks to Hashem that she now received more than her share. She knew that the twelve *Shevatim* would be born from Yaacov's four wives, which means that each wife should give birth to three sons. When her fourth son was born, she understood, and thanked Hashem, that she had received more than her fair portion.

However, Leah having a fourth child meant that one of the other wives would now have less than their fair amount of children. Although *hakaras hatov* is always admirable, thanking Hashem for receiving something at another person's expense is improper, and is not the way that a Jew lives. Hashem punished her for this *hodaah* by not allowing her any more children at that time.

> וְאַחַר יָלְדָה בַת וַתִּקְרָא אֶת שְׁמָהּ דִּינָה:
>
> AND AFTERWARDS, SHE BORE A DAUGHTER, AND SHE NAMED HER DINAH. (BEREISHIS 30:21)

---

11   I later saw this approach in the *Kli Yakar*.

Dinah was Leah's seventh child. Throughout the *parashah*, the Torah has told us that Leah named each one of her children, and gives us the reason why this name was chosen. Yet, the reason for Dinah's name is omitted by the Torah, and left for Rashi to provide. Why?

Rashi explains that while Leah was pregnant, she calculated that her having another boy would mean that her sister Rachel would only give birth to one *Shevet*, which was less than the *Shefachos*. She therefore *davened* that she should have a girl, to save Rachel this hurt. When the child was born, Leah named her Dinah, stating that this baby was a girl from Leah's considering judgment (דִּין) upon herself. It follows that if the reason for Dinah's name would have been made public, Rachel would have been hurt as well. In line with the way that Leah named Dinah, the Torah therefore does not openly say the reason for Dinah's name either.[12]

וַיִּזְכֹּר אֱלֹקִים אֶת רָחֵל וַיִּשְׁמַע אֵלֶיהָ אֱלֹקִים וַיִּפְתַּח אֶת רַחְמָהּ:

AND HASHEM REMEMBERED RACHEL, AND HASHEM LISTENED TO HER, AND HE OPENED HER WOMB. (BEREISHIS 30:22)

Rashi explains that Hashem "remembered" what Rachel did; she told her sister Leah the *simanim*, so she wouldn't be shamed by Yaacov.

Rachel's *mesiras nefesh* happened several years earlier. What caused Hashem to "remember" this episode now?

We just discussed in the previous *pasuk* that Leah asked Hashem that the child that she was carrying be turned into a girl, for, if she would have another boy, Rachel would bear less *Shevatim* than the *Shefachos*. Leah's foregoing bearing an additional *Shevet* to which she was entitled in order that Rachel be spared the shame of having less than the *Shefachos*, "reminded" Hashem of another act of self-sacrifice

---

12 I later saw this explanation in the *Sefer Nachalas Yaacov*.

that had happened between these two sisters, in the other direction, of Rachel having told Leah the *simanim*.

The reciprocity of *chessed* between Rachel and Leah is truly amazing. Let us absorb its lesson by implementing it into our lives as well.

> וַיָּקׇם יַעֲקֹב וַיִּשָּׂא אֶת בָּנָיו וְאֶת נָשָׁיו עַל הַגְּמַלִּים:
>
> SO YAACOV ROSE, AND HE LIFTED UP HIS SONS
> AND HIS WIVES UPON THE CAMELS. (BEREISHIS 31:17)

Rashi points out that the *pasuk* is telling us that Yaacov helped the men onto the camels before the women. Esav, however, did the opposite.

What are we meant to learn from this order? What is the difference in the way that the families were placed onto the camels?

Yaacov did it this way for reasons of modesty. The men and boys went up first so they would not have to see their mothers climb the camels. Their already being there upon the camels precluded them from seeing their mother or aunt in a potentially immodest situation.

This insight also shows why Yaacov acted differently in *Parashas Vayishlach*, when he was helping his family cross the Yabok River, where the Torah says "וַיִּקַּח אֶת שְׁתֵּי נָשָׁיו וְאֶת שְׁתֵּי שִׁפְחוֹתָיו וְאֶת אַחַד עָשָׂר יְלָדָיו וַיַּעֲבֹר אֵת מַעֲבַר יַבֹּק — he took his two wives and his two maidservants and his eleven children, and he crossed the ford of the Yabok." Why didn't Yaacov take his sons first over there, as well? The answer is because the situation of crossing the river would not have been made any more modest by bringing his sons first and his wives second. This being the case, Yaacov therefore brought his wives over first, as their position of greater importance dictated should be done.

> זֶה עֶשְׂרִים שָׁנָה אָנֹכִי עִמָּךְ רְחֵלֶיךָ וְעִזֶּיךָ לֹא שִׁכֵּלוּ
> וְאֵילֵי צֹאנְךָ לֹא אָכָלְתִּי:
>
> THESE TWENTY YEARS HAVE I BEEN WITH
> YOU, YOUR EWES AND SHE-GOATS HAVE NOT

MISCARRIED, NEITHER HAVE I EATEN THE RAMS OF YOUR FLOCKS. (BEREISHIS 31:38)

This *pasuk* is the first time in the *parashah* that the word רְחֵלֶיךָ is used for sheep, instead of the usual צֹאנֶךָ. Yaacov is letting Lavan have it for the way that he has mistreated and cheated him over the past twenty years. By using the phrase רְחֵלֶיךָ, Yaacov is hinting to Lavan that this mistreatment wasn't only when it came to the way he was paid, but he was also cheated in regard to רָחֵל, his wife.

וְיַעֲקֹב הָלַךְ לְדַרְכּוֹ וַיִּפְגְּעוּ בוֹ מַלְאֲכֵי אֱלֹקִים:

AND YAACOV WENT ON HIS WAY, AND ANGELS OF HASHEM MET HIM. (BEREISHIS 32:2)

When Yaacov began traveling to Lavan twenty years earlier, he saw *Malachim* in his dream. Now, when he is leaving Lavan to return home, he meets them in broad daylight. What is the reason for the difference?

When Yaacov left his parents' home to travel to Charan, he first stopped off in *Yeshivas Shem V'Ever* to learn Torah for fourteen years to prepare for his stay with Lavan, during which time he was so absorbed with Torah that he didn't once lay down for the night. After he left the yeshiva, and continued his travel to Charan, he was on such a high level that Hashem even allowed him a glimpse of the spiritual *Malachim* going up and down the ladder.

Twenty years later Yaacov began to return home. He had spent twenty years living with Lavan the *Rasha*, and yet could still proudly tell Esav "עִם לָבָן הָרָשָׁע גַּרְתִּי וְתַרְיַ"ג מִצְוֹת שָׁמַרְתִּי וְלֹא לָמַדְתִּי מִמַּעֲשָׂיו הָרָעִים — I lived with Lavan and nevertheless kept the 613 *mitzvos*, and have not learned from Lavan's bad ways." The *madreigah* that Yaacov was on after learning Torah for so many years was incredible. However, keeping the same Torah under the pressure and influence of living next to a *rasha* for twenty years is a much greater accomplishment. On this level upon his return, Yaacov merited seeing the *Malachim* during the day.

Vayishlach

הַצִּילֵנִי נָא מִיַּד אָחִי מִיַּד עֵשָׂו כִּי יָרֵא אָנֹכִי אֹתוֹ פֶּן יָבוֹא וְהִכַּנִי אֵם עַל בָּנִים:

PLEASE DELIVER ME FROM THE HAND OF MY BROTHER, FROM THE HAND OF ESAV, FOR I AM AFRAID OF HIM, LEST HE COME AND STRIKE ME, AND STRIKE A MOTHER WITH CHILDREN. (BEREISHIS 32:12)

Why did Yaacov *daven* that he be saved "מִיַּד אָחִי מִיַּד עֵשָׂו — from *the hand of* my brother, from *the hand of* Esav"? Why didn't he simply ask that he be saved from "מֵאָחִי עֵשָׂו — from my brother Esav"?

When Yaacov came to Yitzchak for the *Berachos*, Yitzchak commented "הַקֹּל קוֹל יַעֲקֹב וְהַיָּדַיִם יְדֵי עֵשָׂו — "The voice is the voice of Yaacov, but the hands are the hands of Esav." The Midrash (as brought in the *Sefer Oznayim LaTorah*) explains that this teaches us that when the voice of Yaacov is heard in the *beis medrash*, the hands of Esav will have no power. But, when the "voice of Yaacov" is absent from the *beis medrash*, the "hands of Esav" will rule. Although Yaacov proudly stated that he perfectly kept the *mitzvos* while living with Lavan for twenty years, he could not claim that he had spent this time filling the *beis medrash* with the "voice of Yaacov." Yaacov therefore *davened* that he be saved from Esav's literal upper "hand," for he knew that now was a time that the now-powerful "hands of Esav" could be used against him.

וַיָּלֶן שָׁם בַּלַּיְלָה הַהוּא ...

SO HE LODGED THERE ON THAT NIGHT...
(BEREISHIS 32:14)

Why is Yaacov's going to sleep worthy of the Torah's mention? Surely he did many other things over his day, which the Torah leaves out!

Yaacov had done what he could in terms of preparing for war with Esav. And, unlike most of us who suffer sleepless nights wondering what will be with the many problems that we face during the day, the Torah is telling us that after completing his *hishtadlus*, Yaacov was able to sleep without worry. If our *emunah* was also closer to what it should be, we too would prepare ourselves as best as possible and then sleep like a baby, knowing that the rest is in Hashem's Hands.

Interestingly, *pasuk* 22 again tells us that "וַתַּעֲבֹר הַמִּנְחָה עַל פָּנָיו וְהוּא לָן בַּלַּיְלָה הַהוּא בַּמַּחֲנֶה — so the gift passed on before him, and he lodged that night in the camp." Yaacov sent his gift to Esav, and again went to sleep peacefully. Although the confrontation that he was dreading would be tomorrow, Yaacov's incredible *bitachon* still let him sleep soundly.

עִזִּים מָאתַיִם וּתְיָשִׁים עֶשְׂרִים רְחֵלִים מָאתַיִם וְאֵילִים עֶשְׂרִים: גְּמַלִּים מֵינִיקוֹת וּבְנֵיהֶם שְׁלֹשִׁים פָּרוֹת אַרְבָּעִים וּפָרִים עֲשָׂרָה אֲתֹנֹת עֶשְׂרִים וַעְיָרִם עֲשָׂרָה:

TWO HUNDRED SHE-GOATS AND TWENTY HE-GOATS, TWO HUNDRED EWES AND TWENTY RAMS, THIRTY NURSING CAMELS WITH THEIR YOUNG, FORTY COWS AND TEN

BULLS, TWENTY SHE-DONKEYS AND TEN
HE-DONKEYS. (BEREISHIS 32:15–16)

Why does the Torah spend such length detailing the gift that Yaacov gave Esav? Also, Rashi explains that our *pasuk* is telling us that Yaacov sent the right amount of male animals needed to mate with the females. Why is this important, that the Torah makes mention of them?

Yaacov was an אִישׁ תָּם, a complete person, which means that everything that he did was one hundred percent. His gift to Esav was no exception. Let us imagine an example of an "incomplete gift," of someone giving us a present that needs batteries, but without the batteries. And, to further our frustration, we can't find any batteries in the house! Besides for the inherent problem of the giver giving an "incomplete" present, he is forcing the recipient to spend time and money to "complete" the gift and make it usable.

Yaacov was sensitive to this problem, and, as part of his lifetime *avodah* of perfection, he made sure to supply the females with the right amount of male animals, to allow his gift to be one that was perfect. This message, of Yaacov's perfection, is what the Torah is telling us in these *pesukim*.

וַיִּתֵּן בְּיַד עֲבָדָיו עֵדֶר עֵדֶר לְבַדּוֹ וַיֹּאמֶר אֶל עֲבָדָיו
עִבְרוּ לְפָנַי וְרֶוַח תָּשִׂימוּ בֵּין עֵדֶר וּבֵין עֵדֶר:

AND HE GAVE EACH HERD INTO THE HANDS
OF HIS SERVANTS INDIVIDUALLY, AND HE SAID
TO HIS SERVANTS, "PASS ON AHEAD OF ME
AND MAKE A SPACE BETWEEN ONE HERD AND
ANOTHER HERD." (BEREISHIS 32:17)

Rashi explains that the reason why Yaacov instructed his servants to be sure to make a space between each flock of animals, was "כְּדֵי לְהַשְׂבִּיעַ עֵינוֹ שֶׁל אוֹתוֹ רָשָׁע — in order to satisfy that *rasha's* eye." Why does Rashi refer to Esav as "אוֹתוֹ רָשָׁע — that *rasha*" in this context, instead of simply calling Esav by name?

Many people don't consider how their bad *middos* — their *hakpados*, their idiosyncrasies, and their need for absolute perfection under all circumstances — affect other people. Yaacov knew that he had to do whatever it took to satisfy Esav with this present. So he spent extra time, time which could have unquestionably been put to better use, arranging its presentation to make sure that Esav's greedy eye would be satisfied.

We need to be careful about what we impose on other people. Are we difficult and uncompromising? Do we make someone do it again because it is not to our complete satisfaction? Rashi is telling us that someone who causes other people to waste time and go through stress, just because *he* needs things to be just perfect, is nothing but a *rasha*.

> וַיָּקָם בַּלַּיְלָה הוּא וַיִּקַּח אֶת שְׁתֵּי נָשָׁיו וְאֶת שְׁתֵּי שִׁפְחֹתָיו וְאֶת אַחַד עָשָׂר יְלָדָיו וַיַּעֲבֹר אֵת מַעֲבַר יַבֹּק:
>
> AND HE AROSE DURING THAT NIGHT, AND HE TOOK HIS TWO WIVES AND HIS TWO MAIDSERVANTS AND HIS ELEVEN CHILDREN, AND HE CROSSED THE FORD OF THE YABOK. (BEREISHIS 32:23)

Yaacov took his eleven children across the river. But where was Dinah, his twelfth child? Rashi explains that he had hidden her in a box, so Esav would not see her and want to marry her. Yaacov was later punished for doing this, for perhaps Dinah would have guided Esav to *teshuvah*, by her later being kidnapped by Shechem.

How was Dinah's being kidnapped and violated by Shechem an appropriate *middah keneged middah* punishment for Yaacov's hiding her from Esav?

Yaacov tried to protect Dinah from Esav's influences by locking her in a box and creating a situation where they would never meet, and never have the challenge of having to deal with Esav. Hashem showed Yaacov that it was wrong to shelter Dinah from the outside world to this degree. Hashem created a situation where Dinah actually "went out," curious to see the other girls in the land, and became very vulnerable. [See below, (34:1): "וַתֵּצֵא דִינָה ... לִרְאוֹת בִּבְנוֹת הָאָרֶץ" — Dinah... went out to look about, at the daughters of the land."]

> וַיָּשֶׂם אֶת הַשְּׁפָחוֹת וְאֶת יַלְדֵיהֶן רִאשֹׁנָה וְאֶת לֵאָה וִילָדֶיהָ אַחֲרֹנִים וְאֶת רָחֵל וְאֶת יוֹסֵף אַחֲרֹנִים:
>
> AND HE PLACED THE MAIDSERVANTS AND THEIR CHILDREN FIRST AND LEAH AND HER CHILDREN AFTER THEM, AND RACHEL AND YOSEF AFTER THEM. (BEREISHIS 33:2)

Why is Yosef, unlike any of his siblings, mentioned by name in this *pasuk*?

The Torah in *Parashas Vayeitzei* (30:25) tells us that Yaacov asked Lavan for permission to return home immediately after Yosef was born, for as Rashi explains, the *navi* Ovadiah compares Yaacov to a spark and Yosef to a flame (*Ovadiah* 1:18). Yaacov understood that only he would be able to confront and defeat Esav's "house filled with straw." With this in mind, Yaacov divided up all the children by their mothers, but mentions Yosef by name, to send Esav a message that he is not to be challenged.

> וַיָּבֹא יַעֲקֹב שָׁלֵם עִיר שְׁכֶם ...
>
> AND YAACOV CAME, COMPLETE, TO THE CITY OF SHECHEM... (BEREISHIS 33:18)

Rashi explains that Yaacov was indeed "שָׁלֵם — complete" in all areas. He was physically complete, for his hip injury had been healed. He was complete in his wealth, for he was not at all lacking even after having given Esav a tremendous present. Finally, he was complete in his Torah learning, for he had not forgotten any of his Torah while in Lavan's house.

How could Yaacov have possibly been "שָׁלֵם בְּמָמוֹנוֹ — complete in his wealth"? He gave many, many animals to Esav; they were gone!

Yaacov was "שָׁלֵם בְּמָמוֹנוֹ — complete in his wealth" because he did not feel that he had lost out from his tremendous largesse. He felt complete with his wealth after the gift, as much as he did before. Yaacov in fact told this to Esav, "כִּי חַנַּנִי אֱלֹקִים וְכִי יֶשׁ לִי כֹל — For Hashem has favored me, for I have everything."

> וַתֵּצֵא דִינָה בַת לֵאָה אֲשֶׁר יָלְדָה לְיַעֲקֹב לִרְאוֹת בִּבְנוֹת הָאָרֶץ:
>
> DINAH, THE DAUGHTER OF LEAH, WHOM SHE HAD BORNE TO YAACOV, WENT OUT TO LOOK ABOUT, AT THE DAUGHTERS OF THE LAND. (BEREISHIS 34:1)

The Torah here refers to Dinah as "Leah's daughter." Rashi explains that their relationship is mentioned because Dinah, in "going out" to see the daughters of the land, had acted like her mother Leah, who the Torah had said (30:16) had "gone out" to meet Yaacov on his way home from work.

What is the comparison? Dinah "went out" for wrongful, or at least non-productive, reasons. Leah "went out" to meet her husband, in her wanting to give birth to more of the twelve *Shevatim*!

While Leah had good intentions, "going out" to meet Yaacov may have been slightly immodest for a person of her stature. Once Leah "established" that "going out" is something that is acceptable, Dinah, her daughter, picked up on it and did the same, even without the same good reason.

> וַיֹּאמֶר יַעֲקֹב אֶל שִׁמְעוֹן וְאֶל לֵוִי עֲכַרְתֶּם אֹתִי ...
>
> YAACOV SAID TO SHIMON AND TO LEVI, "YOU HAVE TROUBLED ME..." (BEREISHIS 34:30)

Why does the Torah describe Yaacov's statement as being "אֶל שִׁמְעוֹן וְאֶל לֵוִי — to Shimon and to Levi," instead of "אֶל שִׁמְעוֹן וְלֵוִי — to Shimon and Levi," as is generally the case when multiple people are being addressed?

The Torah is telling us that Yaacov addressed Shimon and Levi each as individuals, and was holding each of them equally responsible for what happened. Had the *pasuk* said "אֶל שִׁמְעוֹן וְלֵוִי — to Shimon and Levi," — putting them together — we may have understood that Shimon was more accountable, for he was older, or because he was called by Yaacov first. Speaking to both of them as individuals shows us they were equally accountable.

> וַיְהִי בִּשְׁכֹּן יִשְׂרָאֵל בָּאָרֶץ הַהִוא וַיֵּלֶךְ רְאוּבֵן
> וַיִּשְׁכַּב אֶת בִּלְהָה פִּילֶגֶשׁ אָבִיו וַיִּשְׁמַע יִשְׂרָאֵל
> וַיִּהְיוּ בְנֵי יַעֲקֹב שְׁנֵים עָשָׂר:
>
> AND IT CAME TO PASS WHEN YISRAEL
> SOJOURNED IN THAT LAND, AND REUVEN
> WENT, AND HE LAY WITH BILHAH, HIS
> FATHER'S CONCUBINE, AND YISRAEL HEARD
> OF IT, AND THE SONS OF YAACOV WERE
> TWELVE. (BEREISHIS 35:22)

Why do the words "וַיִּשְׁכַּב אֶת בִּלְהָה פִּילֶגֶשׁ אָבִיו — and he lay with Bilhah, his father's concubine," have two sets of *trop*? Also, this *pasuk* is written in a *Sefer Torah* with a very wide space in the middle, which is denoted in our *Chumashim* with a letter פ. Why?

Rashi explains that Reuven did not actually do anything physically inappropriate with his father's wife. He only moved Yaacov's bed from Bilhah's tent into his mother's. The extra *trop* and uncommon space show us that this *pasuk* is not meant to be read at face value. We must read between the lines, because something else is going on beyond what the *pasuk* overtly says.

Vayeishev
וַיֵּשֶׁב

> וַיִּרְאוּ אֶחָיו כִּי אֹתוֹ אָהַב אֲבִיהֶם מִכָּל אֶחָיו וַיִּשְׂנְאוּ אֹתוֹ וְלֹא יָכְלוּ דַּבְּרוֹ לְשָׁלֹם:
>
> AND HIS BROTHERS SAW THAT THEIR FATHER LOVED HIM MORE THAN ALL HIS BROTHERS, SO THEY HATED HIM, AND THEY WERE UNABLE TO SPEAK WITH HIM PEACEFULLY. (BEREISHIS 37:4)

Why does the Torah use the expression "וְלֹא יָכְלוּ דַּבְּרוֹ לְשָׁלֹם," which literally means "they were unable to speak to him *to peace*." Wouldn't "וְלֹא יָכְלוּ דַּבְּרוֹ בְּשָׁלֹם" — and they were unable to speak to him *with peace*" make more sense?

The Gemara (*Berachos* 64a) advises how a person should take leave of another person. He should not say "לֵךְ בְּשָׁלוֹם," for we find that David told Avshalom "לֵךְ בְּשָׁלוֹם," and Avshalom was hanged shortly thereafter. Rather, a person should tell his friend "לֵךְ לְשָׁלוֹם," like Yisro told Moshe, who soon became the leader of the Jewish people.

The *Shevatim* hated Yosef so much that "וְלֹא יָכְלוּ דַּבְּרוֹ לְשָׁלֹם"; they were unable to speak nicely to him and bless him, by telling him "לֵךְ לְשָׁלוֹם" when they parted ways. They could only tell him "לֵךְ בְּשָׁלוֹם."

> וַיִּרְאוּ אֶחָיו כִּי אֹתוֹ אָהַב אֲבִיהֶם מִכָּל אֶחָיו וַיִּשְׂנְאוּ אֹתוֹ ... וַיַּחֲלֹם יוֹסֵף חֲלוֹם וַיַּגֵּד לְאֶחָיו וַיּוֹסִפוּ עוֹד שְׂנֹא אֹתוֹ ... וַיֹּאמְרוּ לוֹ אֶחָיו הֲמָלֹךְ תִּמְלֹךְ עָלֵינוּ אִם מָשׁוֹל תִּמְשֹׁל בָּנוּ וַיּוֹסִפוּ עוֹד שְׂנֹא אֹתוֹ ... וַיַּחֲלֹם עוֹד חֲלוֹם אַחֵר ... וַיִּגְעַר בּוֹ אָבִיו ... וַיְקַנְאוּ בוֹ אֶחָיו וְאָבִיו שָׁמַר אֶת הַדָּבָר:
>
> AND HIS BROTHERS SAW THAT THEIR FATHER LOVED HIM MORE THAN ALL HIS BROTHERS, SO THEY HATED HIM... AND YOSEF DREAMED A DREAM AND TOLD HIS BROTHERS, AND THEY CONTINUED TO HATE HIM... SO HIS BROTHERS SAID TO HIM, "WILL YOU REIGN OVER US, OR WILL YOU GOVERN US?" AND THEY CONTINUED FURTHER TO HATE HIM... AND HE AGAIN DREAMED ANOTHER DREAM... AND HIS FATHER REBUKED HIM... SO HIS BROTHERS ENVIED HIM, BUT HIS FATHER AWAITED THE MATTER. (BEREISHIS 37:4–5,8,10,11)

The Torah tells us several times that Yosef's brother's hated him, and hated him even more. Yet in *pasuk* 11, after Yaacov got upset with Yosef and understood Yosef's dreams in a way that was similar to how the *Shevatim* had understood it, we are told that the brothers were jealous. Was their jealousy in addition to their hatred, or did it replace their hatred?

When we look at Yosef's two dreams closely, we see that he essentially dreamt the same dream twice, but with different subjects; the sun and the moon instead of sheaves of wheat. This repetition indicates (as Yosef told Pharaoh in *Parashas Mikeitz* 41:32) that the message that the dreams were saying would soon be fulfilled. Perhaps the brothers understood this as well, and now understood the reason for Yosef's previous behavior towards them, and the favoritism that

Yaacov had shown towards Yosef. At this point, their hatred metamorphosed into jealousy.

> וְעַתָּה לְכוּ וְנַהַרְגֵהוּ וְנַשְׁלִכֵהוּ בְּאַחַד הַבֹּרוֹת ...
> וַיֹּאמֶר אֲלֵהֶם רְאוּבֵן אַל תִּשְׁפְּכוּ דָם הַשְׁלִיכוּ אֹתוֹ
> אֶל הַבּוֹר הַזֶּה אֲשֶׁר בַּמִּדְבָּר ...

> SO NOW, LET US KILL HIM, AND WE WILL CAST
> HIM INTO ONE OF THE PITS... AND REUVEN
> SAID TO THEM, "DO NOT SHED BLOOD! CAST
> HIM INTO THIS PIT WHICH IS IN THE DESERT ..."
> (BEREISHIS 37:20,22)

When the *Shevatim* wanted to kill Yosef and throw his body into a pit, they were not particular about which pit they would use. Yet, when Reuven suggests that they not be the ones to kill him, but instead cast him into a pit and leave him to die in the desert, he specified that we throw him into "this pit." Why couldn't they have left Yosef to die in any of the many pits in the desert? What was specific about this one?

Reuven had suggested that the *Shevatim* leave Yosef to die instead of actively killing him because he planned on coming back to save Yosef after the others had left. He thus suggested "this pit," so he would know where Yosef was. Had the brothers just thrown Yosef into just any pit in the desert, Reuven would not be able to find him.

> וַיֵּשְׁבוּ לֶאֱכָל לֶחֶם וַיִּשְׂאוּ עֵינֵיהֶם וַיִּרְאוּ וְהִנֵּה
> אֹרְחַת יִשְׁמְעֵאלִים בָּאָה מִגִּלְעָד וּגְמַלֵּיהֶם נֹשְׂאִים
> נְכֹאת וּצְרִי וָלֹט הוֹלְכִים לְהוֹרִיד מִצְרָיְמָה:

> AND THEY SAT DOWN TO EAT A MEAL, AND THEY
> LIFTED THEIR EYES AND SAW, AND BEHOLD, A
> CARAVAN OF YISHMAELITES WAS COMING FROM
> GILEAD, AND THEIR CAMELS WERE CARRYING

> SPICES, BALM, AND LOTUS, GOING TO TAKE IT
> DOWN TO MITZRAYIM. (BEREISHIS 37:25)

Rashi explains that the caravans traveling through the desert usually transported foul-smelling merchandise like kerosene and tar. Hashem made this particular caravan who took Yosef carry good-smelling spices, in order to make the journey to Mitzrayim more pleasant for Yosef the *Tzadik*.

Even when a *tzadik* has to go through a rough time, there is a lot that we can learn from the way he is treated. Hashem gave Yosef the "gift" of not having to suffer a bad smell on the way to Mitzrayim. Similarly, we find that Moshe, as an infant in a basket in the Nile, didn't have to deal with a bad smell, either. Noach, on the other hand, did. [See Rashi to *Bereishis* 6:4.] It would seem that although he was a *tzadik*, he wasn't quite on the level to merit this extra-special treatment.

We find a similar idea in the *Midbar*, when the Jewish people collected their portion of *Mahn* each day. The righteous received their quota at their doorstep, the middle of the road people had to walk a bit to find their portion, and the *resha'im* had to go *shlep* even farther for their food. This shows us that Hashem provides us with many ways of gauging where our relationship with Him is holding. We just have to open our eyes a bit. Beyond seeing the general story of what happens to us, we need to appreciate the details of when things go just a little bit easier or more pleasant.

> וַיְשַׁלְּחוּ אֶת כְּתֹנֶת הַפַּסִּים וַיָּבִיאוּ אֶל אֲבִיהֶם וַיֹּאמְרוּ זֹאת מָצָאנוּ הַכֶּר נָא הַכְּתֹנֶת בִּנְךָ הִוא אִם לֹא:
>
> AND THEY SENT THE FINE COAT, AND THEY
> BROUGHT IT TO THEIR FATHER, AND THEY
> SAID, "WE HAVE FOUND THIS; NOW RECOGNIZE
> WHETHER IT IS YOUR SON'S COAT OR NOT."
> (BEREISHIS 37:32)

The *Shevatim* of course knew that this torn and bloodied coat belonged to Yosef. Why then did they give it to Yaacov and ask him if he recognized it?

It would appear that the *Shevatim* wanted Yaacov to think that Yosef had been torn to death by a wild animal, but did not want to actually tell a lie. So, they set up the situation in a way that Yaacov would draw his own conclusions. It would further appear that they learned this approach from Yaacov himself, from when he went in to "steal" the *berachos* from Yitzchak. When Yitzchak asked him who he was, Yaacov did not directly answer, but instead said "אָנֹכִי, עֵשָׂו בְּכֹרֶךָ" — I, Esav is your firstborn," with a pause after "I," which, explains Rashi, could also be understood "I am the one who is bringing this food. And, Esav is your firstborn." Similarly, Yaacov covered his arms with hairy goatskin, so Yitzchak would think he was Esav without Yaacov actually having to tell him, and compromise speaking only the truth. In the same way, the brothers did not want to lie, and acted like Yaacov by letting him draw his own conclusions from what they put in front of him.

וַתִּתְפְּשֵׂהוּ בְּבִגְדוֹ לֵאמֹר שִׁכְבָה עִמִּי וַיַּעֲזֹב בִּגְדוֹ
בְּיָדָהּ וַיָּנָס וַיֵּצֵא הַחוּצָה:

SO SHE GRABBED HIM BY HIS GARMENT, SAYING, "LIE WITH ME!" BUT HE LEFT HIS GARMENT IN HER HAND AND FLED AND WENT OUTSIDE. (BEREISHIS 39:12)

Why does the Torah use the dual expression of "וַיָּנָס" — he fled" and "וַיֵּצֵא הַחוּצָה — he went outside"?

A story is told about an elderly *talmid chacham* who suddenly found himself alone in a room with an older woman who was not particularly attractive. When he realized what had happened, he bolted out the door, literally as if there was a fire in the house. People later asked him why the rush; he is old, and she was unattractive. He answered that the *Yetzer Hara* is very capable; he can make me young, and her attractive.

This insight is all the more true by Yosef, who was young, and Potifar's wife, who was very attractive. Yosef knew that the only way to withstand the temptation was to leave his cloak in her hands and literally run out as quickly as he could. This hasty and immediate flight from the room is what the Torah is describing in using this dual expression.

וְהִנֵּה אֹרְחַת יִשְׁמְעֵאלִים ... נְשֹׂאִים נְכֹאת וּצְרִי וָלֹט הוֹלְכִים לְהוֹרִיד מִצְרָיְמָה:
וַיַּפְקִדֵהוּ עַל בֵּיתוֹ וְכָל יֶשׁ לוֹ נָתַן בְּיָדוֹ...
וַיִּתֵּן שַׂר בֵּית הַסֹּהַר בְּיַד יוֹסֵף אֵת כָּל הָאֲסִירִם אֲשֶׁר בְּבֵית הַסֹּהַר...

BEHOLD, A CARAVAN OF YISHMAELITES WAS COMING ... CARRYING SPICES, BALM, AND LOTUS, GOING TO TAKE IT DOWN TO MITZRAYIM. (BEREISHIS 37:25)
POTIFAR APPOINTED HIM OVER HIS HOUSE, AND ALL HE HAD HE GAVE INTO HIS HAND. (BEREISHIS 39:4)
THE PRISON WARDEN PLACED ALL THE PRISONERS WHO WERE IN THE PRISON INTO YOSEF'S HAND... (BEREISHIS 39:22)

Yosef was sold to a caravan of traveling Arabs, sold as a slave upon reaching Mitzrayim, and put in jail shortly thereafter. At the same time, we find that whenever Yosef found himself at the bottom, he was always "at the top of the bottom." Hashem wanted that Yosef be brought to Mitzrayim, and sent him in a sweet-smelling caravan instead of a wagon filled with pitch. When Hashem's plan was for Yosef to work in Potifar's house, he didn't clean the stables, but was instead made his chief of staff. When Yosef was supposed to be in jail, he was also put in charge.

Yosef is our first exposure to *galus*. Much of our *galus* has been horrible to the Jewish people. We have been sold and enslaved, imprisoned and killed. Yet, right now, we thankfully live in great comfort, and relative wealth. The kindnesses that Hashem showed Yosef throughout his many ordeals remind us that the fact that things are going our way, and may even be pleasant, doesn't mean that we are not "imprisoned." A *mashal* to this idea is a prisoner in a white-collar prison without bars on the windows, who would be foolish to think that the fact that he is not surrounded by bars means that he is a free man. Just like Yosef understood that he was in Mitzrayim away from his family even when he was relatively comfortable, we must remember that the relative comfort that we enjoy doesn't mean that things around us are how they are really supposed to be. Right now, the Jewish people are in a comfortable, white-collar prison.

Mikeitz
מִקֵּץ

וַתֹּאכַלְנָה הַפָּרוֹת ... וַתִּבְלַעְנָה הַשִּׁבֳּלִים ...
The cows ate... the stalks of grain swallowed up... (Bereishis 41:4,7)

The Torah uses different terminologies when discussing Pharaoh's dreams. In the first we are told "וַתֹּאכַלְנָה הַפָּרוֹת" — the cows *ate*," and in the second "וַתִּבְלַעְנָה הַשִּׁבֳּלִים" — the ears of grain *swallowed up*." Why the difference?

Cows eat, and stalks of grain typically absorb — that is to say, they "swallow within themselves" — water and sunlight. The Torah thus uses the term specific to each object when discussing how they brought other objects into their bodies in Pharaoh's dreams.

וְשָׁם אִתָּנוּ נַעַר עִבְרִי עֶבֶד לְשַׂר הַטַּבָּחִים וַנְּסַפֶּר לוֹ וַיִּפְתָּר לָנוּ אֶת חֲלֹמֹתֵינוּ אִישׁ כַּחֲלֹמוֹ פָּתָר:
And there with us was a Hebrew lad, a slave of the chief slaughterer, and we told him, and he interpreted our dreams for us; for each of us, he interpreted according to his dream. (Bereishis 41:12)

Rashi points out that the *Sar HaMashkim* spoke disparagingly of Yosef in every way possible. He is a lad, that is to say, a fool unworthy of greatness. He is a Hebrew who doesn't even understand our language, and is a slave who may not become a ruler in Mitzrayim nor even wear royal garb. Why all this slander? Why did the *Sar HaMashkim* speak badly of Yosef to Pharaoh when he knew that Yosef, who had correctly interpreted his dream, was in fact incredibly capable?

One answer to this question is as Rabbi Wein famously says, that no good deed goes unpunished. The sense of being indebted to another person is so uncomfortable, that the recipient will often do whatever they can to discredit the person who helped them, so they no longer feel beholden.

A second approach is that the *Sar HaMashkim* was scared of what Yosef would do to him if he became ruler of Mitzrayim. We know from the end of the previous *parashah* that Yosef had asked the *Sar HaMashkim* to remember him by putting a good word in for him when he returned to the royal palace. The *Sar HaMashkim* did not, and instead quickly put all of the good that Yosef had done for him out of his mind. Now, two years later, when the *Sar HaMashkim* saw that no one else could interpret Pharaoh's dream, he realized that he had to tell the king about Yosef. He knew that Yosef would successfully interpret Pharaoh's dream, and would also be rewarded for doing so. But, he also knew that he was supposed to have mentioned Yosef two years earlier. The *Sar HaMashkim* was thus scared that Yosef would take revenge on him as soon as he would rise to a position of power. As an attempt to avoid that, the *Sar HaMashkim* kept playing down Yosef's importance, and reminded Pharaoh about his inability to rule to make sure that despite any accurate interpretation Yosef may offer, he could never be raised to a position of prominence.

> וְקָמוּ שֶׁבַע שְׁנֵי רָעָב אַחֲרֵיהֶן וְנִשְׁכַּח כָּל הַשָּׂבָע בְּאֶרֶץ מִצְרָיִם וְכִלָּה הָרָעָב אֶת הָאָרֶץ: וְלֹא יִוָּדַע הַשָּׂבָע בָּאָרֶץ מִפְּנֵי הָרָעָב הַהוּא אַחֲרֵי כֵן כִּי כָבֵד הוּא מְאֹד:
>
> AND SEVEN YEARS OF FAMINE WILL ARISE AFTER THEM, AND ALL THE PLENTY WILL BE FORGOTTEN IN THE LAND OF MITZRAYIM, AND THE FAMINE WILL DESTROY THE LAND. AND THE PLENTY WILL NOT BE KNOWN BECAUSE OF THAT FAMINE THAT FOLLOWS, FOR IT WILL BE VERY SEVERE. (BEREISHIS 41:30–31)

What does "וְלֹא יִוָּדַע הַשָּׂבָע בָּאָרֶץ מִפְּנֵי הָרָעָב הַהוּא אַחֲרֵי כֵן — the plenty will not be known because of that famine that follows" add to the phrase "וְנִשְׁכַּח כָּל הַשָּׂבָע בְּאֶרֶץ מִצְרָיִם — all the plenty will be forgotten in the land of Mitzrayim"? When a wealthy person loses his fortune, the memories of his former wealth remain. He can dream that he will regain his affluence, or, even if this is unlikely, fondly reminisce with happy memories when he thinks about the pleasant experiences of the good old days. Someone who was always poor, however, cannot even do this, for he has no memories of ever being well-to-do. Yosef told Pharaoh that not only will the actual plenty be a thing of the past — "will be forgotten" — but it will not "even be known"; the famine's intensity will be so severe and overpowering, that even the good memories of those times will be forgotten as well.

> וַיִּקְרָא פַרְעֹה שֵׁם יוֹסֵף צָפְנַת פַּעְנֵחַ וַיִּתֶּן לוֹ אֶת אָסְנַת בַּת פּוֹטִי פֶרַע כֹּהֵן אֹן לְאִשָּׁה וַיֵּצֵא יוֹסֵף עַל אֶרֶץ מִצְרָיִם:
>
> AND PHARAOH NAMED YOSEF "TZOFNAS PANEACH," AND HE GAVE HIM ASNAS THE

> DAUGHTER OF POTI PHERA, THE GOVERNOR OF ON, AS A WIFE, AND YOSEF WENT FORTH OVER THE LAND OF MITZRAYIM. (BEREISHIS 41:45)

If Pharaoh just changed Yosef's name to "Tzofnas Paneach," why does the end of the *pasuk* say "וַיֵּצֵא יוֹסֵף — *Yosef* went forth"? Furthermore, we see in subsequent *pesukim* (*pasuk* 55) that Pharaoh himself did not use the new name he gave Yosef, but continued calling him Yosef as well!

We know that the Jewish people in Mitzrayim did not change three things; their language, dress, and names. Perhaps Pharaoh's first step at assimilating Yosef into Egyptian society was to give him a new name. And, in stating "וַיֵּצֵא יוֹסֵף — *Yosef* went forth," we see that Yosef resisted this new name from the beginning. So much so, that even Pharaoh dropped this idea, and reverted to calling him Yosef. It is most certain that Yosef's extra fortitude in this area enabled the rest of the B'nei Yisrael to follow suit shortly thereafter for our entire stay in Mitzrayim.

We may understand a different answer to this question from Rashi's comment to *Divrei Hayamim II* 36:4, (brought in *Mosif Rashi*), that the purpose of naming Yosef was only to show that total power, to the extent that he could even rename a person. This being the case, it follows that this extra name was not meant to be actually used.

> וַיֹּאמֶר אֲלֵהֶם יַעֲקֹב אֲבִיהֶם אֹתִי שִׁכַּלְתֶּם יוֹסֵף אֵינֶנּוּ וְשִׁמְעוֹן אֵינֶנּוּ וְאֶת בִּנְיָמִן תִּקָּחוּ עָלַי הָיוּ כֻלָּנָה:
>
> AND THEIR FATHER YAACOV SAID TO THEM, "YOU HAVE BEREAVED ME — YOSEF IS GONE, AND SHIMON IS GONE, AND YOU WANT TO TAKE BINYAMIN! ALL THESE TROUBLES HAVE COME UPON ME!" (BEREISHIS 42:36)

Yaacov tells his sons that not only has he lost Yosef and Shimon, how could they possibly take Binyamin also, and concludes by saying "עָלַי הָיוּ כֻלָּנָה — All these troubles have come upon me!"

In *Parashas Toldos* (27:13), the Vilna Gaon famously explains that when Rivkah told Yaacov that he need not be afraid of Yitzchak cursing him, because "עָלַי קִלְלָתְךָ בְּנִי," the word עָלַי is the *roshei teivos* for עֵשָׂיו, לָבָן, יוֹסֵף; you need not be concerned about harm from any area other than these three.

Perhaps Yaacov was telling his sons this *remez* when he refused to send Binyamin with them to Mitzrayim. I know that I am only supposed to be challenged with Esav, Lavan, and Yosef. But I now see that I am having troubles with Shimon, and now you want Binyamin, as well. This should not be happening. Since this, said Yaacov, is not part of the plan, there is no reason why I should allow Binyamin to go along with you.

> וַיֹּאמֶר רְאוּבֵן אֶל אָבִיו לֵאמֹר אֶת שְׁנֵי בָנַי תָּמִית אִם לֹא אֲבִיאֶנּוּ אֵלֶיךָ תְּנָה אֹתוֹ עַל יָדִי וַאֲנִי אֲשִׁיבֶנּוּ אֵלֶיךָ:
>
> AND REUVEN SPOKE TO HIS FATHER, SAYING, "YOU MAY PUT MY TWO SONS TO DEATH IF I DON'T BRING BINYAMIN TO YOU. PUT HIM INTO MY HANDS AND I WILL RETURN HIM TO YOU."
>
> (BEREISHIS 42:37)

> וַיֹּאמֶר יְהוּדָה אֶל יִשְׂרָאֵל אָבִיו שִׁלְחָה הַנַּעַר אִתִּי וְנָקוּמָה וְנֵלֵכָה וְנִחְיֶה וְלֹא נָמוּת גַּם אֲנַחְנוּ גַם אַתָּה גַּם טַפֵּנוּ:
>
> AND YEHUDAH SAID TO YISRAEL, HIS FATHER, "SEND THE LAD WITH ME, AND WE WILL GET UP AND GO, AND WE WILL LIVE AND NOT DIE, BOTH WE AND YOU AND ALSO OUR YOUNG CHILDREN."
>
> (BEREISHIS 43:8)

Reuven and Yehudah offered to take responsibility for Binyamin, to convince Yaacov to agree that the brothers could take him to Mitzrayim. Why were Reuven and Yehudah the only *Shevatim* who offered?

Reuven and Yehudah were the two brothers who played the biggest role in *Mechiras Yosef*. It was Reuven's idea to put Yosef in the pit, which led to his being sold, and Yehudah was the one who actually had the idea to sell him. It would also seem that Reuven, as the *bechor*, and Yehudah, as the *Melech*, were also the most culpable for a different reason, for they could have convinced the other brothers to stop how they were acting towards Yosef, had they wanted to do so. These two brothers thus offered the most responsibility with Binyamin, as a way to atone for the lack of responsibility that they had previously shown towards Yosef.

VAYIGASH

וַנֹּאמֶר אֶל אֲדֹנִי יֶשׁ לָנוּ אָב זָקֵן וְיֶלֶד זְקֻנִים קָטָן וְאָחִיו מֵת וַיִּוָּתֵר הוּא לְבַדּוֹ לְאִמּוֹ וְאָבִיו אֲהֵבוֹ:

AND WE SAID TO MY MASTER, "WE HAVE AN OLD FATHER AND A YOUNG CHILD OF HIS OLD AGE, AND HIS BROTHER IS DEAD, AND HE IS LEFT ALONE OF HIS MOTHER, AND HIS FATHER LOVES HIM." (BEREISHIS 44:20)

Yehudah told Yosef that "his brother is dead," which of course he did not know to be the case. Rashi explains that the fear that Yehudah felt caused him to say something that wasn't true. Yehudah was afraid that if he were to tell Yosef that this other brother is still alive, Yosef would have demanded that he too be brought before him.

Yehudah's saying that this brother was dead would have been a perfect opportunity for Yosef to interrogate him about what he had said, as he had done with every statement the brothers had made until this point. Why did Yosef hold back?

Yosef had already seen the *mesiras nefesh* that Yehudah had for Binyamin, and the genuine remorse that he felt over selling Yosef. He didn't need to do any more.

וַיֹּאמֶר יוֹסֵף אֶל אֶחָיו אֲנִי יוֹסֵף הַעוֹד אָבִי חָי ...

AND YOSEF SAID TO HIS BROTHERS, "I AM YOSEF. IS MY FATHER STILL ALIVE?"... (BEREISHIS 45:3)

Why did Yosef ask the brothers if his father was still alive, after Yehudah had just mentioned their father several *pesukim* earlier?

Yosef was not asking his brothers if Yaacov was still alive, physically. His question to them was, "Is *my* father still alive?" Is our father the same father as I left him many years ago, or has he changed into an altogether different person?

Yaacov had a very similar reaction when the *Shevatim* returned and told him that Yosef is still alive, and is the ruler of Mitzrayim. Yaacov, the Torah tells us, refused to believe them (45:26). Only when he saw the wagons that Yosef had sent) did Yaacov accept this good news (45: 27). When Yaacov was first told that Yosef was found and is the ruler of Mitzrayim, he couldn't believe that this is the same Yosef whom he knew many years earlier. Only after seeing the wagons, which alluded to the last *sugya* of *eglah arufah* that they had learned together, did Yaacov rejoice. The wagons showed Yaacov that Yosef had not at all slipped in his *avodas Hashem*, and he now realized that his Yosef was indeed still alive.

וְהַקֹּל נִשְׁמַע בֵּית פַּרְעֹה לֵאמֹר בָּאוּ אֲחֵי יוֹסֵף וַיִּיטַב בְּעֵינֵי פַרְעֹה וּבְעֵינֵי עֲבָדָיו:

AND THE VOICE WAS HEARD IN PHARAOH'S HOUSE, SAYING, "YOSEF'S BROTHERS HAVE COME!" AND IT PLEASED PHARAOH AND HIS SERVANTS. (BEREISHIS 45:16)

Why were Pharaoh and his servants pleased that Yosef's family had arrived? What did they care?

We know that in Mitzrayim, a slave was not allowed to rule (Rashi 41:12). When the Egyptians heard that Yosef's brothers came and saw who they were, they realized that although Yosef may have once been sold, he was in truth far from a slave, and in fact came from a very distinguished background. Instead of feeling guilty about bending their laws to allow Yosef to rule, they were now secure in their viceroy, and his legitimacy.[13]

קְנֵה אֹתָנוּ וְאֶת אַדְמָתֵנוּ בַּלָּחֶם ... וְתֶן זֶרַע
Buy us and our farmland for food... and give us seed... (Bereishis 47:19)

What good would giving seeds to the people accomplish, asks Rashi. When Yosef sent word to Yaacov to join him in Mitzrayim, he had told him that, as part of the famine, "כִּי זֶה שְׁנָתַיִם הָרָעָב בְּקֶרֶב הָאָרֶץ וְעוֹד חָמֵשׁ שָׁנִים אֲשֶׁר אֵין חָרִישׁ וְקָצִיר — For already two years of famine have passed in the midst of the land, and there will be neither plowing nor harvest for another five years." What use are seeds if farming is impossible?

In answer, Rashi explains that indeed, another five years of famine remained. But, when Yaacov came to Mitzrayim, the famine miraculously stopped in his merit. These five years of famine did not occur until after Yaacov's death (see Ramban to 47:18).

Why wasn't this break in the famine a fallacy in Yosef's interpretation of Pharaoh's dream? Yosef had said that there would be seven years of plenty followed by seven years of famine!

When describing Pharaoh's dreams, the Torah tells us "וַתֹּאכַלְנָה הַפָּרוֹת רָעוֹת הַמַּרְאֶה וְדַקֹּת הַבָּשָׂר ... וַיִּיקַץ פַּרְעֹה, וַיִּישַׁן וַיַּחֲלֹם שֵׁנִית... — The cows of ugly appearance and lean of flesh devoured ... then Pharaoh awoke. And he fell asleep and dreamed again..." (41:4). What does Pharaoh's awakening in the middle of his dreams represent?

Perhaps this break in the dreams indicates a break in their actualization. While most of the dream would soon come true, and the years of plenty followed by the first years of hunger began almost immediately, this break tells us that some years of famine would in fact be delayed.

---

13 I later saw this approach in the Ramban and in the *Ohr Hachaim*.

VAYECHI
וַיְחִי

וַיִּקְרְבוּ יְמֵי יִשְׂרָאֵל לָמוּת וַיִּקְרָא לִבְנוֹ לְיוֹסֵף וַיֹּאמֶר לוֹ ... אַל נָא תִקְבְּרֵנִי בְּמִצְרָיִם:

WHEN THE TIME DREW NEAR FOR YISRAEL TO DIE, HE CALLED HIS SON YOSEF AND SAID TO HIM ... "PLEASE DO NOT BURY ME IN MITZRAYIM."

(BEREISHIS 48:29)

Rashi explains that Yaacov turned to Yosef to make sure that he was buried in Eretz Yisrael because as the Egyptian viceroy he would be able to get this job done.

Rashi is telling us that we should not think that Yaacov's turning to Yosef to assign him with the mission of burying him came from favoritism, that he preferred that specifically he, and not the other brothers, bury him. Rather, says Rashi, the only reason that Yaacov asked Yosef to do this was because it was the most effective way to get the job done.

Keeping this in mind can be a lesson for us as well, when it seems that we are being passed over for a job that we know that we can do just as well as the person who was ultimately chosen. Very often, the reason why one person was chosen over another is not a question of better or worse, but simply because the person making the decision is more comfortable with his choice; in that he knows the job will get done the particular way that he wants.

> וַיִּקְרְבוּ יְמֵי יִשְׂרָאֵל לָמוּת וַיִּקְרָא לִבְנוֹ לְיוֹסֵף וַיֹּאמֶר לוֹ אִם נָא מָצָאתִי חֵן בְּעֵינֶיךָ שִׂים נָא יָדְךָ תַּחַת יְרֵכִי וְעָשִׂיתָ עִמָּדִי חֶסֶד וֶאֱמֶת אַל נָא תִקְבְּרֵנִי בְּמִצְרָיִם: וְשָׁכַבְתִּי עִם אֲבֹתַי וּנְשָׂאתַנִי מִמִּצְרַיִם וּקְבַרְתַּנִי בִּקְבֻרָתָם וַיֹּאמַר אָנֹכִי אֶעֱשֶׂה כִדְבָרֶךָ:

> WHEN THE TIME DREW NEAR FOR YISRAEL TO DIE, HE CALLED HIS SON YOSEF AND SAID TO HIM … "PLEASE DO NOT BURY ME IN MITZRAYIM. I WILL LIE WITH MY FOREFATHERS, AND YOU SHALL CARRY ME OUT OF MITZRAYIM, AND YOU SHALL BURY ME IN THEIR GRAVE." AND HE SAID, "I WILL DO AS YOU SAY." (BEREISHIS 47:29-30)

Yaacov made Yosef swear that he would not be buried in Mitzrayim, and that he would be buried in Eretz Yisrael with his forefathers in the *Me'aras HaMachpelah*. Why did Yaacov need to specifically mention that he not be buried in Mitzrayim? His being buried in *Me'aras HaMachpelah* meant that he wouldn't be in Mitzrayim. Why state it overtly?

Rashi tells us three reasons why Yaacov didn't want to be buried in Mitzrayim. He knew that the ground would turn into lice during *Makas Kinim*, irritating his body. Also people buried in *Chutz La'Aretz* will have to painfully roll to Eretz Yisrael to achieve *Techiyas HaMesim*. And finally, he did not want the Egyptians to make him into a god, which would have happened had he been buried there. These three reasons are reasons why Yaacov specifically did not want to be buried in Mitzrayim. Because Yaacov had reasons to *not* be buried in Mitzrayim, and reasons to *be* buried in Eretz Yisrael — to be with his forefathers — asking Yosef to bury him in Eretz Yisrael would not have told him the entire story. Yaacov therefore asked Yosef to *not* bury him in Mitzrayim, and to bury him in *Me'aras HaMachpelah*.

וַיַּרְא יִשְׂרָאֵל אֶת בְּנֵי יוֹסֵף וַיֹּאמֶר מִי אֵלֶּה: וַיֹּאמֶר
יוֹסֵף אֶל אָבִיו בָּנַי הֵם אֲשֶׁר נָתַן לִי אֱלֹקִים בָּזֶה
וַיֹּאמַר קָחֶם נָא אֵלַי וַאֲבָרֲכֵם:

THEN YISRAEL SAW YOSEF'S SONS, AND HE SAID, "WHO ARE THESE?" YOSEF SAID TO HIS FATHER, "THEY ARE MY SONS, WHOM HASHEM GAVE ME HERE." SO HE SAID, "NOW BRING THEM NEAR TO ME, SO THAT I MAY BLESS THEM." (BEREISHIS 48:8–9)

Rashi explains that Yaacov felt the Shechinah leaving him as he was about to bless Yosef's children, for he foresaw that *resha'im* would eventually be born from them. Who are these people who will conceive evildoers, he asked Yosef, who are not worthy of my blessing? Yosef answered that they are my children, and showed Yaacov his *kesuvah*. How did showing his father his *kesuvah* qualify his sons for a *berachah*?

Yosef did not need to search back too far to find *resha'im* in Yaacov's family; his brother Esav and uncle Yishmael. Yet, Hashem still blessed their fathers, Yitzchak and Avraham. Perhaps Yosef's showing Yaacov his own *kesuvah*, which showed that his marriage was perfect, and in fact included his father Yaacov's name, was a reminder that unworthy descendants do not invalidate their parents and grandparents, who are still worthy to receive a *berachah* on their own accord.

וַיַּרְא יִשְׂרָאֵל אֶת בְּנֵי יוֹסֵף וַיֹּאמֶר מִי אֵלֶּה: וַיֹּאמֶר
יוֹסֵף אֶל אָבִיו בָּנַי הֵם אֲשֶׁר נָתַן לִי אֱלֹקִים בָּזֶה
וַיֹּאמַר קָחֶם נָא אֵלַי וַאֲבָרֲכֵם:

THEN YISRAEL SAW YOSEF'S SONS, AND HE SAID, "WHO ARE THESE?" YOSEF SAID TO HIS FATHER,

> "THEY ARE MY SONS, WHOM HASHEM GAVE ME HERE." SO HE SAID, "NOW BRING THEM NEAR TO ME, SO THAT I MAY BLESS THEM." (BEREISHIS 48:8–9)

When Yaacov asked Yosef "מִי אֵלֶּה — 'Who are these'" about the people standing in front of him, Yosef responded "בָּנַי הֵם אֲשֶׁר נָתַן לִי אֱלֹקִים — 'They are my sons, whom Hashem has given me.'" This answer is almost identical to the way that Yaacov himself responded to a similar question many years earlier. In *Parashas Vayishlach*, Esav also asked Yaacov "מִי אֵלֶּה — 'Who are these'," referring to Yaacov's family. Like Yosef would do many years later, Yaacov answered "הַיְלָדִים אֲשֶׁר חָנַן אֱלֹקִים אֶת עַבְדֶּךָ — the children with whom Hashem has graced your servant."

Imagine the *nachas* that Yaacov felt when he heard Yosef answer his question in the same way as he did many years earlier. Seeing and knowing that a child has absorbed the life-lessons that his parents have tirelessly worked to impart is music to every parent's ears.

> וַיְבָרֶךְ אֶת יוֹסֵף וַיֹּאמַר ...
>
> AND HE BLESSED YOSEF... (BEREISHIS 48:15)

If Yaacov was giving a *berachah* to Efraim and Menasheh, why does the *pasuk* begin "וַיְבָרֶךְ אֶת יוֹסֵף — he blessed Yosef"?

The Torah is teaching us that when a person receives a *berachah* for his children, he is receiving a *berachah* for himself, as well.[14]

> וַיְמָאֵן אָבִיו וַיֹּאמֶר יָדַעְתִּי בְנִי יָדַעְתִּי גַּם הוּא יִהְיֶה לְעָם וְגַם הוּא יִגְדָּל וְאוּלָם אָחִיו הַקָּטֹן יִגְדַּל מִמֶּנּוּ וְזַרְעוֹ יִהְיֶה מְלֹא הַגּוֹיִם:
>
> BUT HIS FATHER REFUSED, AND HE SAID, "I KNOW, MY SON, I KNOW; HE TOO WILL BECOME A PEOPLE, AND HE TOO WILL BE GREAT. BUT HIS

---

14 I later saw this idea in the Rashbam, *Ohr Hachaim*, and Ramban.

> YOUNGER BROTHER WILL BE GREATER THAN HE, AND HIS CHILDREN'S FAME WILL FILL THE NATIONS." (BEREISHIS 48:19)

Rashi explains that Yaacov placed his right hand on Efraim's head because his descendants, for example Yehoshua bin Nun, would be greater than those of Menashe.

If Efraim was in fact potentially greater than Menashe, shouldn't Yaacov have given the stronger *berachah* to Menashe? He is the one who needed the extra help!

The Gemara (*Kiddushin* 29b) tells us that when a father only has enough money to allow himself to learn Torah, or to send his son to learn Torah, he, as the one spending the money, is allowed precedence. However, if his son has more potential than he does, then the son should be sent to learn Torah instead. This Gemara thus explains why Yaacov gave the stronger *berachah* to Efraim. Since Efraim had more potential for greatness, Yaacov focused his *berachah* on the place where it would be more effective.

My Rosh Yeshiva, Rav Chaim Kreiswirth *zatzal*, felt that if a person has the choice between being *mekarev* someone who is not *frum*, or turning a *ben Torah* into a *talmid chacham*, he should do the latter. Perhaps his source is this Gemara that we just discussed. This too explains Yaacov's giving Efraim the stronger *berachah*.

> וַיְבָרֲכֵם בַּיּוֹם הַהוּא לֵאמוֹר בְּךָ יְבָרֵךְ יִשְׂרָאֵל לֵאמֹר יְשִׂמְךָ אֱלֹקִים כְּאֶפְרַיִם וְכִמְנַשֶּׁה וַיָּשֶׂם אֶת אֶפְרַיִם לִפְנֵי מְנַשֶּׁה:
>
> SO HE BLESSED THEM ON THAT DAY, SAYING, "WITH YOU, YISRAEL WILL BLESS, SAYING, 'MAY HASHEM MAKE YOU LIKE EFRAIM AND LIKE MENASHE,'" AND HE PLACED EFRAIM BEFORE MENASHE. (BEREISHIS 48:20)

Why do we *bentch* our sons to be like Menashe and Efraim, instead of like Avraham, Yitzchak, and Yaacov? One of the answers to this question that is often given is that Efraim and Menashe were born in the *galus* of Mitzrayim, in a place that was inhospitable and even alien to any growth in *ruchniyus*. Yet, they still grew up to be great people. Our sons as well, are growing up in a world far from *kedushah*, so we bless them that they should excel and become spiritually great, although they are living in such an environment.

If this is true, we should find a different *berachah* to give our daughters! While some of the *Imahos* may have been born outside of Eretz Yisrael, they didn't grow up in the pit of *tumah* called Mitzrayim, like Menashe and Efraim!

The answer is that the respective *berachos* that we give our sons and our daughters reflect their roles in life. A man's responsibility of supporting his family means that he will one day be forced to go out, and deal with the outside society for one reason or another. We thus bless them with the fortitude of being like Efraim and Menashe, who had no choice but to deal with the Egyptian population and all of its decadence.

Our daughters, however, are in charge of making the home into a sanctuary free from the dangers of the "outside." To do this they need not venture out and mingle. Instead they must be vigilant about what comes through the doors of their home. We therefore bless them that they should be like Sarah, Rivkah, Rachel, and Leah, who excelled in making their homes into palaces of *ruchniyus*, free of all outside influences.

וַיִּקְרָא יַעֲקֹב אֶל בָּנָיו וַיֹּאמֶר הֵאָסְפוּ וְאַגִּידָה לָכֶם
אֵת אֲשֶׁר יִקְרָא אֶתְכֶם בְּאַחֲרִית הַיָּמִים:

YAACOV CALLED FOR HIS SONS AND SAID,
"GATHER AND I WILL TELL YOU WHAT WILL
HAPPEN TO YOU AT THE END OF DAYS."

(BEREISHIS 49:1)

Rashi explains that Yaacov wished to tell his sons when the End of Days would be. However, the Shechinah left him, preventing him from doing so. Unable to tell them, he then instead began to bless them. Why did he choose to specifically bless them, at this time?[15]

The reason that Yaacov wanted to reveal when the End of Days would finally occur was to help his children, and the B'nei Yisrael as a whole, endure the *galus*. It is easier to hold out when you know when the ordeal will be over. Hashem, however, prevented him from doing so. So, Yaacov did something else to help us through *galus*: he gave his children *berachos*, which gave them the tools they needed to persevere.

> בְּסֹדָם אַל תָּבֹא נַפְשִׁי בִּקְהָלָם אַל תֵּחַד כְּבֹדִי כִּי בְאַפָּם הָרְגוּ אִישׁ וּבִרְצֹנָם עִקְּרוּ שׁוֹר:
>
> LET MY SOUL NOT ENTER THEIR COUNSEL; MY HONOR, YOU SHALL NOT JOIN THEIR ASSEMBLY, FOR IN THEIR WRATH THEY KILLED A MAN, AND WITH THEIR WILL THEY UPROOTED A BULL. (BEREISHIS 49:6)

Yaacov's claim on Shimon and Levi was not that they killed out an entire city. Indeed, many commentaries (see, for example, Ramban) explain that the city of Shechem in fact deserved the death penalty! Rather, Yaacov's *mussar* was that they acted rashly, without thinking. Drastic measures, like wiping out a city, may sometimes be necessary. However, it is never acceptable to do something out of anger.

When someone wrongs us and a response is necessary, are we being driven by a sense of rationality and responsibility, or anger? Are we careful to punish our children out of love, and not anger? Decisions, whatever they may be, must always be well thought out and clear of bias.

---

15   I heard this question from Rav Michoel Maimon.

וַיֹּאמֶר אֲלֵהֶם יוֹסֵף אַל תִּירָאוּ כִּי הֲתַחַת אֱלֹקִים אָנִי:

But Yosef said to them, "Do not be afraid; am I instead of Hashem?" (Bereishis 50:19)

After the *Shevatim* returned from Yaacov's funeral, they were scared that Yosef would take revenge on them, for having sold him. Yosef cried when he heard their concerns, and told the brothers "אַל תִּירָאוּ כִּי הֲתַחַת אֱלֹקִים אָנִי — Do not be afraid; am I instead of Hashem?" How did this answer calm the brothers' fears of Yosef's retribution?

In *Parashas Vayeitzei* (30:1–2) Rachel demanded children from Yaacov. Yaacov responded "הֲתַחַת אֱלֹקִים אָנֹכִי אֲשֶׁר מָנַע מִמֵּךְ פְּרִי בָטֶן — Am I instead of Hashem, Who has withheld from you the offspring of the womb?" When the *Shevatim* heard Yosef saying exactly what their father had said many years earlier, they felt better, for two reasons. Firstly, they saw that Yosef had totally inculcated their father Yaacov's *hashkafah*, in which revenge of course plays no role. Also, they understood that Yosef was expressing the same powerlessness that Yaacov had in regard to giving Rachel children, in regard to taking revenge on his brothers. Yosef was telling them that even if he would have wanted to take revenge on them, he was totally incapable of doing so, for only Hashem can make such a decision.

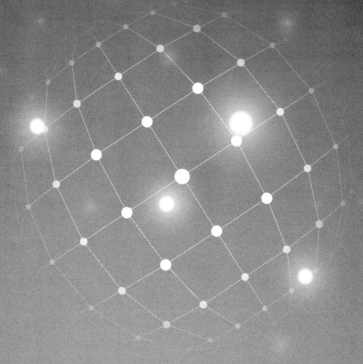

Shemos

שְׁמוֹת

SHEMOS
שְׁמוֹת

> וַיֹּאמֶר בְּיַלֶּדְכֶן אֶת הָעִבְרִיּוֹת וּרְאִיתֶן עַל הָאָבְנָיִם אִם בֵּן הוּא וַהֲמִתֶּן אֹתוֹ וְאִם בַּת הִוא וָחָיָה:
>
> AND HE SAID, "WHEN YOU DELIVER THE HEBREW WOMEN, AND YOU SEE ON THE BIRTHSTOOL, IF IT IS A SON, YOU SHALL PUT HIM TO DEATH, BUT IF IT IS A DAUGHTER, SHE SHALL REMAIN ALIVE."
>
> (SHEMOS 1:16)

Why did Pharaoh include "וְאִם בַּת הִוא וָחָיָה — but if it is a daughter, she shall remain alive" as part of his decree? The decree was to kill the boys; why mention the girls at all? Also, if Pharaoh wanted to wipe out the Jewish people, why didn't he also decree that the girls be killed as well, so they would not reproduce?

Perhaps "וְאִם בַּת הִוא וָחָיָה — but if it is a daughter, she shall remain alive" indeed wasn't coming to limit the decree to the boys, but was in fact a decree unto itself. We know that the Mitzrim were steeped in immorality. Beyond wanting the Jewish boys dead, we may explain that Pharaoh also wanted the Jewish girls alive, and well fed, so they could be used by the Egyptians.

> וַיֹּאמֶר בְּיַלֶּדְכֶן אֶת הָעִבְרִיּוֹת וּרְאִיתֶן עַל הָאָבְנָיִם אִם בֵּן הוּא וַהֲמִתֶּן אֹתוֹ וְאִם בַּת הִוא וָחָיָה: וַתִּירֶאןָ הַמְיַלְּדֹת אֶת הָאֱלֹקִים וְלֹא עָשׂוּ כַּאֲשֶׁר דִּבֶּר אֲלֵיהֶן מֶלֶךְ מִצְרָיִם וַתְּחַיֶּיןָ אֶת הַיְלָדִים:
>
> AND HE SAID, "WHEN YOU DELIVER THE HEBREW WOMEN, AND YOU SEE ON THE BIRTHSTOOL, IF IT IS A SON, YOU SHALL PUT HIM TO DEATH, BUT IF IT IS A DAUGHTER, SHE SHALL REMAIN ALIVE." THE MIDWIVES, HOWEVER, FEARED HASHEM; SO THEY DID NOT DO AS THE KING OF MITZRAYIM HAD SPOKEN TO THEM, BUT THEY GAVE LIFE TO THE CHILDREN. (SHEMOS 1:16–17)

Why does the Torah state "וַתְּחַיֶּיןָ אֶת הַיְלָדִים — but the midwives gave life to the children," instead of "but the midwives allowed the boys to remain alive"?

The Gemara explains that Shifrah and Puah did not just hold back from killing the baby boys as they were instructed to do, but in fact nurtured the babies until they were older children. This is what the *pasuk* is telling us, that they actually gave life to the boys.

This is an incredible lesson to us. We often pat ourselves on the back after having done a mitzvah that was slightly more difficult than we are used to. Do we ask ourselves if we could have done more? Was there something that we could have done that would have enhanced the mitzvah, making it even more special?

> וַיִּפֶן כֹּה וָכֹה וַיַּרְא כִּי אֵין אִישׁ וַיַּךְ אֶת הַמִּצְרִי וַיִּטְמְנֵהוּ בַּחוֹל:
>
> HE TURNED THIS WAY AND THAT WAY, AND HE SAW THAT THERE WAS NO MAN; SO HE

STRUCK THE MITZRI AND HID HIM IN THE SAND. (SHEMOS 2:12)

Rashi explains that "וַיַּרְא כִּי אֵין אִישׁ — he saw that there was no man" means that Moshe looked into the *Mitzri's* future to see if any converts would one day descend from him. When he saw that there weren't any, he killed him as punishment for hitting the Jew.

Why did Moshe do this? *Beis Din* never takes someone's future into account if the halachah, based on the facts on the ground, is that this person should be killed.

Indeed, it is impossible for a human *Beis Din* to see into the future of someone about whom they are considering the death penalty. The *Beis Din Shel Maalah*, on the other hand, has a whole different system. Hashem may delay or spare punishment because of something that this person will do in the future, because of a righteous descendant, or because this person has to be in a certain place at a certain time in the future in order that someone else be helped. Rashi tells us that Moshe Rabbeinu killed the *Mitzri* using Hashem's *Shem Hameforash* (2:14). This supernatural manner essentially killed him with the power of the *Beis Din Shel Maalah*. This being the case, it was necessary for Moshe to see if any good would come out of this person before he could be killed.

וַיִּפֶן כֹּה וָכֹה וַיַּרְא כִּי אֵין אִישׁ וַיַּךְ אֶת הַמִּצְרִי וַיִּטְמְנֵהוּ בַּחוֹל:

HE TURNED THIS WAY AND THAT WAY, AND HE SAW THAT THERE WAS NO MAN; SO HE STRUCK THE MITZRI AND HID HIM IN THE SAND. (SHEMOS 2:12)

In gauging the consequences of the *Mitzri's* death by considering potential future descendants, Moshe Rabbeinu is teaching us an important lesson. Would there be repercussions from what he was about to do, would future Jews be lost? We must understand that everything that we do has aftereffects. Some are larger and some smaller. Some are short term, some are long term, and some are *very* long term. And, we must weigh these outcomes *before* taking any action.

My Rosh Yeshiva, Rav Aryeh Rottman, *shlita*, would literally agonize over a decision that he had to make, when considering whether to expel a *bachur* from the Yeshiva. He explained that when we expel a *bachur*, we don't only tell him that he is no longer wanted in the Yeshiva. We are also telling his children and grandchildren that you don't belong here, together with us.

וְעַתָּה הִנֵּה צַעֲקַת בְּנֵי יִשְׂרָאֵל בָּאָה אֵלָי וְגַם רָאִיתִי אֶת הַלַּחַץ אֲשֶׁר מִצְרַיִם לֹחֲצִים אֹתָם:

AND NOW, BEHOLD, THE CRY OF THE B'NEI YISRAEL HAS COME TO ME, AND I HAVE ALSO SEEN THE OPPRESSION THAT THE EGYPTIANS ARE OPPRESSING THEM. (SHEMOS 3:9)

Hashem told Moshe that I have taken notice of the B'nei Yisrael's cries, and have seen how they are being oppressed. Now, the *pasuk* that discusses Hashem's originally "noticing" the Jewish people's situation is "וַיֵּאָנְחוּ בְנֵי יִשְׂרָאֵל מִן הָעֲבֹדָה וַיִּזְעָקוּ וַתַּעַל שַׁוְעָתָם אֶל הָאֱלֹקִים מִן הָעֲבֹדָה" — the B'nei Yisrael groaned from the labor, and they cried out, and their cry ascended to Hashem from the labor"; the terrible labor is mentioned *before* their crying out to Hashem, which is of course how the events chronologically occurred (*Shemos* 2:23). Why does our *pasuk*, which tells us of how Hashem related to the B'nei Yisrael's situation, mention "the cry of the B'nei Yisrael has come to Me," *before* "I have also seen the oppression that the Egyptians are oppressing them"?

Hashem, of course, knew all along that the B'nei Yisrael were suffering at the hands of the Mitzrim. Yet, He only "saw" it, and began the process of *geulah*, after the Jews began to cry out to Him. We also see this pattern in 2:24, that "וַיִּשְׁמַע אֱלֹקִים אֶת נַאֲקָתָם וַיִּזְכֹּר אֱלֹקִים אֶת בְּרִיתוֹ וכו'" — Hashem heard their cry, and Hashem remembered His covenant..."; first He heard their cry, and only after did He "remember" His covenant.[16]

A person cannot expect Hashem to help him simply because Hashem is aware of what is happening in his life; Hashem is indeed the reason why these troubles are taking place! Rather, he must *daven* for what he needs and want, both for himself and for his family. Only then will Hashem examine his situation and respond.

> וַיִּחַר אַף ה' בְּמֹשֶׁה וַיֹּאמֶר הֲלֹא אַהֲרֹן אָחִיךָ הַלֵּוִי ... וְגַם הִנֵּה הוּא יֹצֵא לִקְרָאתֶךָ וְרָאֲךָ וְשָׂמַח בְּלִבּוֹ:
>
> AND HASHEM'S WRATH WAS KINDLED AGAINST MOSHE, AND HE SAID, "IS THERE NOT AHARON YOUR BROTHER, THE LEVI? ... BEHOLD, HE IS COMING FORTH TOWARD YOU, AND WHEN HE SEES YOU, HE WILL REJOICE IN HIS HEART."
>
> (SHEMOS 4:14)

Rashi explains that Aharon's reward for being truly happy about Moshe's rise to greatness — literally "וְשָׂמַח בְּלִבּוֹ" — he will rejoice in his heart" — was that he would ultimately merit wearing the *Choshen* on his heart. What is the connection between Aharon's being happy for Moshe, and wearing the *Choshen*?

Moshe had just become the Jewish leader. Who wouldn't be happy for him, that he had reached this position? Unfortunately, there are many people who are unable to share someone else's joy; someone who is envious, hurt, or frightened, or has other *negiyos* that cloud his ability to connect to his friend, or even brother's joy.

Even when his younger brother became the Jewish leader, Aharon was entirely happy for him, unclouded by any personal *negiyos*. In this way he showed that he was able to realize and connect with the truth outside him. Through his doing so, Aharon merited to be the

---

16   Rav Michoel Maimon showed me this second *pasuk*.

one who would wear the *Choshen*, which is where people would turn when Hashem's direction, which is absolute and unclouded truth, was needed. Just as Aharon's total absence of *negiyos* let him appreciate another person's joy, it also gave him the unclouded vision necessary to appreciate Hashem's message.

וַיֹּאמֶר ה' אֶל מֹשֶׁה בְּמִדְיָן לֵךְ שֻׁב מִצְרָיִם כִּי מֵתוּ כָּל הָאֲנָשִׁים הַמְבַקְשִׁים אֶת נַפְשֶׁךָ:

HASHEM SAID TO MOSHE IN MIDYAN, "GO, RETURN TO MITZRAYIM, FOR ALL THE PEOPLE WHO SOUGHT YOUR LIFE HAVE DIED." (SHEMOS 4:19)

Rashi explains that "the people who sought your life" who have died are Dasan and Aviram. Although they were still alive, they had become impoverished, and Chazal (*Nedarim* 64b) tell us that "הֶעָנִי חָשׁוּב כַּמֵּת — a pauper is considered as dead."

How was Dasan's and Aviram's becoming impoverished the prompt for Moshe to return to Mitzrayim? We can understand that Pharaoh's death would open a window of opportunity to return and free the Jews. But why Dasan's and Aviram's?

It would seem that the reason why a pauper is likened to someone who is dead is because when a person has money, other people listen to what he has to say. Few people pay attention to the opinions of a poor person. Perhaps the change of fortune that happened to Dasan and Aviram was a key to Moshe's success. As long as they were wealthy and thus influential, they would do whatever they could to stop him from fulfilling his mission of helping the B'nei Yisrael.

Unfortunately, our worst enemies often come from where we would least expect it: within our own camp. Sometimes it is from those among us who can kill a worthwhile mission. Hashem therefore arranged that Dasan and Aviram should lose their wealth, so they would no longer be paid attention to, and would not be able to thwart Moshe in his quest to free the Jewish people from Mitzrayim.

VA'EIRA
וָאֵרָא

וַיְדַבֵּר ה' אֶל מֹשֶׁה וְאֶל אַהֲרֹן וַיְצַוֵּם אֶל בְּנֵי יִשְׂרָאֵל וְאֶל פַּרְעֹה מֶלֶךְ מִצְרָיִם לְהוֹצִיא אֶת בְּנֵי יִשְׂרָאֵל מֵאֶרֶץ מִצְרָיִם:

So Hashem spoke to Moshe and to Aharon, and He commanded them concerning the B'nei Yisrael and concerning Pharaoh, the king of Mitzrayim, to let the B'nei Yisrael out of the land of Mitzrayim. (Shemos 6:13)

Why did Hashem have to tell Moshe and Aharon to order the B'nei Yisrael to leave Mitzrayim? Isn't it clear that everyone wanted to leave, on their own?

Perhaps one reason why Hashem commanded the Jews to do something that they would do anyways is based on the Gemara (*Kiddushin* 31a), which says "גָּדוֹל מְצֻוֶּה וְעוֹשֶׂה יוֹתֵר מִמִּי שֶׁאֵינוֹ מְצֻוֶּה וְעוֹשֶׂה — it is greater to do something when commanded, than to do something voluntarily." Hashem wanted to give the B'nei Yisrael more *sechar*, so He *commanded* them to leave Mitzrayim.[17]

---

17   R' Duvie Merenstein suggested this approach.

We may suggest a different approach based on the *pasuk* at the beginning of *Parashas Beshalach* which tells us that only a fifth of the B'nei Yisrael left Mitzrayim, for four-fifths had died in the *Makah* of *Choshech* (13:18). These Jews, explain Rashi, didn't want to leave Mitzrayim (10:22). It now makes a lot of sense that Hashem had to tell Moshe and Aharon to command the Jews to leave Mitzrayim, for many of them simply didn't want to go.

וַיַּעַשׂ מֹשֶׁה וְאַהֲרֹן כַּאֲשֶׁר צִוָּה ה' אֹתָם כֵּן עָשׂוּ:

MOSHE AND AHARON DID, AS HASHEM
COMMANDED THEM, SO THEY DID. (SHEMOS 7:6)

Why is it so noteworthy that Moshe and Aharon did what Hashem told them, that the Torah has to mention it?

The way that human nature works is that we will only do something that we think can make a difference, and not when we realize that we are only wasting our time. When telling Moshe and Aharon to go to Pharaoh, several *pesukim* earlier, Hashem had told them (*pasuk* 3), "וַאֲנִי אַקְשֶׁה אֶת לֵב פַּרְעֹה וְהִרְבֵּיתִי אֶת אֹתֹתַי וְאֶת מוֹפְתַי בְּאֶרֶץ מִצְרָיִם — but I will harden Pharaoh's heart, and I will increase My signs and My wonders in the land of Mitzrayim." This means that Moshe and Aharon were going in to Pharaoh knowing that Pharaoh would not listen to them. And even so, they still went to speak with — have a real conversation with — Pharaoh, as if they didn't know what his answer would be.

וּמֹשֶׁה בֶּן שְׁמֹנִים שָׁנָה וְאַהֲרֹן בֶּן שָׁלֹשׁ וּשְׁמֹנִים
שָׁנָה בְּדַבְּרָם אֶל פַּרְעֹה:

AND MOSHE WAS EIGHTY YEARS OLD, AND
AHARON WAS EIGHTY-THREE YEARS OLD WHEN
THEY SPOKE TO PHARAOH. (SHEMOS 7:7)

This *pasuk* is teaching us an important *yesod*, that it sometimes takes a long time for a person's life-mission to become clear. Moshe was now eighty, and Aharon was eighty-three. It was only now, in the final third of their life, that their *tachlis*, the impact that they would make on Klal Yisrael, would be achieved. Very often we feel unaccomplished or unfulfilled because we feel that we have not yet found what we are supposed to be doing. Don't worry so much! It could be that the right time hasn't yet come.

וַיָּבֹא מֹשֶׁה וְאַהֲרֹן אֶל פַּרְעֹה וַיַּעֲשׂוּ כֵן כַּאֲשֶׁר צִוָּה ה' וַיַּשְׁלֵךְ אַהֲרֹן אֶת מַטֵּהוּ לִפְנֵי פַרְעֹה וְלִפְנֵי עֲבָדָיו וַיְהִי לְתַנִּין:

THEREUPON, MOSHE AND AHARON CAME TO PHARAOH, AND THEY DID SO, AS HASHEM HAD COMMANDED; AHARON CAST HIS STAFF BEFORE PHARAOH AND BEFORE HIS SERVANTS, AND IT BECAME A SERPENT. (SHEMOS 7:10)

Why is it so noteworthy that Moshe and Aharon did what Hashem told them by coming to Pharaoh, that the Torah feels it necessary to mention it?

Hashem sent Moshe and Aharon to Pharaoh many times. Sometimes it was to demand that the Jewish people be let free, and sometimes it was to warn him of an upcoming *makah*. In this *pasuk*, it doesn't appear that the purpose of their being sent to Pharaoh was for anything beyond performing a *mofes* for him, of turning a staff into a serpent.

We are often asked to do what we think is an inconsequential chore. And, understandably, we are reluctant to do it, either because we look at it as relatively meaningless, or because we feel that it does not befit our stature or position. Even in the event that we do fulfill this request, our performance will be somewhat lacking, either in focus, enthusiasm, or in our attention to precision and detail. Here, Moshe and Aharon were only sent to turn a staff into a snake, which is something that almost anyone could have done. Yet, when Hashem told Moshe and Aharon to do it, they fulfilled their mission to the fullest, like any mission that Hashem had charged them.

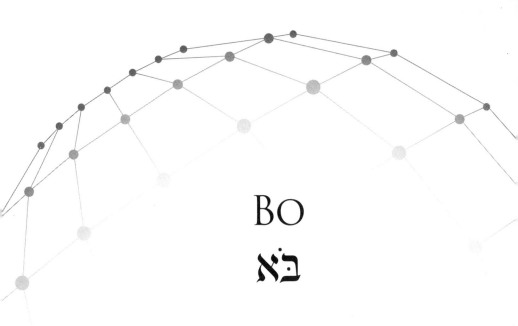

BO
בֹּא

וַיֵּלְכוּ וַיַּעֲשׂוּ בְּנֵי יִשְׂרָאֵל כַּאֲשֶׁר צִוָּה ה' אֶת מֹשֶׁה וְאַהֲרֹן כֵּן עָשׂוּ:

SO THE B'NEI YISRAEL WENT AND DID; AS HASHEM COMMANDED MOSHE AND AHARON, SO THEY DID. (SHEMOS 12:28)

Again, why does the Torah make a point of telling us that the B'nei Yisrael listened to every single detail (see Rashi) that Moshe and Aharon instructed them?

The previous twenty-seven *pesukim* describe the many, many *halachos* of Pesach, for example *korban Pesach*, not eating or owning *chametz*, and the Seder. The Jews were finally about to leave Mitzrayim after over two hundred years, and *shechting* a sheep and eating matzah at a Seder were probably the last things on their minds. The Torah is telling us that despite their incredible urge to just walk out, the B'nei Yisrael listened to Moshe and Aharon in performing every single facet of Pesach, as we continue to do each year.

> וּבְנֵי יִשְׂרָאֵל עָשׂוּ כִּדְבַר מֹשֶׁה וַיִּשְׁאֲלוּ מִמִּצְרַיִם
> כְּלֵי כֶסֶף וּכְלֵי זָהָב וּשְׂמָלֹת:
>
> AND THE B'NEI YISRAEL DID ACCORDING TO MOSHE'S ORDER, AND THEY BORROWED FROM THE EGYPTIANS SILVER OBJECTS, GOLDEN OBJECTS, AND GARMENTS. (SHEMOS 12:35)

What is so remarkable that the Jewish people took gifts from the Egyptians, that the Torah makes a point of mentioning it?

The Seforno (11:2) explains that the B'nei Yisrael may have been scared to listen to Moshe and take valuables from the Mitzrim, for this would give the Mitzrim more reason to chase after them. The Torah is thus telling us that instead of just running towards the freedom that had eluded them for so long, they listened to Moshe Rabbeinu, even at the expense of their lives.

We may suggest another answer. After having been enslaved for so many years and literally at the cusp of freedom, Moshe told the B'nei Yisrael to go and "borrow" jewelry and other valuables from the Mitzrim. The Jews could have been troubled by this request for several reasons. Why are we asking to borrow valuables, instead of asking to keep them? Also, with freedom so close, why bother with asking for jewelry? We just want to leave Mitzrayim! Despite these reservations, the B'nei Yisrael did not hesitate, and did what was asked of them.

> וַיִּסְעוּ בְנֵי יִשְׂרָאֵל מֵרַעְמְסֵס סֻכֹּתָה כְּשֵׁשׁ מֵאוֹת
> אֶלֶף רַגְלִי הַגְּבָרִים לְבַד מִטָּף: וְגַם עֵרֶב רַב עָלָה
> אִתָּם וְצֹאן וּבָקָר מִקְנֶה כָּבֵד מְאֹד:
>
> THE B'NEI YISRAEL JOURNEYED FROM RAMSES TO SUCCOS, ABOUT SIX HUNDRED THOUSAND ON FOOT, THE MEN, BESIDES THE YOUNG CHILDREN. AND ALSO, A MIXED MULTITUDE WENT UP WITH

THEM, AND FLOCKS AND CATTLE, VERY MUCH
LIVESTOCK. (SHEMOS 12:37-38)

The first *pasuk* discusses the people who traveled from Ramses to Succos, and the second *pasuk* discusses the animals, the enormous amounts of flocks and livestock. The second *pasuk* also discusses the *Erev Rav*. Wouldn't it more appropriate to group the *Erev Rav* with the *people*, in the first *pasuk*, and not with the animals, in the second?

We know that Hashem was not pleased with Moshe's decision to convert the *Erev Rav*. Putting them together with the animals, which are a great burden to care for, shows us that Hashem is conveying that the *Erev Rav* were not an asset, but at the best something to be *schlepped* along. Indeed, they proved themselves to be very difficult for the Jews throughout their years in the *Midbar*.

BESHALACH
בְּשַׁלַּח

וַיִּקַּח מֹשֶׁה אֶת עַצְמוֹת יוֹסֵף עִמּוֹ...

MOSHE TOOK YOSEF'S BONES WITH HIM...
(SHEMOS 13:19)

What is added by the Torah's telling us that Moshe took Yosef's bones "עִמּוֹ — *with him*"?

The Gemara (*Sotah* 13a) contrasts how Moshe acted when leaving Mitzrayim, with the way that the rest of the Jewish people acted. Moshe was involved in a mitzvah of finding and taking Yosef's bones. The other Jews, however, occupied themselves with taking Egyptian silver and gold. Rav Schwab asks a question on this comparison; collecting Egyptian booty was also a mitzvah, as Hashem had commanded the Jews to request valuables from the Mitzrim. Why, then, is Moshe praised and the Jews faulted?

It is true that the rest of the B'nei Yisrael were also fulfilling Hashem's instruction. However, they chose to be busy with a mitzvah whose rewards are quite obvious, while Moshe chose a mitzvah which is *chessed shel emes*, whose entire reward is eternal, for which there is no reward in this world. This is what the Torah means when telling us that Moshe took Yosef's bones "עִמּוֹ — *with him*"; Moshe took the complete mitzvah *with him* after his death, to a place where we cannot take silver and gold.

> וַיֵּט מֹשֶׁה אֶת יָדוֹ עַל הַיָּם וַיּוֹלֶךְ ה' אֶת הַיָּם בְּרוּחַ קָדִים עַזָּה כָּל הַלַּיְלָה וַיָּשֶׂם אֶת הַיָּם לֶחָרָבָה וַיִּבָּקְעוּ הַמָּיִם:
>
> AND MOSHE STRETCHED OUT HIS HAND OVER THE SEA, AND HASHEM LED THE SEA WITH THE STRONG EAST WIND ALL NIGHT, AND HE MADE THE SEA INTO DRY LAND AND THE WATERS SPLIT. (SHEMOS 14:21)

Rashi explains that "וַיִּבָּקְעוּ הַמָּיִם — the waters split" tells us that all of the waters in the world also split, at the time of *Krias Yam Suf*.

Perhaps Rashi understood this deeper insight from reading the *pasuk*, which says "וַיּוֹלֶךְ ה' אֶת הַיָּם בְּרוּחַ קָדִים עַזָּה כָּל הַלַּיְלָה וַיָּשֶׂם אֶת הַיָּם לֶחָרָבָה — Hashem led the sea with the strong east wind all night, and He made the sea into dry land." If the intense blowing wind is what turned the Yam Suf into dry land, what water remained to split, which "וַיִּבָּקְעוּ הַמָּיִם — the waters split" is referring to? Thus, Rashi explains that indeed, "וַיִּבָּקְעוּ הַמָּיִם — the waters split" does not mean the Yam Suf, but means the other waters of the world.

> וַיֹּאמֶר ה' אֶל מֹשֶׁה נְטֵה אֶת יָדְךָ עַל הַיָּם וְיָשֻׁבוּ הַמַּיִם ...
>
> THEREUPON, HASHEM SAID TO MOSHE, "STRETCH OUT YOUR HAND OVER THE SEA, AND LET THE WATER RETURN UPON THE MITZRIM..." (SHEMOS 14:26)

Why did Moshe have to do something to return the Yam Suf to its normal flow?

The Yam Suf returning to itself was not just a return back to nature, but was the way that the Egyptian armies, who entered the water after the

B'nei Yisrael, were drowned. So, in telling Moshe to return the water to its normal flow, Hashem was actually telling him to bring on the last and most devastating *makah*. This, like the other *Makos*, required an action.

> וַתִּקַּח מִרְיָם הַנְּבִיאָה אֲחוֹת אַהֲרֹן אֶת הַתֹּף בְּיָדָהּ
> וַתֵּצֶאןָ כָל הַנָּשִׁים אַחֲרֶיהָ בְּתֻפִּים וּבִמְחֹלֹת:

> MIRIAM, THE PROPHETESS, AHARON'S SISTER,
> TOOK A TAMBOURINE IN HER HAND, AND
> ALL THE WOMEN CAME OUT AFTER HER WITH
> TAMBOURINES AND WITH DANCES. (SHEMOS 15:20)

When commenting on the words "וַתִּקַּח מִרְיָם הַנְּבִיאָה — Miriam, the prophetess, took," Rashi explains that Miriam is called "אֲחוֹת אַהֲרֹן — Aharon's sister" because she experienced prophecy at the time when she was still only Aharon's sister, before Moshe Rabbeinu was born. Why does Rashi tell us this when explaining "וַתִּקַּח מִרְיָם הַנְּבִיאָה," instead of explaining "אֲחוֹת אַהֲרֹן"? Moreover, why is she called "אֲחוֹת אַהֲרֹן — Aharon's sister" specifically in the context of this *pasuk*? Why is her relationship to him significant here and now?

Rashi wants to emphasize that Miriam was a prophet in her own right, and not just because she was Aharon's sister. This information is now pertinent because her prophecy then declared that her parents would soon bear the מוֹשִׁיעָן שֶׁל יִשְׂרָאֵל, the Rescuer of the Jewish people, which, now at *Krias Yam Suf*, finally occurred.

> וַיֹּאמֶר אִם שָׁמוֹעַ תִּשְׁמַע לְקוֹל ה' אֱלֹקֶיךָ וְהַיָּשָׁר
> בְּעֵינָיו תַּעֲשֶׂה וְהַאֲזַנְתָּ לְמִצְוֹתָיו וְשָׁמַרְתָּ כָּל חֻקָּיו
> כָּל הַמַּחֲלָה אֲשֶׁר שַׂמְתִּי בְמִצְרַיִם לֹא אָשִׂים עָלֶיךָ
> כִּי אֲנִי ה' רֹפְאֶךָ:

> AND HE SAID, IF YOU HEARKEN TO THE VOICE
> OF HASHEM, YOUR GOD, AND YOU DO WHAT IS

proper in His eyes, and you listen closely to His commandments and observe all His statutes, all the diseases that I have visited upon Mitzrayim I will not visit upon you, for I, Hashem, heal you. (Shemos 15:26)

Why is this declaration, which states that our listening to Hashem will prevent the diseases of Mitzrayim from happening to us, specifically said here, by *Krias Yam Suf*?

Perhaps this is the ideal time to warn the Jewish people of this, for they have just seen what happened to the Mitzrim for disobeying Hashem, much as the Gemara explains that someone who sees a *sotah's* disgrace should do something to ensure that he will never fall into that pitfall (*Sotah* 2a).

וַיֹּאמֶר ה' אֶל מֹשֶׁה הִנְנִי מַמְטִיר לָכֶם לֶחֶם מִן הַשָּׁמָיִם וְיָצָא הָעָם וְלָקְטוּ דְּבַר יוֹם בְּיוֹמוֹ לְמַעַן אֲנַסֶּנּוּ הֲיֵלֵךְ בְּתוֹרָתִי אִם לֹא:

So Hashem said to Moshe, Behold! I am going to rain down for you bread from heaven, and the people shall go out and gather what is needed for the day, so that I can test them, whether or not they will follow My Torah. (Shemos 16:4)

Why is the *Mahn* the test that Hashem uses to see whether or not we will follow His Torah?

Rashi explains that the way B'nei Yisrael was tested with the *Mahn* was whether or not they observed the two *mitzvos* that the *Mahn* involved. These *mitzvos* were that they were not to leave any for the next day, and must not go out on Shabbos to collect *Mahn*. These two *mitzvos* show *bitachon* in Hashem. A person could not store food for tomorrow, but had to depend that Hashem would give him food tomorrow just as

He gave him today. And, the Gemara tells us that observing Shabbos is equal to keeping all the *mitzvos (Yerushalmi Niddah* 3:9). By not going out to collect *Mahn* on Shabbos, the B'nei Yisrael showed that they are following the entire Torah.[18]

> וַיֹּאמֶר מֹשֶׁה וְאַהֲרֹן אֶל כָּל בְּנֵי יִשְׂרָאֵל עֶרֶב
> וִידַעְתֶּם כִּי ה' הוֹצִיא אֶתְכֶם מֵאֶרֶץ מִצְרָיִם:
>
> MOSHE AND AHARON SAID TO ALL THE B'NEI YISRAEL, "THIS EVENING, YOU SHALL KNOW THAT HASHEM BROUGHT YOU OUT OF THE LAND OF MITZRAYIM." (SHEMOS 16:6)

Rashi explains that in *pasuk* 3 the Jewish people had complained, and had blamed Moshe and Aharon for taking them out of Mitzrayim to die in the desert. Now, said Moshe and Aharon, the appearance of quail to eat will show you that Hashem in fact was the One Who took you out.

How does the quail show that Hashem took them out of Mitzrayim? If Moshe and Aharon could somehow miraculously free the Jews from Mitzrayim, why couldn't they also make quail appear in the desert?

The answer is that there are only two people in the world who will give something to someone even when they were rudely asked for it, or if the beseecher doesn't need it or deserve it: a father, and a mother. B'nei Yisrael's request for meat in the desert was inappropriate for several reasons. They were in the desert, where luxuries such as meat are unheard of. And they had their own cattle, which they could have slaughtered to provide them with meat. Yet, they instead chose to complain to Hashem.

Moshe was telling the B'nei Yisrael that after you see that Hashem "gave in" to your inappropriate request and gave you the meat you complained for, you will now realize that it was in fact Hashem Who took

---

18   See also *Kli Yakar*.

you out of Mitzrayim, for only our Father in Heaven would entertain such an inappropriate request from his children.

> וַיַּעֲשׂוּ כֵן בְּנֵי יִשְׂרָאֵל וַיִּלְקְטוּ הַמַּרְבֶּה וְהַמַּמְעִיט:
>
> AND THE B'NEI YISRAEL DID SO, THEY GATHERED, BOTH THE ONE WHO GATHERED MUCH AND THE ONE WHO GATHERED LITTLE. (SHEMOS 16:17)

Why is it so noteworthy that the B'nei Yisrael gathered the *Mahn* as they were told, that the Torah feels it necessary to mention?

The previous *pasuk* told us that every person received the same amount of *Mahn*, of an *omer's* measurement per person. This means that when the Jews went to gather *Mahn*, each person had to take this amount for each member of his family. While it may sound easy to do, the fact is that different people eat different amounts. It is hard for a father to gather exactly an *omer* for his sixteen-year-old ravenous growing teenage boy, his petite three-year-old daughter, and for all of the other members of his family, in various shapes and sizes. The Torah is praising the B'nei Yisrael that, despite the apparent "illogic" of this instruction, they did not make their own *cheshbonos* of how much *Mahn* to bring home, but gathered the *Mahn* in the manner that Hashem had told them.

> וַיֹּאמֶר מֹשֶׁה אֶל יְהוֹשֻׁעַ בְּחַר לָנוּ אֲנָשִׁים וְצֵא הִלָּחֵם בַּעֲמָלֵק ...
>
> SO MOSHE SAID TO YEHOSHUA, "SELECT MEN FOR US, AND GO OUT AND FIGHT AGAINST AMALEK..."
> (SHEMOS 17:9)

Rashi points out that Moshe said, "בְּחַר לָנוּ אֲנָשִׁים — Select men for us." This terminology of "לָנוּ — for us," teaches us the important lesson discussed in the Mishnah (*Avos* 4:12), that "יְהִי כְבוֹד תַּלְמִידְךָ חָבִיב עָלֶיךָ כְּשֶׁלָּךְ — your *talmid's* honor should be as dear to you as your own."

Rav Hutner *zatzal* asks an interesting question. Why is specifically the war with Amalek, where Yehoshua was given the job of choosing soldiers able to battle Amalek, the place where the Torah imparts this lesson of honoring a student? Why isn't this lesson taught under the more conventional circumstances of times of peace, when less pressing issues were on Moshe Rabbeinu's mind?

The reason why a time of war is used to illustrate a *rebbi's* honor for his student is not *despite* the fact that the stakes are so high, but rather *because* the stakes are so high. The battle against Amalek was a matter of life and death, and Moshe knew that choosing the right soldiers could very well make the difference between victory and defeat. Moshe could have easily told Yehoshua to step aside for a minute and "let me take care of this one, you can come back tomorrow," to decide on lesser issues. But he didn't. Moshe showed that he fully trusted his *talmid* to make the proper decision, even with the most important of issues. In this way, he showed an example of the ultimate honor, the honor of viewing the student as a qualified equal, that a *rebbi* can show his *talmid*. This phenomenal lesson is something that every parent, teacher, or leader can and must take to heart.

YISRO
יִתְרוֹ

וַיִּשְׁמַע יִתְרוֹ ...

NOW YISRO HEARD... (SHEMOS 18:1)

Rashi explains that Yisro had seven names, yet only explains the meaning of three of them. Why? Also, Rashi has previously told us about Yisro's seven names, in *Parashas Shemos* (4:18). Why does he repeat it, here?

In *Parashas Shemos*, Rashi told us about Yisro's names as an introduction to the personality whom we were meeting for the first time. Here, when Yisro came to join the Jewish people, Rashi repeated the list in order to explain the three names that are relevant to our *parashah*; "יֶתֶר — Yeser," for a *parashah* was *added* to the Torah due to him, "יִתְרוֹ — Yisro," for a letter was *added* to his name when he became a Jew, and "חוֹבָב — Chovav", for he *loved* the Torah.

וַיֹּאמֶר אֶל מֹשֶׁה אֲנִי חֹתֶנְךָ יִתְרוֹ בָּא אֵלֶיךָ ...

AND HE SAID TO MOSHE, "I, YISRO, YOUR FATHER-IN-LAW, AM COMING TO YOU..."
(SHEMOS 18:6)

It seems odd that Yisro said "אֲנִי חֹתֶנְךָ יִתְרוֹ — I, Yisro, your father-in-law." Did Moshe have another father-in-law that Yisro had to identify himself by name? Or, did Moshe call Yisro by his first name? Saying "אֲנִי חֹתֶנְךָ — I, your father-in-law," should have been enough!

The *roshei teivos* of the words "אֲנִי חֹתֶנְךָ יִתְרוֹ" spells "אָחִי — my brother." Yisro was not asking Moshe that he greet him out of honor and respect, but rather out of their close relationship.[19]

> וַיִּשְׁמַע יִתְרוֹ כֹהֵן מִדְיָן חֹתֵן מֹשֶׁה אֵת כָּל אֲשֶׁר
> עָשָׂה אֱלֹקִים לְמֹשֶׁה וּלְיִשְׂרָאֵל עַמּוֹ כִּי הוֹצִיא ה'
> אֶת יִשְׂרָאֵל מִמִּצְרָיִם ... וַיְסַפֵּר מֹשֶׁה לְחֹתְנוֹ אֵת
> כָּל אֲשֶׁר עָשָׂה ה' לְפַרְעֹה וּלְמִצְרַיִם עַל אוֹדֹת
> יִשְׂרָאֵל אֵת כָּל הַתְּלָאָה אֲשֶׁר מְצָאָתַם בַּדֶּרֶךְ
> וַיַּצִּלֵם ה':

NOW MOSHE'S FATHER-IN-LAW, YISRO, THE CHIEFTAIN OF MIDYAN, HEARD ALL THAT HASHEM HAD DONE FOR MOSHE AND FOR YISRAEL HIS PEOPLE, THAT HASHEM HAD TAKEN YISRAEL OUT OF MITZRAYIM... MOSHE TOLD HIS FATHER-IN-LAW ALL THAT HASHEM HAD DONE TO PHARAOH AND TO THE EGYPTIANS ON ACCOUNT OF YISRAEL, AND ABOUT ALL THE HARDSHIPS THAT HAD BEFALLEN THEM ON THE WAY, AND THAT HASHEM HAD SAVED THEM. (SHEMOS 18:1,8)

Rashi explains that the events that Yisro heard about were *Krias Yam Suf*, and the war with Amalek. Again, when explaining *pasuk* 8, Rashi explains that the events about which Moshe told Yisro when he came

---

19 For example, see the *Beis Halevi* in *Parashas Vayishlach* (32:12), who explains that "אָח," is a terminology indicating relationship.

to the B'nei Yisrael were *Krias Yam Suf* and the war with Amalek. The reason why Moshe recounted these events was in order to draw his heart closer to the Torah.

Why did Moshe tell Yisro things about which he already knew? Wouldn't telling him new ideas be a better way to bring him closer to the Torah?

It is true that Yisro already knew all the facts. But hearing it from a different perspective is hearing a whole new story. A new perspective makes an impact on a person far beyond the way that he originally knew it.

Hearing the same information again can make an impact on a person in several ways. Relating current events is called news. But telling over these same episodes with the intent of drawing someone's heart closer to Torah is a whole different story. Moshe related the miracles that happened in a way that showed Hashem's love, care, and the lessons that He wants us to learn from these stories.

Another way that hearing the same story twice makes a greater impact on a person is when it is heard straight from the source, from Moshe Rabbeinu, instead of hearing it second- or third-hand. When Yisro heard that, it gave him a sense of excitement that he did not have before.

וַיִּשְׁמַע מֹשֶׁה לְקוֹל חֹתְנוֹ וַיַּעַשׂ כֹּל אֲשֶׁר אָמָר:

MOSHE OBEYED HIS FATHER-IN-LAW, AND HE DID ALL THAT HE SAID. (SHEMOS 18:24)

This *pasuk* is an incredible compliment to Moshe Rabbeinu. Moshe was the king, and the greatest prophet who ever lived. Yet he was still quick to accept a good suggestion from his father-in-law, who was a convert and former idol worshipper. Imagine the CEO of an international corporation taking advice from his father-in-law the janitor. This *pasuk* is a picture of Moshe's humility at its best.

We find another example of Moshe's humility in these *pesukim*, as well. The *parashah* opens by telling us "וַיִּשְׁמַע יִתְרוֹ כֹהֵן מִדְיָן חֹתֵן מֹשֶׁה אֵת כָּל

אֲשֶׁר עָשָׂה אֱלֹקִים לְמֹשֶׁה וּלְיִשְׂרָאֵל עַמּוֹ... — Yisro... heard all that Hashem had done for Moshe and for Yisrael His people." Indeed, Moshe Rabbeinu played the key role in all of the events that Yisro had heard about. But, when Moshe tells these events to Yisro, *pasuk* 8 says, "וַיְסַפֵּר מֹשֶׁה לְחֹתְנוֹ אֵת כָּל אֲשֶׁר עָשָׂה ה' לְפַרְעֹה וּלְמִצְרַיִם עַל אוֹדֹת יִשְׂרָאֵל... — Moshe told his father-in-law all that Hashem had done to Pharaoh and to the Egyptians." In his absolute humility, Moshe Rabbeinu totally left himself out of the picture.

> וְהָיָה כָּל הַדָּבָר הַגָּדֹל יָבִיאוּ אֵלֶיךָ וְכָל הַדָּבָר הַקָּטֹן יִשְׁפְּטוּ הֵם ...
>
> ANY LARGE MATTER THEY SHALL BRING TO YOU, AND THEY SHALL JUDGE EVERY SMALL MATTER THEMSELVES ... (SHEMOS 18:22)

> אֶת הַדָּבָר הַקָּשֶׁה יְבִיאוּן אֶל מֹשֶׁה וְכָל הַדָּבָר הַקָּטֹן יִשְׁפּוּטוּ הֵם ...
>
> THE DIFFICULT MATTER THEY WOULD BRING TO MOSHE, BUT WOULD JUDGE ANY SMALL MATTER THEMSELVES... (SHEMOS 18:26)

Moshe made a small change to Yisro's idea. Yisro had suggested that the cases be divided between Moshe and the other *dayanim*, in a way they would take "כָּל הַדָּבָר הַקָּטֹן — every small matter," and Moshe would judge "כָּל הַדָּבָר הַגָּדֹל — any large matter." Moshe, however, implemented that he be sent not "כָּל הַדָּבָר הַגָּדֹל — any large matter," but every "דָּבָר הַקָּשֶׁה — difficult matter." To Yisro and the world he was coming from, the difference between a case for Moshe, and a case that could be handled by someone else, was the amount of money under discussion; was it a dispute over a small amount or a halachic question that affected millions of dollars? Moshe, however, taught us otherwise, that the bottom line in any *din Torah* is reaching the proper halachah. A relatively open and shut question involving large amounts of money may be handled by one of the other *dayanim*, but a complex case of just a few dollars must sometimes be taken to Moshe himself.

> וַיֹּאמֶר ה' אֶל מֹשֶׁה לֵךְ אֶל הָעָם וְקִדַּשְׁתָּם הַיּוֹם וּמָחָר וְכִבְּסוּ שִׂמְלֹתָם:
>
> AND HASHEM SAID TO MOSHE, "GO TO THE PEOPLE AND PREPARE THEM TODAY AND TOMORROW, AND THEY SHALL WASH THEIR CLOTHING." (SHEMOS 10:19)

Rashi (*Devarim* 8:4) tells us that the *Ananei Hakavod* washed and pressed the Jews' clothing. Why, then, did Moshe have to tell them to wash their clothing in preparation for Matan Torah? They were already clean!

The purpose of washing their clothing was not so the clothing would be clean. Washing the clothing was in order to involve the B'nei Yisrael in the preparations for Matan Torah. A vital part of receiving and growing in Torah is doing something to make one's self ready to receive and grow from the Torah that one is about to learn.

> וְכָל הָעָם רֹאִים אֶת הַקּוֹלֹת וְאֶת הַלַּפִּידִם וְאֵת קוֹל הַשֹּׁפָר וְאֶת הָהָר עָשֵׁן וַיַּרְא הָעָם וַיָּנֻעוּ וַיַּעַמְדוּ מֵרָחֹק: וַיֹּאמְרוּ אֶל מֹשֶׁה דַּבֵּר אַתָּה עִמָּנוּ וְנִשְׁמָעָה וְאַל יְדַבֵּר עִמָּנוּ אֱלֹקִים פֶּן נָמוּת:
>
> AND ALL THE PEOPLE SAW THE VOICES AND THE TORCHES, THE SOUND OF THE SHOFAR, AND THE SMOKING MOUNTAIN, AND THE PEOPLE SAW AND TREMBLED; SO THEY STOOD FROM AFAR. THEY SAID TO MOSHE, "YOU SPEAK WITH US, AND WE WILL HEAR, BUT LET HASHEM NOT SPEAK WITH US LEST WE DIE." (SHEMOS 20:15–16)

When Hashem originally told Moshe to take the Jews out of Mitzrayim, he refused on the grounds that he was unable to speak and could not approach Pharaoh. Why didn't Moshe also use this answer when the Jews told him that he, and not Hashem, should tell them the *Aseres Hadibros*?

Perhaps Rashi already answered this question in the same *pasuk* that describes the B'nei Yisrael's great fear, that "וְכָל הָעָם רֹאִים אֶת הַקּוֹלֹת וְאֶת הַלַּפִּידִם וְאֵת קוֹל הַשֹּׁפָר וְאֶת הָהָר עָשֵׁן — and all the people saw the voices and the torches, the sound of the shofar, and the smoking mountain." Rashi explains that "*all* the people saw..." tells us that the blind were able to see, and other infirmities were also healed. This being the case, Moshe's speech impediment was also cured, and he had no reason to tell the B'nei Yisrael that he could not tell them the *Aseres Hadibros*.

Mishpatim

מִשְׁפָּטִים

כִּי תִקְנֶה עֶבֶד עִבְרִי...

IF YOU BUY A HEBREW SLAVE... (SHEMOS 21:2)

Of all of the laws of *Parashas Mishpatim*, why is *eved ivri* mentioned first?

B'nei Yisrael had just left Mitzrayim, where they were slaves who were mistreated, and the sons and grandsons of slaves who had been mistreated. It was very possible that in the not so distant future, when they would have other people working for them, they would mistreat them almost without thinking. This is the way that things are! At the first possible moment, the Torah makes a point of telling us of the right way that an *eved* is to be treated.[20]

עַיִן תַּחַת עַיִן שֵׁן תַּחַת שֵׁן יָד תַּחַת יָד רֶגֶל תַּחַת רָגֶל:

AN EYE INSTEAD OF AN EYE, A TOOTH INSTEAD OF A TOOTH, A HAND INSTEAD OF A HAND, A FOOT INSTEAD OF A FOOT.

(SHEMOS 21:24)

---

20 I later saw this idea in the *Sefer Lemaan Achai Ve'reiai*.

A person must pay his victim for injuring any part of his body. Why, then, does the Torah enumerate specifically these four items, the eye, the tooth, the hand, and the foot?

The *roshei teivos* of these four words — עַיִן, שֵׁן, יָד, רֶגֶל — spell the word "עָשִׁיר — a wealthy person." The definition of a wealthy person is someone who does not need another person's assistance, be it financially, physically, emotionally, or otherwise. These four examples of injuries take away a person's "wealth," or independence. A blind person is forever dependent on others for guidance. Similarly, someone who cannot chew their food, get things, or walk on their own is missing this basic freedom.

On the flip side, the Torah is telling us another message. What do we need to be considered wealthy? Just these four things: eyes, teeth, hands, and feet.

> אִם כֶּסֶף תַּלְוֶה אֶת עַמִּי אֶת הֶעָנִי עִמָּךְ לֹא תִהְיֶה
> לוֹ כְּנֹשֶׁה לֹא תְשִׂימוּן עָלָיו נֶשֶׁךְ:

> WHEN YOU LEND MONEY TO MY PEOPLE, TO
> THE POOR PERSON WHO IS WITH YOU, YOU
> SHALL NOT BEHAVE TOWARD HIM AS A LENDER;
> YOU SHALL NOT IMPOSE INTEREST UPON
> HIM. (SHEMOS 22:24)

Rashi explains that the Torah says "הֶעָנִי עִמָּךְ — to the poor person who is with you," to tell us that when lending money to someone else, a person should feel that he is a poor person.

Why specifically here does the Torah tell us to put ourselves into the shoes of the person who needs money?

Helping people with money can be a very sensitive area. Some people in need are not ashamed to ask and receive. Other people would rather starve than ask someone else for assistance. The Torah is telling us to imagine that we were poor: to position ourselves to be sensitive not only to the amount of money that he needs to get by, but just as importantly, to the person's emotional needs as well. *Chessed* isn't just "filling a hole." When done in the wrong way, it can create as many new problems as it solves.

> וְאַנְשֵׁי קֹדֶשׁ תִּהְיוּן לִי וּבָשָׂר בַּשָּׂדֶה טְרֵפָה לֹא תֹאכֵלוּ לַכֶּלֶב תַּשְׁלִכוּן אֹתוֹ:

> AND YOU SHALL BE HOLY PEOPLE TO ME, AND FLESH TORN IN THE FIELD YOU SHALL NOT EAT; YOU SHALL THROW IT TO THE DOG. (SHEMOS 22:7)

We generally try to become holy by doing holy things, like *davening* and learning Torah. How does refraining from doing something, like refraining from the *treif* meat discussed in this *pasuk*, make us holy?

Imagine a scenario of a person who bought a large animal to *shecht*, and then finds out that it has a problem with its lungs and is not kosher. Instead of just looking the other way "this one time," the man throws the meat to the dogs and suffers the entire loss. Denying ourselves the temptation to cut corners and do something wrong, stands up to the *Yetzer Hara*, and shows him who's boss. That — living with Hashem instead of with the *Yetzer Hara* — is *kedushah*!

Terumah
תְּרוּמָה

וְזֹאת הַתְּרוּמָה אֲשֶׁר תִּקְחוּ מֵאִתָּם זָהָב וָכֶסֶף וּנְחֹשֶׁת: וּתְכֵלֶת וְאַרְגָּמָן וְתוֹלַעַת שָׁנִי וְשֵׁשׁ וְעִזִּים: וְעֹרֹת אֵילִם מְאָדָּמִים וְעֹרֹת תְּחָשִׁים וַעֲצֵי שִׁטִּים: שֶׁמֶן לַמָּאֹר בְּשָׂמִים לְשֶׁמֶן הַמִּשְׁחָה וְלִקְטֹרֶת הַסַּמִּים: אַבְנֵי שֹׁהַם וְאַבְנֵי מִלֻּאִים לָאֵפֹד וְלַחֹשֶׁן:

AND THIS IS THE OFFERING THAT YOU SHALL TAKE FROM THEM: GOLD, SILVER, AND COPPER; BLUE, PURPLE, AND CRIMSON WOOL; LINEN AND GOAT HAIR; RAM SKINS DYED RED, TACHASH SKINS, AND ACACIA WOOD; OIL FOR LIGHTING, SPICES FOR THE ANOINTING OIL AND FOR THE INCENSE; SHOHAM STONES AND FILLING STONES FOR THE EPHOD AND FOR THE CHOSHEN. (SHEMOS 25:3–7)

Pesukim 3–5 do not explain the how each material would be used, while *pesukim* 6 and 7 do. Why the difference?

The first three *pesukim* discuss materials that would be immediately used for the Mishkan's construction, which would be clear to all. The items in the final two *pesukim* — the oil, the spices, and the stones — were not construction materials to build the Mishkan, but things that would be used in the future for the *avodah*: the *Menorah*, the *ketores*, and the *bigdei kehunah*. Only these items were explained, as their purpose was not self-evident.

וְזֹאת הַתְּרוּמָה אֲשֶׁר תִּקְחוּ מֵאִתָּם זָהָב וָכֶסֶף וּנְחֹשֶׁת: וּתְכֵלֶת וְאַרְגָּמָן וְתוֹלַעַת שָׁנִי וְשֵׁשׁ וְעִזִּים: וְעֹרֹת אֵילִם מְאָדָּמִים וְעֹרֹת תְּחָשִׁים וַעֲצֵי שִׁטִּים: שֶׁמֶן לַמָּאֹר בְּשָׂמִים לְשֶׁמֶן הַמִּשְׁחָה וְלִקְטֹרֶת הַסַּמִּים: אַבְנֵי שֹׁהַם וְאַבְנֵי מִלֻּאִים לָאֵפֹד וְלַחֹשֶׁן:

> AND THIS IS THE OFFERING THAT YOU SHALL TAKE FROM THEM: GOLD, SILVER, AND COPPER; BLUE, PURPLE, AND CRIMSON WOOL; LINEN AND GOAT HAIR; RAM SKINS DYED RED, TACHASH SKINS, AND ACACIA WOOD; OIL FOR LIGHTING, SPICES FOR THE ANOINTING OIL AND FOR THE INCENSE; SHOHAM STONES AND FILLING STONES FOR THE EPHOD AND FOR THE CHOSHEN. (SHEMOS 25:3–7)

The materials mentioned in the *pesukim* appear to be going in a declining order of value, first expensive metals, and then materials, then skins and wooden beams. Then the Torah mentioned the precious gems that would be used for the *Ephod* and *Choshen*. Shouldn't these valuable stones have been mentioned closer to the beginning of the list, together with the gold and silver?

The way that Hashem looks at a person who gives tzedakah isn't only based on the amount of money that the person gave but also include the manner in which he gave it, and based on his income and expenses, how difficult it was for him to part with this money. It is possible that someone of more modest means will get more *sechar* for giving one hundred dollars than a wealthy man will get for giving ten thousand dollars; when this smaller amount was given more magnanimously, or included a greater degree of self-sacrifice.

Hashem wanted the B'nei Yisrael to donate to the Mishkan in the most ideal way, which included intangibilities other than the size and value of the donation. [Rashi in fact hints to this idea, for he explains that the word "לִי" — for Me" in "וְיִקְחוּ לִי תְּרוּמָה" — and you should accept for Me an offering," means "לִשְׁמִי" — focused towards Me," showing us that the mitzvah of giving to the Mishkan included the level of *kavanah* (*Shemos* 25:2).] The less valuable materials of skins and wooden beams are therefore mentioned "out of order," between the expensive metals and precious gems. This tells us that the gauge of importance of donations to the Mishkan includes factors other than the amount of money that the material cost.

> בְּטַבְּעֹת הָאָרֹן יִהְיוּ הַבַּדִּים לֹא יָסֻרוּ מִמֶּנּוּ:
>
> THE POLES OF THE ARON SHALL BE IN THE RINGS; THEY SHALL NOT BE REMOVED FROM IT. (SHEMOS 25:15)

The *Aron* had poles to allow it to be carried. So why couldn't they be removed when the Jewish people had reached their destination? Also, when we think about it, Chazal tell us the *Aron* carried itself, and even carried the people whose job was to carry it (*Sotah* 35b). So why did the *Aron* need poles at all?[21]

We may ask a similar question concerning the *Shulchan*. Rashi explains that the *Shulchan* was built in a way that the *lechem hapanim* would not sit too close together, to allow space for air to circulate so the loaves would not become moldy (*Shemos* 25:29). Now, the Gemara tells us that the *lechem hapanim* was left out for an entire week, and miraculously stayed warm and fresh the entire time. If this miracle was anyway happening, why was it necessary to ensure enough space between the loaves?

---

21   I heard this question from R' Baruch Levine.

Hashem wanted these miracles, of the *Aron's* carrying itself and of the *lechem hapanim's* remaining fresh, to occur. At the same time, He gave us the opportunity to "help," so that we may feel as if we are the ones making these things work effectively. These two elements of our trying our best and Hashem's helping us out, or better put, Hashem's perfectly taking care of things, and His giving us the chance to feel like we are playing a role, are not limited to the Mishkan, but to every day of our lives. The lesson is obvious; we may think that *we* are the ones who are being successful. But in truth it is Hashem giving us success, and the feeling of accomplishment.

The poles always remained on the *Aron* to remind us of this important lesson: that the efforts that we expend are really unnecessary. At moments that we feel that *we* have accomplished something significant, we just have to think of the *Aron's* ever-present poles, or study this *pasuk* discussing them. We will remember that these poles are here even though they are really unnecessary, just like our personal efforts at reaching success.

וְעָשִׂיתָ מְנֹרַת זָהָב ...

AND YOU SHALL MAKE A MENORAH OF PURE GOLD... (SHEMOS 25:31)

The *gematria* of the word מְנוֹרָה is 301, the same as the word "אֵשׁ — fire." The Menorah was "made" from fire, and was used to carry fire.

Tetzaveh
תְּצַוֶּה

וְאַתָּה תְּצַוֶּה אֶת בְּנֵי יִשְׂרָאֵל וְיִקְחוּ אֵלֶיךָ שֶׁמֶן זַיִת זָךְ כָּתִית לַמָּאוֹר לְהַעֲלֹת נֵר תָּמִיד:

AND YOU SHALL COMMAND THE B'NEI YISRAEL, AND THEY SHALL TAKE TO YOU PURE OLIVE OIL, CRUSHED FOR LIGHTING, TO KINDLE THE LAMPS CONTINUALLY. (SHEMOS 27:20)

When Moshe Rabbeinu was arguing with Hashem to forgive the B'nei Yisrael for making the *Eigel*, he argued: "וְעַתָּה אִם תִּשָּׂא חַטָּאתָם וְאִם אַיִן מְחֵנִי נָא מִסִּפְרְךָ אֲשֶׁר כָּתָבְתָּ — And now, if You forgive their sin. But if not, erase me now from Your book, which You have written" (*Shemos* 32:32). In punishment, Hashem omitted his name from one *parashah* in the Torah, *Parashas Tetzaveh*. Why specifically *Parashas Tetzaveh*?

Parashas Tetzaveh discusses the *bigdei Kehunah*. We know that Moshe was originally supposed to be the Kohen Gadol, but he lost this privilege when he didn't want to be the one to take the Jewish people out of Mitzrayim. Perhaps in His Mercy, Hashem arranged that the omission of Moshe's name be in a *parashah* which anyway does not focus on him, but rather focuses on Aharon and his children, in order that the absence of Moshe's name be felt less and be less painful to him.[22]

We may also suggest another approach. *Parashas Tetzaveh* is read almost a full year after hearing about Moshe's argument in *Parashas Ki Sisa*, that he was ready to be erased from the Torah if necessary. This long wait from *Ki Sisa* to the *parashah* before it, the next year, shows us that Hashem is not eager to punish. We procrastinate when we are not looking forward to doing something, but know we have to do it. So does Hashem, so to speak. He will only punish when absolutely necessary, which in our case, is that a full year of *parshios* has just about passed, and He has promised Moshe that his name would be omitted from a *parashah*. This reluctance to punish is part of Hashem's great *chessed*, which often gives us time for *teshuvah*.

וְאַתָּה הַקְרֵב אֵלֶיךָ אֶת אַהֲרֹן אָחִיךָ וְאֶת בָּנָיו אִתּוֹ מִתּוֹךְ בְּנֵי יִשְׂרָאֵל לְכַהֲנוֹ לִי אַהֲרֹן נָדָב וַאֲבִיהוּא אֶלְעָזָר וְאִיתָמָר בְּנֵי אַהֲרֹן:

And you bring close to yourself your brother Aharon, and his sons with him, from among the B'nei Yisrael to serve Me as Kohanim: Aharon, Nadav, and Avihu, Elazar, and Isamar, Aharon's sons. (Shemos 28:1)

Hashem commands Moshe to bring Aharon and his sons towards him, to make them into Kohanim. Why does the Torah say "אַהֲרֹן אָחִיךָ וְאֶת בָּנָיו אִתּוֹ — your brother Aharon, and his sons with him," then specify their names — Aharon, Nadav, and Avihu, Elazar, and Isamar — and finally, again say that these people are "בְּנֵי אַהֲרֹן — Aharon's sons"?

I once saw a *sefer* which explained that the Torah in this *pasuk* calls Aharon "אָחִיךָ — your brother," as a reprimand to Moshe, to remind him

---

22 I later saw this approach in the *Baal Haturim*.

that the *Kehunah* was originally supposed to be his, and only went to Aharon because he had refused Hashem's instruction of leading B'nei Yisrael. Perhaps this approach also explains why Aharon's sons are mentioned. This too is part of Hashem's reprimand to Moshe; not only would he have been a Kohen, but the *Kehunah* would have been in his family forever, and passed down to *his* children, instead of Aharon's.

> וְאַתָּה הַקְרֵב אֵלֶיךָ אֶת אַהֲרֹן אָחִיךָ וְאֶת בָּנָיו אִתּוֹ מִתּוֹךְ בְּנֵי יִשְׂרָאֵל לְכַהֲנוֹ לִי אַהֲרֹן נָדָב וַאֲבִיהוּא אֶלְעָזָר וְאִיתָמָר בְּנֵי אַהֲרֹן:
>
> AND YOU BRING CLOSE TO YOURSELF YOUR BROTHER AHARON, AND HIS SONS WITH HIM, FROM AMONG THE B'NEI YISRAEL TO SERVE ME AS KOHANIM: AHARON, NADAV, AND AVIHU, ELAZAR, AND ISAMAR, AHARON'S SONS. (SHEMOS 28:1)

This *pasuk* is discussing the way that Hashem instructed Moshe to inaugurate Aharon and his sons as Kohanim. Why did Hashem tell Moshe to "הַקְרֵב אֵלֶיךָ אֶת אַהֲרֹן אָחִיךָ וְאֶת בָּנָיו — bring close *to yourself* your brother Aharon and his sons"? *Kehunah* is an added closeness to Hashem. Why, then, didn't Hashem say, "הַקְרֵב אֵלַי אֶת אַהֲרֹן אָחִיךָ וְאֶת בָּנָיו — bring close *to Me* your brother Aharon and his sons"?

Moshe Rabbeinu was the prototypical *eved Hashem*, from whom we learn what serving Hashem means. Hashem told Moshe to bring Aharon and his sons close to *him*, so he could educate them. Being close to Moshe would enable Aharon and his children to watch Moshe's every move and see that it was *lesheim Shamayim*, which was an excellent preparation for their becoming Kohanim. This was true by Aharon and his sons, and is certainly true in regard to us. The way that we may become better *ovdei Hashem* is by becoming closer to *rabbonim* and *talmidei chachamim*, where we can then watch and emulate their behavior.

וְהֵם יִקְחוּ אֶת הַזָּהָב וְאֶת הַתְּכֵלֶת וְאֶת הָאַרְגָּמָן
וְאֶת תּוֹלַעַת הַשָּׁנִי וְאֶת הַשֵּׁשׁ:

THEY SHALL TAKE THE GOLD, THE BLUE,
PURPLE, AND CRIMSON WOOL, AND THE
LINEN. (SHEMOS 28:5)

Rashi explains that the people being referred to in "וְהֵם יִקְחוּ אֶת הַזָּהָב וכו' — *they* shall take the gold etc.," are the *chachmei lev*, the artisans who were to make the *bigdei Kehunah*. These people, explains Rashi, were to directly receive the donations of the materials mentioned in this *pasuk* — "the gold, the blue, purple, and crimson wool, and the linen," — from the people donating them. Now, in the beginning of *Parashas Terumah*, we find that Hashem spoke to Moshe and told him "תִּקְחוּ אֶת תְּרוּמָתִי — *you* shall take My offering," implying that he was to oversee the entire donation and collection process (25:2). Why were the *bigdei Kehunah* different that their materials were to be given directly to the *chachmei lev* who would use them without their first going through a middleman overseeing the donations?

We discussed earlier (page 157) that the reason why Moshe's name was specifically omitted from *Parashas Tetzaveh* is because this *parashah* discusses the *bigdei Kehunah*, which were taken away from Moshe for initially refusing Hashem's instruction that he take the Jewish people out of Mitzrayim. Since Moshe's name would in any case be left out of one *parashah*, Hashem spared him the pain of being mentioned in the context of the *bigdei Kehunah*, which he had lost.

Perhaps this is also why Hashem allowed the *bigdei Kehunah* materials to be given directly to the *chachmei lev* artisans who would use them, instead of first giving them to Moshe. This too would spare Moshe the hurt of being involved in making the special clothing that he could have worn, and lost.

Ki Sisa
כִּי תִשָּׂא

וּשְׁמַרְתֶּם אֶת הַשַּׁבָּת כִּי קֹדֶשׁ הִוא לָכֶם מְחַלְלֶיהָ מוֹת יוּמָת ...

THEREFORE, KEEP THE SHABBOS, FOR IT IS A SACRED THING FOR YOU. THOSE WHO DESECRATE IT SHALL SURELY BE PUT TO DEATH...

(SHEMOS 31:14)

When speaking about Shabbos, the Torah mentions "מְחַלְלֶיהָ — those who desecrate it," referring to someone who does *melachah* — writing, cooking, or building, for example — on the holy day. Rashi, however, gives a deeper insight in *chillul Shabbos*, by explaining that מְחַלְלֶיהָ means "הַנּוֹהֵג בָּהּ חוֹל בִּקְדֻשָּׁתָהּ — those who treat its sanctity as ordinary." In explaining "מְחַלְלֶיהָ" in this way, Rashi is telling us the meaning behind *melachos* being forbidden, namely, that it is inherently wrong to act on Shabbos, a day which is holy and special, in the same way as he acts during the week.

By extension, understanding that acting in a weekday manner on Shabbos desecrates it, shows us the great need to make sure that the things that we do on Shabbos are different than how we act and spend our time during the week, even when not technically doing a *melachah*.

162 A Deeper Dimension

A daily routine that is similar to a weekday also makes Shabbos "ordinary," and desecrates the *kedushah* of Shabbos.

וַיִּפֶן וַיֵּרֶד מֹשֶׁה מִן הָהָר וּשְׁנֵי לֻחֹת הָעֵדֻת בְּיָדוֹ
לֻחֹת כְּתֻבִים מִשְּׁנֵי עֶבְרֵיהֶם מִזֶּה וּמִזֶּה הֵם
כְּתֻבִים: וְהַלֻּחֹת מַעֲשֵׂה אֱלֹקִים הֵמָּה וְהַמִּכְתָּב
מִכְתַּב אֱלֹקִים הוּא חָרוּת עַל הַלֻּחֹת:

AND MOSHE TURNED AND WENT DOWN
FROM THE MOUNTAIN BEARING THE TWO
TABLETS OF THE TESTIMONY IN HIS HAND,
TABLETS INSCRIBED FROM BOTH THEIR SIDES;
ON ONE SIDE AND ON THE OTHER SIDE THEY
WERE INSCRIBED. NOW, THE TABLETS WERE
HASHEM'S WORK, AND THE INSCRIPTION WAS
HASHEM'S INSCRIPTION, ENGRAVED ON THE
TABLETS. (SHEMOS 32:15–16)

Hashem told Moshe that the B'nei Yisrael were worshipping *avodah zarah* while he was still standing upon Har Sinai. Why then did Moshe take the *Luchos* down with him?

We may also ask a second question. As we know, Moshe broke the *Luchos*. Why then does the Torah spend several *pesukim* describing the *Luchos*; "inscribed from both their sides; on one side and on the other side they were inscribed... the tablets were Hashem's work, and the inscription was Hashem's inscription, engraved on the tablets"? What is the point of knowing the details of something that would soon be broken?

Perhaps Moshe took the *Luchos* down from Har Sinai with him to show them to the Jewish people, so they would see the infinite difference between the beauty and overwhelming superiority of Hashem's *Luchos*, and the *Eigel*, which they had made through the powers of *kishuf* and *tumah*. Right now, reasoned Moshe, the B'nei Yisrael are distracted, and have been drawn to the *Eigel*, because that is all that they have.

But, once they see the *Luchos*, they will realize the mistake of worshipping the "cheap imitation", and will quickly cast it aside and return to Hashem. The Torah details the spiritual characteristics of the *Luchos*, in order to highlight the qualities that Moshe had hoped would make an impression on the B'nei Yisrael.

However, Moshe's plan didn't work. When he descended the mountain and saw the Jewish Camp, he saw that it was simply too late to stop their moral decline. Moshe saw that not only had the B'nei Yisrael made an *Eigel*, but "וַיַּרְא אֶת הָעֵגֶל וּמְחֹלֹת" — he saw the Eigel *and the dances"* (32:19). The *Eigel* had so captivated the Jewish people that they did not only make an *avodah zarah* and bow to it, but were even enthusiastically dancing around it. When he saw this, Moshe realized that he was too late. It is true that the *Luchos* were superior in every way. But the stupor that the B'nei Yisrael were in simply did not permit them to appreciate these qualities and stop their moral decline. At that point, Moshe understood that the only impression that he could possibly make on the B'nei Yisrael was by breaking the *Luchos*.

וַיִּקַּח אֶת הָעֵגֶל אֲשֶׁר עָשׂוּ וַיִּשְׂרֹף בָּאֵשׁ וַיִּטְחַן עַד אֲשֶׁר דָּק ...

THEN HE TOOK THE EIGEL THEY HAD MADE, BURNED IT IN FIRE, GROUND IT TO FINE POWDER... (SHEMOS 32:20)

The *Eigel* was of course made out of gold. How then did Moshe burn it and grind its ashes? Gold does not burn; it melts!

In his comments to *pasuk* 5, Rashi explains that Aharon saw that the golden calf statue had come to life. Similarly, the *Midrash Tanchuma* tells us that the *Eigel* roared as it jumped about (32:19). This shows us that while the calf was originally made out of gold, it now had the characteristics of a real animal. With this, we can understand how Moshe was able to burn the *Eigel* and grind its ashes, for here too it burned, just like a real animal.

נֹצֵר חֶסֶד לָאֲלָפִים ...

PRESERVING CHESSED FOR THOUSANDS OF GENERATIONS... (SHEMOS 34:7)

When written in a *Sefer Torah*, the word נֹצֵר is written with a large letter נ. Why?

When discussing how to count the Jewish people in our *parashah* Hashem instructed "וְנָתְנוּ אִישׁ כֹּפֶר נַפְשׁוֹ לַה'" — let each one give Hashem an atonement for his soul" (30:12). The *Baal Haturim* points out that the word "וְנָתְנוּ — and he shall give," is a palindrome, that reading these letters forwards or backwards spells the same word.[23] This teaches us that tzedakah money goes "forwards and backwards"; that is to say, that the money a person gives to tzedakah will not be lost, but will eventually come back to him.

Similarly, the letter נ, spelled נ-ו-ן, is also a palindrome. Perhaps the נ in the phrase "נֹצֵר חֶסֶד — preserving *chessed*" is written bigger, to highlight a similar lesson regarding *chessed*. A person who spends time helping another person — whether visiting the sick, learning Torah with someone on a weaker level, or doing one of the many, many, different *chassadim* which can take up many hours of a person's time — will not lose by doing so. On the contrary, Hashem saves the reward for him or his progeny, for two thousand generations.

כִּי לֹא תִשְׁתַּחֲוֶה לְאֵל אַחֵר ...

FOR YOU SHALL NOT PROSTRATE YOURSELF BEFORE ANOTHER GOD... (SHEMOS 34:14)

When written in a *Sefer Torah*, the word אַחֵר is written with a large letter ר. Why?

The Midrash tells us that if in this *pasuk*, a person even mistakenly changes the letter ר of אַחֵר to a ד, perhaps by adding a bit too much ink

---

23   I heard this *Baal Haturim* from Rabbi Paysach Krohn.

to the letter's top right corner, he is essentially destroying the world, for he has entirely changed its meaning (*Vayikra Rabba* 19:2). Altering the letter ד to a ר changes the *pasuk*'s translation from "you shall not prostrate yourself before another god," to "you shall not bow down to the G-d Who is One," *chas veshalom*. Maybe this is the reason why the Torah enlarged the letter ד, to emphasize how important this letter is.

We may also suggest another approach. The letter ר is spelled ר-י-ש, which means "head." Perhaps, by enlarging the ר, the Torah is telling us that besides for of course not bowing down to another god — an idol — we must not even tip our head in its direction, for even the slightest positive movement can indicate that there is some credence, *chas veshalom*, to an entity other than Hashem.

וַיַּרְא אַהֲרֹן וְכָל בְּנֵי יִשְׂרָאֵל אֶת מֹשֶׁה וְהִנֵּה קָרַן עוֹר פָּנָיו וַיִּירְאוּ מִגֶּשֶׁת אֵלָיו:

AHARON AND ALL THE B'NEI YISRAEL SAW MOSHE AND BEHOLD! THE SKIN OF HIS FACE HAD BECOME RADIANT, AND THEY WERE AFRAID TO COME NEAR HIM. (SHEMOS 34:30)

וּבְבֹא מֹשֶׁה לִפְנֵי ה' לְדַבֵּר אִתּוֹ יָסִיר אֶת הַמַּסְוֶה עַד צֵאתוֹ וְיָצָא וְדִבֶּר אֶל בְּנֵי יִשְׂרָאֵל אֵת אֲשֶׁר יְצֻוֶּה:

WHEN MOSHE WOULD COME BEFORE HASHEM TO SPEAK WITH HIM, HE WOULD REMOVE THE MASK UNTIL HIS DEPARTURE, THEN HE WOULD LEAVE AND TELL B'NEI YISRAEL WHAT HE HAD BEEN COMMANDED. (SHEMOS 34:34)

The Torah tells us in *pasuk* 30 that Moshe Rabbeinu's face shone. Why is this repeated in *pasuk* 34?

We often listen to a *shiur*, *daven* at a *kever*, or even go to Eretz Yisrael, and become very inspired. We want to keep this feeling alive. However, this burst of inspiration and dedication is unfortunately generally short-lived.

The Torah is telling us that that was not the case with Moshe Rabbeinu. The *karnei hod* that he had when he came down from Har Sinai never left him. Moshe was able to capture a *madreigah*, and stay with it.

Vayakhel

קְחוּ מֵאִתְּכֶם תְּרוּמָה לַה' כֹּל נְדִיב לִבּוֹ יְבִיאֶהָ אֵת תְּרוּמַת ה' זָהָב וָכֶסֶף וּנְחֹשֶׁת: וּתְכֵלֶת וְאַרְגָּמָן וְתוֹלַעַת שָׁנִי וְשֵׁשׁ וְעִזִּים: וְעֹרֹת אֵילִם מְאָדָּמִים וְעֹרֹת תְּחָשִׁים וַעֲצֵי שִׁטִּים: וְשֶׁמֶן לַמָּאוֹר וּבְשָׂמִים לְשֶׁמֶן הַמִּשְׁחָה וְלִקְטֹרֶת הַסַּמִּים: וְאַבְנֵי שֹׁהַם וְאַבְנֵי מִלֻּאִים לָאֵפוֹד וְלַחֹשֶׁן:

Take from yourselves an offering for Hashem; every generous-hearted person shall bring it, namely, Hashem's offering: gold, silver, and copper; and blue, purple, and crimson wool; and linen and goat hair; and ram skins dyed red, tachash skins, and acacia wood; and oil for lighting, and spices for the anointing oil and for the incense; and Shoham stones and filling stones for the Ephod and for the Choshen. (Shemos 35:5–9)

These *pesukim* are filled with words beginning with the letter ו, connecting each new phrase to the one before it. The *Ohr Hachaim* explains that many uses of the "וְהַחִיבּוּר — connector ו" teaches us that אֶחָד הַמַּרְבֶּה וְאֶחָד הַמַּמְעִיט, וּבִלְבַד שֶׁיְּכַוֵּין לִבּוֹ לְשָׁמַיִם, whether a person gives a lot or a little, the imperative is that his heart's *kavanah* is Heavenward.[24] By starting each phrase with a letter ו, the Torah is showing us that from Hashem's perspective, all of the gifts are the same; a person who altruistically donated wool is the same as someone else who altruistically donated gold.

We may suggest another idea alluded to by the repetition of the letter ו. There are fifteen words beginning with a "וְהַחִיבּוּר — connector ו," in these *pesukim*. Similarly, the morning *berachah* of אֱמֶת וְיַצִּיב, said immediately after *krias shema*, also has fifteen words starting with וְהַחִיבּוּר: וְיַצִּיב, וְנָכוֹן, וְקַיָּם.... The Ramo explains that since the *gematria* of the letter ו is 6, fifteen times the letter ו is 90 (*Orach Chaim* 61:3). And, when we factor in the "reading it," we have 91. Now, continues the Ramo, 91 is the combined *gematria* of Hashem's two Names of "י-ה-ו-ה" (26) and "א-ד-נ-י" (65). The Torah therefore is telling us that Hashem's Names were present in the Mishkan's materials.

> וַיָּבֹאוּ הָאֲנָשִׁים עַל הַנָּשִׁים כֹּל נְדִיב לֵב הֵבִיאוּ חָח
> וָנֶזֶם וְטַבַּעַת וְכוּמָז כָּל כְּלִי זָהָב וְכָל אִישׁ אֲשֶׁר
> הֵנִיף תְּנוּפַת זָהָב לַה':

THE MEN CAME WITH THE WOMEN; EVERY GENEROUS HEARTED PERSON BROUGHT BRACELETS AND EARRINGS AND RINGS AND BUCKLES, ALL KINDS OF GOLDEN OBJECTS, AND EVERY MAN WHO WAVED A WAVING OF GOLD TO HASHEM. (SHEMOS 35:22)

Why was it necessary for the men to go along, when the women donated their jewelry to the Mishkan?

---

24 R' Shlomo Gigi showed me this *Ohr Hachaim*.

VAYAKHEL

During the episode of the *Eigel*, Aharon tried to stall, and told the men to go to their wives and ask them for their jewelry. The women did not agree to volunteer. The men, in their great enthusiasm, simply tore the jewelry away from them, in many cases tearing it off their ears. When it came time to donate to the Mishkan, the women enthusiastically volunteered. They brought their husbands with them, to teach them a lesson in proper giving, in donating one's most meaningful possessions to Hashem.

וְהַנְּשִׂאָם הֵבִיאוּ אֵת אַבְנֵי הַשֹּׁהַם ...

AND THE NESI'IM BROUGHT THE SHOHAM STONES. (SHEMOS 35:27)

The *gematria* of the word וְהַנְשִׂאִים, when spelled מָלֵא, is 412. And, the *gematria* of the phrase אַבְנֵי הַשֹּׁהַם is 413.

וְהַנְּשִׂאָם הֵבִיאוּ אֵת אַבְנֵי הַשֹּׁהַם וְאֵת אַבְנֵי
הַמִּלֻּאִים לָאֵפוֹד וְלַחֹשֶׁן:

AND THE NESI'IM BROUGHT THE SHOHAM STONES AND FILLING STONES FOR THE EPHOD AND FOR THE CHOSHEN. (SHEMOS 35:27)

Rashi points out that the word וְהַנְּשִׂאָם is written חָסֵר, without the letter י. This was in criticism of the *Nesi'im*, who, in contrast to the excitement shown by the rest of B'nei Yisrael, did not rush to donate to the Mishkan, explaining that they would give whichever items were missing at the end. To show their *atzlus*, the Torah left a letter י out of their names.

Why was specifically the letter י left out?

The letter י is spelled out י-ו-ד, which is closely related to the word "יָד — hand." The *Nesi'im's* failing was that they didn't *give* to the Mishkan when they were supposed to. To bring out this point, the letter י was left out, symbolizing that their "יָד — hand" had fallen short.

וְעָשָׂה בְצַלְאֵל וְאָהֳלִיאָב וְכֹל אִישׁ חֲכַם לֵב אֲשֶׁר נָתַן ה' חָכְמָה וּתְבוּנָה בָּהֵמָּה לָדַעַת לַעֲשֹׂת אֶת כָּל מְלֶאכֶת עֲבֹדַת הַקֹּדֶשׁ לְכֹל אֲשֶׁר צִוָּה ה':

Betzalel and Oholiav and every wise-hearted man into whom Hashem had imbued wisdom and insight to know how to do, shall do all the work of the holy service, according to all that Hashem has commanded. (Shemos 36:1)

Why is it so noteworthy that Betzalel and his team did what Hashem commanded, that the Torah has to mention it?

The *Ohr Hachaim* asks another question. At the time to which the *pasuk* is referring, the B'nei Yisrael had not yet begun to collect the materials for the Mishkan. What could have Betzalel done, that the Torah praises him for acting as Hashem had commanded? In answer, he explains that much preparation was necessary before the actual work could begin. Tools had to be prepared, and made available for use. These preparations are what the Torah is referring to.

We may understand several things from the *Ohr Hachaim*'s explanation. Betzalel was an architect and master craftsman, and could have certainly justified having an assistant take care of the tools and other prep work. Nevertheless, he understood it proper than he should be involved in every aspect of the Mishkan.

Betzalel's exuberance doubtlessly allowed the Mishkan's construction to proceed in a more expeditious manner. There is no comparison to a project in which all the tools, equipment, and materials are prepared and neatly laid out, to one which must be stopped several times in the middle in order to find the right tool or piece of wood. Betzalel wanted the work on the Mishkan to go as smoothly as possible, and did all he could to make that happen.

וַיְצַו מֹשֶׁה וַיַּעֲבִירוּ קוֹל בַּמַּחֲנֶה לֵאמֹר אִישׁ וְאִשָּׁה
אַל יַעֲשׂוּ עוֹד מְלָאכָה לִתְרוּמַת הַקֹּדֶשׁ וַיִּכָּלֵא
הָעָם מֵהָבִיא:

> So Moshe commanded, and they announced in the camp, saying, "Let no man or woman do any more work for the offering for the Holy." So the people refrained from bringing. (Shemos 36:6)

Onkelous explains that the word וַיִּכָּלֵא means "וּפְסַק — they stopped," telling us that they stopped bringing donations when Moshe told them to stop. Rashi, however, explains differently, that וַיִּכָּלֵא means "they held back."

Rashi is telling us that the B'nei Yisrael wanted to continue giving to the Mishkan, but since the coffers were already full, were prevented from doing so. This may be compared to the willpower of a person on a diet, who sees something that makes his mouth water. Since he is hungry and wants to eat it, he must literally *hold himself back*. The enthusiasm that the Jewish people had for the Mishkan was so intense that ceasing to donate required a conscious and powerful decision.[25]

וַיַּעֲשׂוּ כָל חֲכַם לֵב בְּעֹשֵׂי הַמְּלָאכָה אֶת הַמִּשְׁכָּן
עֶשֶׂר יְרִיעֹת שֵׁשׁ מָשְׁזָר וּתְכֵלֶת וְאַרְגָּמָן וְתוֹלַעַת
שָׁנִי כְּרֻבִים מַעֲשֵׂה חֹשֵׁב עָשָׂה אֹתָם:

> Then all the wise-hearted people of the performers of the work made the Mishkan out of ten curtains, consisting of twisted fine linen, and blue, purple, and crimson wool. A cherubim design, the work of a master weaver he made them. (Shemos 36:8)

---

25 I later saw this approach in the *Sefas Emes*.

Why does the Torah stress that the *chachmei lev* made the curtains for the Mishkan? That was one of the things on their list!

The *Ohr Hachaim* explains that the curtains were not made by one artisan but by many; "וַיַּעֲשׂוּ כָל חֲכַם לֵב ... אֶת הַמִּשְׁכָּן עֶשֶׂר יְרִיעֹת" — all the wise hearted people made the Mishkan out of ten curtains." Normally, such a project would look like it was made by many people, with different shades of color, various stitching, and a less than uniform pattern. The Torah is telling us that the Mishkan's curtains looked perfect. All the pieces were combined to the exact specifications, and the curtains looked as if each one was a product from the same craftsman.

Perhaps we may add the following. Projects which involve many people often come with discord, and argument. At the same time, the better the staff works together, the better the finished product will be. In telling us that the curtains came out exactly as they should, the Torah is not only testifying to the degree of work and precision. The perfect curtains were also a testimony to the cohesiveness, teamwork, and *shalom* of the people involved in making it as well.

Pekudei
פְּקוּדֵי

וּבְצַלְאֵל בֶּן אוּרִי בֶן חוּר לְמַטֵּה יְהוּדָה עָשָׂה אֵת
כָּל אֲשֶׁר צִוָּה ה' אֶת מֹשֶׁה:

BETZALEL, SON OF URI, SON OF CHUR,
OF THE TRIBE OF YEHUDAH, HAD MADE
ALL THAT HASHEM HAD COMMANDED
MOSHE. (SHEMOS 38:22)

Why does the Torah tell us that Betzalel had made "כָּל אֲשֶׁר צִוָּה ה' אֶת מֹשֶׁה — *all* that Hashem had commanded Moshe"? Would we have supposed otherwise?

Rashi explains that Betzalel actually reversed the order in which Moshe told him to build the Mishkan and its *keilim*. Moshe had told Betzalel to first make the *keilim*, and then the Mishkan structure. Betzalel responded that the other way — first the Mishkan and only then the *keilim* — makes more sense. Amazed, Moshe agreed to Betzalel; that is what Hashem had told me!

This conversation is amazing. Betzalel was twelve years old at the time, and yet had the courage to challenge Moshe Rabbeinu, who was the *Melech* of Klal Yisrael, the greatest *Navi* to ever live, and was a man in his mid-eighties. Imagine the inner conflict that Betzalel must have had when he realized Moshe's mistake. Betzalel could have easily done as he was told, and had whom to "blame" and pass the buck; after all, this is what Moshe Rabbeinu told me to do! Yet Betzalel did what he felt was right, despite being at odds with Moshe himself.

> כָּל הַזָּהָב הֶעָשׂוּי לַמְּלָאכָה בְּכֹל מְלֶאכֶת הַקֹּדֶשׁ וַיְהִי זְהַב הַתְּנוּפָה תֵּשַׁע וְעֶשְׂרִים כִּכָּר וּשְׁבַע מֵאוֹת וּשְׁלֹשִׁים שֶׁקֶל בְּשֶׁקֶל הַקֹּדֶשׁ:
>
> ALL THE GOLD THAT HAD BEEN USED FOR THE WORK IN ALL THE WORK OF THE HOLY THE GOLD OF THE WAVING WAS TWENTY NINE TALENTS, SEVEN HUNDRED AND THIRTY SHEKELS, ACCORDING TO THE HOLY SHEKEL. (SHEMOS 38:24)

The *Sefas Emes* asks that we know that a *berachah* only takes effect on something that is hidden from the eye. Why then does the Torah openly record the amounts of gold, silver, and copper than were received and used in the Mishkan?

Perhaps indeed, the Torah is forgoing this extra *berachah* that inconspicuousness brings, in order that no one have any suspicions that any money donated to the Mishkan had been stolen. The Torah is telling us that as important as added *berachah* may be, the need to be above blame is an absolute necessity.

> וַתֵּכֶל כָּל עֲבֹדַת מִשְׁכַּן אֹהֶל מוֹעֵד וַיַּעֲשׂוּ בְּנֵי יִשְׂרָאֵל כְּכֹל אֲשֶׁר צִוָּה ה' אֶת מֹשֶׁה כֵּן עָשׂוּ:
>
> ALL THE WORK OF THE MISHKAN OF THE OHEL MOED WAS COMPLETED; THE B'NEI YISRAEL HAD DONE IT; ACCORDING TO ALL THAT HASHEM HAD COMMANDED MOSHE, SO THEY HAD DONE. (SHEMOS 39:32)

What point is the Torah making when telling us that the B'nei Yisrael completed all of the Mishkan as Hashem had commanded Moshe?

The Seforno explains that literally the entire B'nei Yisrael participated in building the Mishkan, whether through donating money or materials, or by assisting with the actual physical labor. The Torah is testifying that the Mishkan that was built was not the efforts of a few individuals, but was indeed a product of all of Klal Yisrael.

We all know that it is often much more efficient to take care of something alone instead of asking a large team of people to do it. And it often seems that the more people that are involved in something, the less gets done. People end up getting in each other's way, everyone wants certain jobs and not other ones, and it's not always clear whose piece should be put where. We may appreciate the overwhelming feelings of collaboration and unity of purpose that the B'nei Yisrael had to accomplish this task of building the Mishkan. When else in history did everyone participate and something was accomplished in the most beautiful manner?

וַיַּרְא מֹשֶׁה אֶת כָּל הַמְּלָאכָה וְהִנֵּה עָשׂוּ אֹתָהּ
כַּאֲשֶׁר צִוָּה ה' כֵּן עָשׂוּ וַיְבָרֶךְ אֹתָם מֹשֶׁה:

MOSHE SAW THE ENTIRE WORK, AND BEHOLD!
— THEY HAD DONE IT AS HASHEM HAD
COMMANDED, SO HAD THEY DONE. SO MOSHE
BLESSED THEM. (SHEMOS 39:43)

Which special praise is the Torah showering on the B'nei Yisrael, in stating that they built the Mishkan exactly as Hashem had commanded?

Rav Hirsch gives a beautiful explanation to this *pasuk*: "Nowhere could be detected an effort, by adding or leaving out to carry out any idea of improvement, to leave some impression of the artist's own personality on the work. Each and every workman accepted as his highest aim the careful and precise carrying out, not of his own ideas, but the ideas and thoughts which were embodied in the commands of Hashem."

The essence of art is about the "I." How do *I* interpret a bowl of fruit? How can *I* make *my* building unique, thereby distinguishing it from the hundreds of other buildings in town? The *chachmei lev* were commanded to create a Mishkan and its *keilim* according to instructions that are an anathema to a true artist. These skilled craftsmen were relegated to regular construction workers following a blueprint. And, along the same lines, there was nowhere for them to sign their names. Besides for being superbly done, all of their work was done purely for Hashem's sake, without any personal recognition.

> וַיַּרְא מֹשֶׁה אֶת כָּל הַמְּלָאכָה וְהִנֵּה עָשׂוּ אֹתָהּ
> כַּאֲשֶׁר צִוָּה ה' כֵּן עָשׂוּ וַיְבָרֶךְ אֹתָם מֹשֶׁה:

> MOSHE SAW THE ENTIRE WORK, AND BEHOLD!
> — THEY HAD DONE IT AS HASHEM HAD
> COMMANDED, SO HAD THEY DONE. SO MOSHE
> BLESSED THEM. (SHEMOS 39:43)

Why doesn't the Torah say "וַיַּרְא מֹשֶׁה אֶת כָּל הַמְּלָאכָה וְהִנֵּה עָשׂוּ אֹתָהּ כַּאֲשֶׁר צִוָּה אוֹתוֹ ה' — Moshe saw the entire work, and behold! — They had done it as Hashem had commanded *him*, so had they done"?

Moshe Rabbeinu just saw himself as a conduit of transmitting Hashem's Word to the Jewish people; the intermediary was not at all important. When Moshe looked over the entire completed Mishkan, the only thing that he saw was that the blueprints that Hashem had instructed had become a reality.

> וְאֶת בָּנָיו תַּקְרִיב וְהִלְבַּשְׁתָּ אֹתָם כֻּתֳּנֹת: וּמָשַׁחְתָּ
> אֹתָם כַּאֲשֶׁר מָשַׁחְתָּ אֶת אֲבִיהֶם וְכִהֲנוּ לִי וְהָיְתָה
> לִהְיֹת לָהֶם מָשְׁחָתָם לִכְהֻנַּת עוֹלָם לְדֹרֹתָם: וַיַּעַשׂ
> מֹשֶׁה כְּכֹל אֲשֶׁר צִוָּה ה' אֹתוֹ כֵּן עָשָׂה:

> AND YOU SHALL BRING HIS SONS NEAR AND
> CLOTHE THEM WITH TUNICS. AND YOU SHALL

ANOINT THEM, AS YOU HAVE ANOINTED THEIR FATHER, SO THAT THEY MAY SERVE ME AS KOHANIM. AND THIS SHALL BE SO THAT THEIR ANOINTMENT SHALL REMAIN FOR THEM AN EVERLASTING KEHUNAH THROUGHOUT THEIR GENERATIONS. THUS MOSHE DID; ACCORDING TO ALL THAT HASHEM HAD COMMANDED HIM, SO HE DID. (SHEMOS 40:14–16)

Why is it so noteworthy that Moshe did what Hashem told him, that the Torah has to mention it?

Moshe was told to prepare Aharon and his sons to be Kohanim, in a several-step process of bringing them close to him, clothing them in the *bigdei Kehunah*, and anointing them. Imagine how hard this was for Moshe to do. We know that *Moshe* was supposed to have been the Kohen Gadol, and *his* children Kohanim (see Rashi to *Shemos* 4:14)! Yet, we do not find that Moshe asked Hashem to find someone else to consecrate Aharon and his sons or did this mitzvah in any less than perfect way.

Sometime we are put into a very uncomfortable situation, where it is very hard to do the right thing. Let us learn from Moshe Rabbeinu, and focus not on ourselves, but on what Hashem wants us to do.

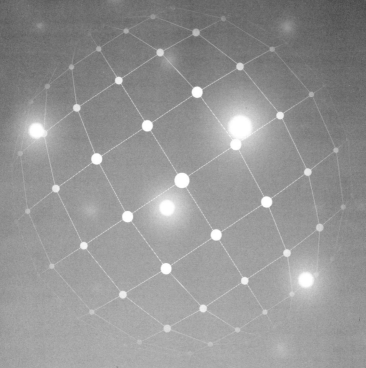

Vayikra

וַיִּקְרָא

VAYIKRA
וַיִּקְרָא

וַיִּקְרָא אֶל מֹשֶׁה...
AND HE CALLED TO MOSHE... (VAYIKRA 1:1)

When written in a *Sefer Torah*, the word וַיִּקְרָא is written with a small letter א. Why?

The Chasam Sofer explains that at Har Sinai, the entire B'nei Yisrael achieved *ruach hakodesh*, which was lost after the *Cheit Ha'Eigel*. The only one who stayed on this level was Moshe Rabbeinu. In his humility, Moshe did not want to call attention to the fact that he was still able to receive Hashem's communication, when everyone else was not. So Moshe wrote a small letter א in the word וַיִּקְרָא, which means "and He called," to make it appear as וַיִּקָּר, meaning "and He chanced upon"; as if to say that Hashem only spoke to Moshe because He "happened" to meet him, instead of His "calling out" to him and specifically requesting a private audience.

The word וַיִּקְרָא appears many times in the Torah. Why is the beginning of *Sefer Vayikra* the place where this lesson is specifically said?

The Midrash tells us that *Sefer Vayikra* is the place where a child traditionally begins learning *Chumash*, for, הַתִּינוֹקוֹת טְהוֹרִין וְהַקָּרְבָּנוֹת טְהוֹרִין יָבוֹאוּ טְהוֹרִין וְיִתְעַסְּקוּ בִּטְהוֹרִין, the children are *tahor*, and *korbanos* are *tahor*; let pure children study about pure *korbanos* (*Vayikra Rabbah* 7:3). Perhaps this is the reason why the lesson of Moshe's humility is said specifically here. Since *Sefer Vayikra* is the first exposure to Torah that a child will have, the Torah conveys this lifelong lesson about humility and sensitivity to others at the first possible moment. When reading literally the first word he comes across in the Torah, a child will ask why this letter א is smaller than the other letters, and receive this lesson.

Another fascinating idea that comes from the Torah's writing וַיִּקְרָא with a small letter א is that when reading his first word of the Torah, the child will already realize that he has a question which needs an answer. What a beautiful lesson to learn on the first day of *cheder*!

אָדָם כִּי יַקְרִיב מִכֶּם קָרְבָּן לַה' ...

WHEN A PERSON FROM AMONG YOU BRINGS AN OFFERING TO HASHEM... (VAYIKRA 1:2)

Rashi explains that this *pasuk* which says "אָדָם כִּי יַקְרִיב מִכֶּם," which may also be read "when a person brings a *korban* from within himself," is discussing a voluntary *korban*.

The word מִכֶּם is a palindrome, that is to say, that reading it backwards or forwards spells the same word. Based on the *Baal Haturim* which we discussed in *Parashas Ki Sisa* (page 164), who explains that the Torah's use of the palindrome וְנָתְנוּ when discussing tzedakah teaches us that the money that a person gives to tzedakah will one day return to him, we may understand that our *pasuk* is extending this idea to any money that is spent on *divrei ruchniyus*. A person who gives Hashem a "voluntary *korban*" even at great personal cost will not lose out, for he will only gain from his experience. Keeping this thought in mind makes it easier for a person to use his hard earned money for a mitzvah, for it is not so hard to part with our money when we know that it is coming right back.

Another message that we may understand in the Torah's using a palindrome to discuss offering a voluntary *korban*, involves the different parts of a person that may motivate him to bring a *korban*. Some people may inwardly know that it is correct to spend money on mitzvah items, but are hesitant to actually do so. Or another person is only bringing a *korban* to show off to others, and is missing the inner sense of altruism. מִכֶּם is teaching us that both ways are still imperfect; a *korban* must be bidirectional, that is, תּוֹכוֹ כְּבָרוֹ וּבָרוֹ כְּתוֹכוֹ, that the person's inner motives are like his outward actions, and outward actions like his inner motives.

TZAV
צַו

צַו אֶת אַהֲרֹן וְאֶת בָּנָיו לֵאמֹר זֹאת תּוֹרַת הָעֹלָה ...
COMMAND AHARON AND HIS SONS, SAYING, "THIS IS THE LAW OF THE BURNT OFFERING..."
(VAYIKRA 6:2)

Rashi explains that the Torah uses the word "צַו — command," which is a terminology that connotes added focus and enthusiasm, when introducing the *korban olah*. The reason for this is because the Kohen administering the *korban olah* didn't get so much out of doing so, for, in contrast to offering a *korban shelamim* or *korban chatas*, where the Kohen received some of the meat, a Kohen who offered an *olah* only received the hides. [I later saw that the *Divrei David* and the *Gur Aryeh* also explain Rashi's terminology of "חֶסְרוֹן כִּיס — loss of money" in this manner, for the Kohen of course did not actually lose any money out of pocket by bringing a *korban olah*.] To counterbalance a Kohen's natural reluctance to "waste" his time offering this *korban*, the Torah introduces this mitzvah with an extra expression of focus.

The Torah is telling the Kohanim a message, that their criteria for deciding whose *korban* to offer from among the several people waiting should not be the one in which they profit the most. Rather, it must only be a decision that is based on efficiency and enhancement of *kavod Shamayim*, even when it comes at their own expense.

צַו אֶת אַהֲרֹן וְאֶת בָּנָיו לֵאמֹר זֹאת תּוֹרַת הָעֹלָה הִוא הָעֹלָה עַל מוֹקְדָה עַל הַמִּזְבֵּחַ כָּל הַלַּיְלָה עַד הַבֹּקֶר ...

COMMAND AHARON AND HIS SONS, SAYING, "THIS IS THE LAW OF THE BURNT OFFERING, IT IS THE BURNT OFFERING ON THE PYRE ON THE MIZBEYACH ALL NIGHT UNTIL MORNING..."
(VAYIKRA 6:2)

When written in a *Sefer Torah*, the word מוֹקְדָה, which is the fires upon which the *korban olah* is offered, is written with a small letter מ. Why?

We just learned that the Torah uses the word "צַו — command," connoting added focus and enthusiasm, when introducing the *korban olah*. The reason for this is because the Kohen administering the *korban olah* didn't especially profit by doing so.

The letter מ is spelled מֵם, which is a word that can be read the same way backwards and forwards. Similar to what we discussed above in *Parashas Ki Sisa* (page 164) and *Parashas Vayikra* (page 182), a palindrome indicates that the monies and efforts that a person invests in something, or loses because he is doing a mitzvah, will one day come back to him. Perhaps, then, the small letter מ is telling the Kohen a message that he should not regret his service offering a *korban olah*, for whatever benefit he would have made working with a different *korban* will one day come back to him in a different way.

קַח אֶת אַהֲרֹן וְאֶת בָּנָיו אִתּוֹ ...

TAKE AHARON AND HIS SONS WITH HIM...
(VAYIKRA 8:2)

This *pasuk* is discussing Hashem's instructions to Moshe, how he should make Aharon the Kohen Gadol, and his sons Kohanim. Rashi explains that "קַח אֶת אַהֲרֹן — take Aharon" means "convince him." Why would Aharon need to be convinced to be the Kohen Gadol, which was the most sacred position in the B'nei Yisrael?

Aharon knew Moshe was originally supposed to be the Kohen Gadol. Perhaps Aharon did not feel comfortable taking this position away from his brother, especially when that same brother was the one who would have to consecrate him in his new role. He thus hesitated to accept the "offer," until Moshe convinced him to do it.

Another possibility is that until this point, the Jewish people were a classless society. Creating a caste of Kohanim, with a Kohen Gadol, would inevitably get some people angry, and jealous, as we later see by Korach. Aharon, who loved peace and pursued it, surely wanted no part of creating this tremendous *machlokes* and resentment. He therefore had to be convinced by Moshe that greater good for everyone would be achieved if he took this job.

A third approach in understanding Aharon's refusal is that he was hesitant to become B'nei Yisrael's representative to plead atonement from Hashem because of his involvement with the *Eigel Hazahav*. [For example, see Ramban who explains that the Mizbeyach appeared to Aharon "כְּתַבְנִית שׁוֹר — in the form of a bull," which was reminiscent of the *Eigel* (9:7).] Therefore, Moshe had to convince Aharon that nevertheless, he was the right person for the right job.

וַיַּעַשׂ אַהֲרֹן וּבָנָיו אֵת כָּל הַדְּבָרִים אֲשֶׁר צִוָּה ה' בְּיַד מֹשֶׁה:

AND AHARON AND HIS SONS DID ALL THE THINGS THAT HASHEM COMMANDED THROUGH MOSHE. (VAYIKRA 8:36)

What praise of Aharon and his sons is the Torah telling us? Why wouldn't they listen to Hashem here?

The praise that the Torah is telling us, explains the Sifra (194), is not that they listened to Hashem, but that Aharon and his sons were just as happy to hear their instructions from Moshe as they would have been to hear from Hashem Himself. The Maharal explains that human nature is such that an important person does not like to be told what to do by other people. Aharon and his sons, however, although they were Kohanim and Moshe was not, took Hashem's instructions "בְּיַד מֹשֶׁה — through Moshe," as easily as they would have taken it from Hashem directly.[26]

We may appreciate this praise of the Kohanim even more when we remember that originally, Moshe was supposed to be the Kohen Gadol, but was punished and lost it. Why should he tell us what to do as Kohanim, the Kohanim could have very well reasoned. The Torah is thus telling us that Aharon's reaction was one of total submission and subservience to Moshe, his younger brother.

---

26   I heard this insight from Rabbi Yisroel Schwartz *shlita*.

SHEMINI
שְׁמִינִי

וַיֹּאמֶר מֹשֶׁה אֶל אַהֲרֹן הוּא אֲשֶׁר דִּבֶּר ה' לֵאמֹר
בִּקְרֹבַי אֶקָּדֵשׁ וְעַל פְּנֵי כָל הָעָם אֶכָּבֵד וַיִּדֹּם אַהֲרֹן:

THEN MOSHE SAID TO AHARON, "THIS IS WHAT HASHEM SPOKE, WHEN HE SAID, 'I WILL BE SANCTIFIED THROUGH THOSE NEAR TO ME, AND BEFORE THE ENTIRE PEOPLE I WILL BE GLORIFIED.'" AND AHARON WAS SILENT. (VAYIKRA 10:3)

Moshe told Aharon that the deaths of his two sons were what Hashem had told him "בִּקְרֹבַי אֶקָּדֵשׁ וְעַל פְּנֵי כָל הָעָם אֶכָּבֵד — 'I will be sanctified through those near to Me, and before the entire People I will be glorified.'" In response, Aharon simply remained silent. Rashi tells us that Aharon's reward for his silence was that he received a direct prophecy from Hashem, telling him the halachah that a Kohen may not go into the Beis Hamikdash after having drunk even a small amount of wine.

One of the reasons why Nadav and Avihu had died was because they drank wine before entering the Mishkan. Wouldn't hearing this halachah, that what they had done was forbidden, rub salt on Aharon's grief over the death of his sons?

For most people, hearing this instruction from Hashem would indeed be hurtful. But for Aharon, it was just the opposite; it was an opportunity. The best reward that Aharon could have received was ensuring that his son's deaths did not go to "waste"; by instead using what had happened to them as an eternal example to teach all future Kohanim the proper way to act in the Beis Hamikdash.

Baruch Hashem we also find this *middah* in people today. There is a family who tragically lost their son to alcoholism and drugs, *rachmanah litzlan*. In the aftermath, they have become the spokesman against teen drinking. They have turned their personal tragedy into a tremendous *kiddush Hashem* and opportunity for others to learn and grow from their mistakes. For this family, a direct message from Hashem about the importance of this campaign is the ultimate compliment they could receive.

> וַיִּקְרָא מֹשֶׁה אֶל מִישָׁאֵל וְאֶל אֶלְצָפָן בְּנֵי עֻזִּיאֵל דֹּד
> אַהֲרֹן וַיֹּאמֶר אֲלֵהֶם קִרְבוּ שְׂאוּ אֶת אֲחֵיכֶם מֵאֵת
> פְּנֵי הַקֹּדֶשׁ אֶל מִחוּץ לַמַּחֲנֶה:

AND MOSHE SUMMONED MISHAEL AND ELTZAFAN, THE SONS OF AHARON'S UNCLE UZIEL, AND SAID TO THEM, "APPROACH THEM, AND RAISE YOUR BROTHERS FROM WITHIN THE KODESH, TO THE OUTSIDE OF THE CAMP." (VAYIKRA 10:4)

Moshe instructed Mishael and Eltzafan that they "קִרְבוּ שְׂאוּ — draw near and raise" the bodies of Nadav and Avihu from within the Kodesh. These two words, קִרְבוּ and שְׂאוּ are words that are often used within the context of *avodah* in the Beis Hamikdash. For example, in 9:7, Moshe told Aharon "קְרַב אֶל הַמִּזְבֵּחַ — *approach* the Mizbeyach," and שְׂאוּ often implies being elevated to a new role, or new level of *kedushah*.

Moshe was not giving his nephews a chore. The Torah is telling us that removing Nadav and Avihu from within the Kodesh was an *avodah*, like any other.

> וַיֹּאמֶר מֹשֶׁה אֶל אַהֲרֹן וּלְאֶלְעָזָר וּלְאִיתָמָר בָּנָיו רָאשֵׁיכֶם אַל תִּפְרָעוּ וּבִגְדֵיכֶם לֹא תִפְרֹמוּ ... וַאֲחֵיכֶם כָּל בֵּית יִשְׂרָאֵל יִבְכּוּ אֶת הַשְּׂרֵפָה אֲשֶׁר שָׂרַף ה' ... וּמִפֶּתַח אֹהֶל מוֹעֵד לֹא תֵצְאוּ ... וַיַּעֲשׂוּ כִּדְבַר מֹשֶׁה:
>
> AND MOSHE SAID TO AHARON AND TO ELAZAR AND TO ISAMAR, HIS SONS, "DO NOT LEAVE YOUR HEADS UNSHORN, AND DO NOT REND YOUR GARMENTS... BUT YOUR BROTHERS, THE ENTIRE HOUSE OF YISRAEL, SHALL CRY OVER THE FIRE THAT HASHEM HAS BURNED... DO NOT GO OUT OF THE ENTRANCE OF THE TENT OF MEETING..." AND THEY DID ACCORDING TO MOSHE'S ORDER. (VAYIKRA 10:6–7)

Why is the Torah making a point of telling us that Aharon and his remaining sons listened to Moshe?

Rashi comments on the instruction of "רָאשֵׁיכֶם אַל תִּפְרָעוּ — do not leave your heads unshorn," that, although a mourner is normally forbidden to take a haircut, Aharon and his sons were to do nothing that would mar Hashem's joy, so to speak, of the Mishkan's inauguration. It even seems that they were not even allowed to let themselves cry over the loss; "*your brothers, the entire House of Yisrael*, shall cry over the fire that Hashem has burned," but you shall not. This level of self-control that Aharon and his remaining sons were commanded and expected to have was literally superhuman. It is indeed a tremendous praise that the Torah testifies that they succeeded in obeying Moshe's command.

Shemini

וַיְדַבֵּר מֹשֶׁה אֶל אַהֲרֹן וְאֶל אֶלְעָזָר וְאֶל אִיתָמָר בָּנָיו הַנּוֹתָרִים ...

AND MOSHE SPOKE TO AHARON AND TO ELAZAR AND TO ISAMAR, HIS SURVIVING SONS...

(Vayikra 10:12)

Rashi explains that Elazar and Isamar are called "Aharon's surviving sons" because they escaped the Heavenly death penalty that had been declared upon them as well. They were only spared due to Moshe's *tefillos*.

Why was Moshe's *tefillah* only effective for Elazar and Isamar, and wasn't able to save Nadav and Avihu, as well?

Rashi explains that one of the reasons why Nadav and Avihu died was because they *paskened* in front of Moshe, their *rebbi* (10:2). Perhaps this breach in *kavod* affected their relationship with Moshe, and was the reason for their not being protected by Moshe's heartfelt *tefillos*. Otherwise, the *tefillos* that Moshe *davened* would have been effective for all of Aharon's sons.

וַיְדַבֵּר מֹשֶׁה אֶל אַהֲרֹן וְאֶל אֶלְעָזָר וְאֶל אִיתָמָר בָּנָיו הַנּוֹתָרִים ...

AND MOSHE SPOKE TO AHARON AND TO ELAZAR AND TO ISAMAR, HIS SURVIVING SONS...

(Vayikra 10:12)

וְאֵת שְׂעִיר הַחַטָּאת דָּרֹשׁ דָּרַשׁ מֹשֶׁה ... וַיִּקְצֹף עַל אֶלְעָזָר וְעַל אִיתָמָר בְּנֵי אַהֲרֹן הַנּוֹתָרִם ...

AND MOSHE THOROUGHLY INVESTIGATED ... AND HE WAS ANGRY WITH ELAZAR AND ISAMAR, AHARON'S SURVIVING SONS... (Vayikra 10:16)

Why does the Torah call Elazar and Isamar "Aharon's surviving sons" a second time, in *pasuk* 16?

We just learned that the reason that Elazar and Isamar are called "Aharon's surviving sons" in *pasuk* 12 is to tell us that they too should have been killed, and were only spared because of Moshe's *tefillah*. In *pasuk* 16, Moshe is upset with Elazar and Isamar. Here they are called "Aharon's surviving sons" for a different reason, to tell us that Moshe expects more from them *because* they are Aharon's surviving sons. A person who goes through a difficult period cannot be the same person as he was before; he must grow from his experiences, and become a different and better person. Moshe was reminding Elazar and Isamar of their now-heightened responsibility.[27]

זֹאת הַחַיָּה אֲשֶׁר תֹּאכְלוּ מִכָּל הַבְּהֵמָה אֲשֶׁר עַל הָאָרֶץ

THESE ARE THE CREATURES THAT YOU
MAY EAT AMONG ALL THE ANIMALS ON
EARTH. (VAYIKRA 11:2)

Rashi explains that "זֹאת הַחַיָּה אֲשֶׁר תֹּאכְלוּ — these are the creatures that you may eat," teaches us that Moshe held each animal, kosher and non-kosher, that he was discussing, and showed it to the B'nei Yisrael. Imagine! The last time that the animals had such an incredible reunion was when they were together in the *Teivah*!

This is even more incredible when we realize that the Jews were in the desert, and animals came from every climate just to be shown. This demonstration tells us how important the laws of *kashrus* are; which is an area that we encounter often, literally every time that we buy food to eat.

כֹּל הוֹלֵךְ עַל גָּחוֹן ... לֹא תֹאכְלוּם כִּי שֶׁקֶץ הֵם:

ANY CREATURE THAT GOES ON ITS BELLY
... YOU SHALL NOT EAT, FOR THEY ARE AN
ABOMINATION. (VAYIKRA 11:42)

---

27   See also *Parashas Noach* (*Bereishis* 9:18), page 45.

Rashi explains that "כֹּל הוֹלֵךְ עַל גָּחוֹן — any creature that goes on its belly" refers to the snake. Why doesn't the Torah just say "don't eat snakes"?

Since the snake is the source of all of the curses and punishments that humanity suffers, the Torah prefers not to mention it explicitly. It therefore just refers to it by referring to its sin and punishment; "the one who crawls on its belly," instead of walking.

Interestingly, when it is written in a *Sefer Torah*, the letter ו in the word גָּחוֹן is written larger than the other letters. My children Shira and Avi pointed out that the letter ו looks like a snake standing upright. Although a direct reference to the *Nachash* is not made, the Torah does hint to it, by describing the way it walks and even the way that it looks.

Tazria
תַזְרִיעַ

אָדָם כִּי יִהְיֶה בְעוֹר בְּשָׂרוֹ שְׂאֵת אוֹ סַפַּחַת אוֹ
בַהֶרֶת וְהָיָה בְעוֹר בְּשָׂרוֹ לְנֶגַע צָרָעַת וְהוּבָא
אֶל אַהֲרֹן הַכֹּהֵן אוֹ אֶל אַחַד
מִבָּנָיו הַכֹּהֲנִים:

IF A PERSON HAS A SE'EIS, A SAPACHAS, OR A BAHERES ON THE SKIN OF HIS FLESH, AND IT FORMS A NEGA OF TZARAAS ON THE SKIN OF HIS FLESH, HE SHALL BE BROUGHT TO AHARON THE KOHEN, OR TO ONE OF HIS SONS, THE KOHANIM. (VAYIKRA 13:2)

Why does the Torah specifically mention Aharon Hakohen when discussing *tzaraas*? Why doesn't the *pasuk* just say that a person with *tzaraas* "shall be brought to one of the Kohanim"?

The *parashah* discusses the *metzora's* purification process. This included several steps. The first step is that he live in solitude outside of the city (13:46), for, explains the Gemara, he created distance between man and wife, or one friend from another, through his speaking *lashon hara* about one person to another (*Arachin* 16b). Therefore, his punishment is that he too must be separated.

Pasuk 14:4 tells us that the next step of a *metzora's* purification process included two birds, cedar wood, a string of red wool, and a low growing plant called hyssop. Rashi explains that the birds were used because a person who speaks *lashon hara* resembles a prattling, chirping bird; cedar wood represents the haughtiness that results in *tzaraas*; and the red string and hyssop are the *shiflus* and modesty with which the *metzora* must now view himself.

However, the *metzora* must still learn the lesson of Aharon Hakohen, whose essence was אוֹהֵב שָׁלוֹם וְרוֹדֵף שָׁלוֹם, constantly trying to repair and reinforce friendships. Aharon's life was the polar opposite of the *metzora's*. The Torah thus instructs that the *metzora* should go to Aharon, and absorb this lifestyle from its master.

How, then can the *metzora* instead go to "one of Aharon's sons, the Kohanim"?

Part of being a Kohen is that Aharon's sons inherited this trait of אוֹהֵב שָׁלוֹם וְרוֹדֵף שָׁלוֹם from their father.[28] By going to one of Aharon's children, the *metzora* is essentially going to Aharon himself. Alternatively, even when this *middah* is not in the genes, growing up in Aharon's home is the best way to fulfill the Mishnah's instruction of "הֱוֵי מִתַּלְמִידָיו שֶׁל אַהֲרֹן אוֹהֵב שָׁלוֹם וְרוֹדֵף שָׁלוֹם, אוֹהֵב אֶת הַבְּרִיּוֹת וּמְקָרְבָן לַתּוֹרָה — be Aharon's *talmidim*; love *shalom*, pursue *shalom*, love Hashem's creations, and bring them closer to Torah" (*Avos* 1:12). Who could better absorb the *limud* and *lemaaseh* of *ahavas habrios* than Aharon's children, who witnessed both on a daily basis?

---

28 R' Shlomo Gigi told me this insight.

Metzora
מְצוֹרָע

וְהִנֵּה נִרְפָּא נֶגַע הַצָּרַעַת מִן הַצָּרוּעַ
THE NEGA OF TZARAAS HAS HEALED IN THE AFFLICTED PERSON. (VAYIKRA 14:3)

The Gemara tells us that *negaim* come for seven different types of wrongful behavior, one of which is צָרוּת הָעַיִן, being stingy (*Arachin* 16a). This behavior is alluded to in the Torah, for "צָרוּעַ — afflicted person," may be read as a contraction of the two words צַר עַיִן.

וְצִוָּה הַכֹּהֵן וְלָקַח לַמִּטַּהֵר שְׁתֵּי צִפֳּרִים חַיּוֹת טְהֹרוֹת וְעֵץ אֶרֶז וּשְׁנִי תוֹלַעַת וְאֵזֹב:
THEN THE KOHEN SHALL ORDER, AND THE PERSON TO BE PURIFIED SHALL TAKE TWO LIVE, CLEAN BIRDS, A CEDAR STICK, A STRIP OF CRIMSON WOOL, AND HYSSOP. (VAYIKRA 14:4)

Rashi explains that the *metzora's* purification procedure uses two birds, for *tzaraas* is a punishment for speaking *lashon hara*, in which the person acted like prattling, chirping birds. Then, Rashi explains why the *metzora* uses a piece of cedar wood; because *tzaraas* occurs in punishment of גַּסוּת הָרוּחַ, haughtiness, alluded to in the towering cedar. What did the *metzora* do wrong? Did he speak *lashon hara*, or was he haughty?

The answer is that these two bad *middos* are related: haughtiness is the cause, and speaking *lashon hara* is the result. Only someone who is full of himself and his own "greatness" can possibly speak ill about another Jew.

> וְלָקַח לַמִּטַּהֵר שְׁתֵּי צִפֳּרִים חַיּוֹת טְהֹרוֹת ...
>
> THE PERSON TO BE PURIFIED SHALL TAKE TWO
> LIVE, CLEAN BIRDS... (VAYIKRA 14:4)

We just learned one reason why the *metzora* uses birds, for a person who spoke *lashon hara* acted like a prattling, chirping bird.

Another similarity between speaking *lashon hara* and birds is that just as birds, which constantly fly from tree to tree, are always wandering about without purpose, a gossipmonger peddles his "wares" from person to person as he continues to pointlessly retell stories about other people.

> וְלָקַח לַמִּטַּהֵר שְׁתֵּי צִפֳּרִים חַיּוֹת טְהֹרוֹת ...
>
> THE PERSON TO BE PURIFIED SHALL TAKE TWO
> LIVE, CLEAN BIRDS... (VAYIKRA 14:4)

Why did the *metzora's* purification procedure need *two* birds? How is it different than any other atonement *korban*, where only *one* bird or animal is used?[29]

Other atonement *korbanos* are brought to atone for the *aveirah* that the person bringing it was involved in. *Lashon hara*, however, is different, for *lashon hara* involves two people; the speaker, and listener. Perhaps the second bird is an atonement on the second person's — the

---

29 I heard this question from Rav Aharon Cohen, from the *Sefas Emes*.

listener's — behalf. This second bird is dipped in the blood of the first, showing that he was contaminated by the *lashon hara* that he heard from the first person, and is then set free, for he was not the primary one at fault in the *aveirah*.

> אֶת הַצִּפֹּר הַחַיָּה יִקַּח אֹתָהּ וְאֶת עֵץ הָאֶרֶז וְאֶת
> שְׁנִי הַתּוֹלַעַת וְאֶת הָאֵזֹב וְטָבַל אוֹתָם וְאֵת הַצִּפֹּר
> הַחַיָּה בְּדַם הַצִּפֹּר הַשְּׁחֻטָה עַל הַמַּיִם הַחַיִּים: וְהִזָּה
> עַל הַמִּטַּהֵר מִן הַצָּרַעַת שֶׁבַע פְּעָמִים וְטִהֲרוֹ וְשִׁלַּח
> אֶת הַצִּפֹּר הַחַיָּה עַל פְּנֵי הַשָּׂדֶה:

> AS FOR THE LIVE BIRD, HE SHALL TAKE IT, AND THEN THE CEDAR STICK, THE STRIP OF CRIMSON WOOL, AND THE HYSSOP, AND, ALONG WITH THE LIVE BIRD, HE SHALL DIP THEM INTO THE BLOOD OF THE SLAUGHTERED BIRD, OVER THE SPRING WATER. HE SHALL THEN SPRINKLE SEVEN TIMES UPON THE PERSON BEING PURIFIED FROM TZARAAS, AND HE SHALL CLEANSE HIM. HE SHALL THEN SEND AWAY THE LIVE BIRD INTO THE OPEN FIELD. (VAYIKRA 14:6–7)

There is a famous story about a *baal lashon hara* who came to the Chofetz Chaim filled with regret, and asked him how he could fix what he had done wrong. The Chofetz Chaim answered that the man should place a feather from his pillow on every doorstep in town. The man did so and returned to the Chofetz Chaim to ask what he should do now. The Chofetz Chaim told him to now go back and collect all of the feathers. The man tried, and came back to the Chofetz Chaim empty handed; the wind had blown away all of the feathers, and he could not even find one. The Chofetz Chaim explained to him that the same thing happens when words leave someone's mouth. Like feathers that are blown away the moment after they are put down, words that are spoken can never be retrieved, and we have no idea where they ended up and the damage that they may have caused.

Perhaps this story gives us another insight into why a *metzora* needed two birds for his *kapparah*, instead of only one, as well as why only one of the birds was *shechted*, and the other set free. The bird that remains alive is dipped and sprinkled in the blood of the other bird. This is *"metamei"* this bird with the stain of *lashon hara*. Then the bird is set free, over the open field. This shows that just as this bird "stained" with "*lashon hara* blood" can never be retrieved, so too the damage caused by the *lashon hara* that this person spoke can never be undone.

Acharei Mos
אַחֲרֵי מוֹת

וְהָיְתָה זֹּאת לָכֶם לְחֻקַּת עוֹלָם לְכַפֵּר עַל בְּנֵי יִשְׂרָאֵל מִכָּל חַטֹּאתָם אַחַת בַּשָּׁנָה וַיַּעַשׂ כַּאֲשֶׁר צִוָּה ה' אֶת מֹשֶׁה:

All this shall be as an eternal statute for you, to effect atonement upon the Children of Yisrael, for all their sins, once each year. And he did as Hashem had commanded Moshe. (Vayikra 16:34)

Why does the Torah have to tell us that Aharon did as Hashem had instructed him? Isn't this obvious?

This *pasuk* is one of the few places where Rashi answers this question outright. Aharon only wore the *bigdei kehunah gedolah* because Hashem told him that he must, and not because he took pride in wearing such expensive and exclusive clothing. For example, when we eat on Erev Yom Kippur because it's a mitzvah, we nevertheless enjoy the tasty food. Aharon was different. He was able to filter out his personal pleasures, until he achieved something incredible. The Torah is making the point that the only enjoyment that Aharon got from wearing these *begadim* was that he accomplished another one of Hashem's *mitzvos*.

כְּמַעֲשֵׂה אֶרֶץ מִצְרַיִם אֲשֶׁר יְשַׁבְתֶּם בָּהּ לֹא תַעֲשׂוּ ...

LIKE THE PRACTICE OF THE LAND OF MITZRAYIM, IN WHICH YOU DWELLED, YOU SHALL NOT DO...
(VAYIKRA 18:3)

Rashi explains that the Mitzrim were the most perverted of nations, and the place where the B'nei Yisrael lived — Goshen — was the worst of all. What was so bad about the land of Goshen?

We know that Yosef chose Goshen as the place where his family would live because it was the most fertile in all of Mitzrayim. The abundant grass there would best serve Yaacov's family's flocks in their chosen profession of shepherding. However, we also know that the Egyptians worshipped the sheep, which means that Goshen was probably the place where the Mitzrim cared for *their* sheep. It was thus the place with the most idols and most *tumah* in all of Mitzrayim.

כְּמַעֲשֵׂה אֶרֶץ מִצְרַיִם אֲשֶׁר יְשַׁבְתֶּם בָּהּ לֹא תַעֲשׂוּ וּכְמַעֲשֵׂה אֶרֶץ כְּנַעַן אֲשֶׁר אֲנִי מֵבִיא אֶתְכֶם שָׁמָּה לֹא תַעֲשׂוּ וּבְחֻקֹּתֵיהֶם לֹא תֵלֵכוּ:

LIKE THE PRACTICE OF THE LAND OF MITZRAYIM, IN WHICH YOU DWELLED, YOU SHALL NOT DO, AND LIKE THE PRACTICE OF THE LAND OF CANAAN, TO WHICH I AM BRINGING YOU, YOU SHALL NOT DO, AND YOU SHALL NOT FOLLOW THEIR CUSTOMS. (VAYIKRA 18:3)

When warning us not to imitate Mitzrayim, the Torah tells us not to follow their practices. Yet, when discussing the land of Canaan, we are warned not to follow their practices, or their customs. Why the addition?

The *pasuk* points out that Eretz Mitzrayim is where we dwelled in the past. Hence, while concern remains that we may follow in their footsteps in regard to their lewd and licentious behavior, there is little chance that we would continue their customs, as we are no longer around them to continue to be influenced. However, during our conquer of Eretz Canaan, we would once again find ourselves living among another nation, and be subject to the influence of both its actions and customs.

> וּמִזַּרְעֲךָ לֹא תִתֵּן לְהַעֲבִיר לַמֹּלֶךְ וְלֹא תְחַלֵּל אֶת שֵׁם אֱלֹקֶיךָ אֲנִי ה':
>
> AND YOU SHALL NOT GIVE ANY OF YOUR OFFSPRING TO PASS THROUGH FOR MOLECH. AND YOU SHALL NOT PROFANE THE NAME OF YOUR GOD. I AM HASHEM. (VAYIKRA 18:21)

Why does the Torah place the prohibition of not giving over one's child to Molech within the prohibitions of *arayos*?

Perhaps the common denominator between Molech and *arayos* is that the Torah phrases the prohibition of Molech וּמִזַּרְעֲךָ לֹא תִתֵּן לְהַעֲבִיר לַמֹּלֶךְ, which literally means "you shall not give your seed to pass it to Molech." *Arayos* are also a literal giving of seed to the wrong place.

In placing these *aveiros* together, the Torah is telling us that in both scenarios — Molech and *arayos* — a person is taking the potential that Hashem has given him to create children and build families, and is wasting it by putting it in a place where it will not be used properly. By *arayos* the *aveirah* is done before the child is born, and by Molech the child is wasted when already alive. However, both *aveiros* result in the same colossal waste of beautiful potential.

Kedoshim
קְדוֹשִׁים

דַּבֵּר אֶל כָּל עֲדַת בְּנֵי יִשְׂרָאֵל וְאָמַרְתָּ אֲלֵהֶם קְדשִׁים
תִּהְיוּ כִּי קָדוֹשׁ אֲנִי ה' אֱלֹקֵיכֶם: אִישׁ אִמּוֹ וְאָבִיו
תִּירָאוּ וְאֶת שַׁבְּתֹתַי תִּשְׁמֹרוּ אֲנִי ה' אֱלֹקֵיכֶם:

Speak to the entire congregation of the B'nei Yisrael, and say to them, You shall be holy, for I, Hashem, your God, am holy. A person shall revere their father and mother, and observe My Shabbos, I am Hashem, your God. (Vayikra 19:2–3)

The Torah instructs us to "be holy," but doesn't tell us how! Rashi explains that the way that we become holy is by staying away from illicit relationships, and from other *aveiros*. Perhaps the next *pasuk*, which discusses honoring our parents and observing Shabbos, gives us another way to be holy. Honoring one's parents is based on *hakaras hatov* for all that we have received from them, which will in turn lead to deepened appreciation of Hashem. And Shabbos is of course "Hashem's day" of the week. Focusing on these two *mitzvos* will help us become holier people, people whose life is more focused on Hashem.

לֹא תִקֹּם וְלֹא תִטֹּר אֶת בְּנֵי עַמֶּךָ וְאָהַבְתָּ לְרֵעֲךָ כָּמוֹךָ אֲנִי ה':

YOU SHALL NEITHER TAKE REVENGE FROM NOR BEAR A GRUDGE AGAINST THE MEMBERS OF YOUR PEOPLE; YOU SHALL LOVE YOUR NEIGHBOR AS YOURSELF. I AM HASHEM. (VAYIKRA 19:18)

The *Chovos Halevavos* tells us in *Shaar Habitachon* that a person should respond kindly to someone who mistreated him, for an insult or physical damage is all from Hashem; the aggressor is only a *shliach*.

Perhaps his source is from our *pasuk*, where, after warning "לֹא תִקֹּם וְלֹא תִטֹּר אֶת בְּנֵי עַמֶּךָ — you shall neither take revenge from nor bear a grudge against the members of your people," the next phrase is "וְאָהַבְתָּ לְרֵעֲךָ כָּמוֹךָ — you shall love your neighbor as yourself."

אַל תְּחַלֵּל אֶת בִּתְּךָ לְהַזְנוֹתָהּ וְלֹא תִזְנֶה הָאָרֶץ וּמָלְאָה הָאָרֶץ זִמָּה:

YOU SHALL NOT PROFANE YOUR DAUGHTER BY MAKING HER A HARLOT, LEST THE LAND FALL INTO HARLOTRY AND THE LAND BE FILLED WITH IMMORALITY. (VAYIKRA 19:29)

What type of father would make his daughter into a harlot?

Perhaps we may translate אַל תְּחַלֵּל not as "you shall not defile," but, "you shall not make ordinary," like the word "חוֹל" — weekday." The Torah is thus telling us, "do not make your daughter regular, into a *zonah*." The opposite of *kodesh* is *chol*, and the opposite of *tzanuah* is *znus*; "half-modest" does not exist, for a person is either in one world, or the other. The Torah is thus telling us that a father must be *mechaneich* his daughter that she is a *bas melech* and nothing less, and her actions and dress should always reflect this.[30]

---

30   See also the *Ohr Hachaim*.

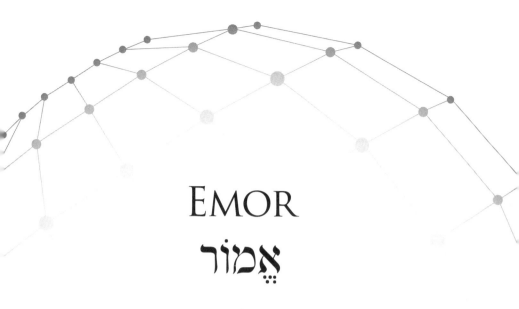

Emor
אֱמוֹר

וּבְקֻצְרְכֶם אֶת קְצִיר אַרְצְכֶם לֹא תְכַלֶּה פְּאַת שָׂדְךָ
בְּקֻצְרֶךָ וְלֶקֶט קְצִירְךָ לֹא תְלַקֵּט לֶעָנִי וְלַגֵּר תַּעֲזֹב
אֹתָם אֲנִי ה' אֱלֹקֵיכֶם:

WHEN YOU REAP THE HARVEST OF YOUR LAND, YOU SHALL NOT COMPLETELY REMOVE THE SIDE OF YOUR FIELD DURING YOUR HARVESTING, AND YOU SHALL NOT GATHER UP THE GLEANINGS OF YOUR HARVEST. YOU SHALL LEAVE THEM FOR THE POOR PERSON AND FOR THE STRANGER. I AM HASHEM, YOUR GOD. (VAYIKRA 23:22)

Rashi explains that in saying "תַּעֲזֹב אֹתָם — you shall leave them," the Torah is telling us that the farmer must *leave* the *peah* (the crop growing on one side of the field) and *leket* (fallen pieces) for the poor people to come and take, and not play any role in deciding how it is collected.

Why is it so important that the *peah* and *leket* are left in the fields for the poor people to take by themselves? Having to harvest the *peah* and walk around collecting the *leket* is difficult, and makes their life harder! Wouldn't it help them more if the farmer would harvest it for them, and leave it in a nice bundle for the *ahni* to pick up?

The Rambam famously explains that the highest form of tzedakah is giving a job to someone in need, so they will now have the means to support themselves. With this perspective, if we would cut the *peah* and foods and give it to the poor, they would feel like they are getting a gift. But when we leave them in the fields, to let the *ahni* work hard to take home *his* wheat, he will feel that he played a role in the harvest, like everyone else.

וַיְדַבֵּר מֹשֶׁה אֶל בְּנֵי יִשְׂרָאֵל וַיּוֹצִיאוּ אֶת הַמְקַלֵּל אֶל מִחוּץ לַמַּחֲנֶה וַיִּרְגְּמוּ אֹתוֹ אָבֶן וּבְנֵי יִשְׂרָאֵל עָשׂוּ כַּאֲשֶׁר צִוָּה ה' אֶת מֹשֶׁה:

AND MOSHE TOLD ALL THIS TO THE B'NEI YISRAEL, SO THEY TOOK THE MEKALLEL OUTSIDE THE CAMP AND STONED HIM, AND THE B'NEI YISRAEL DID JUST AS HASHEM HAD COMMANDED MOSHE. (VAYIKRA 24:23)

Why does the Torah make a point of telling us that the B'nei Yisrael carried out the *Mekallel's* punishment just as Hashem had commanded Moshe?

The Ramban explains that the B'nei Yisrael did not kill the *Mekallel* because of their hatred for him, or because of the trouble that he had caused them. The only reason why they killed him was *leshmah*; in order to rid the evil that was in their midst.

It often happens that we get upset when somone does something wrong. We almost naturally hope that the person will be caught and punished. When we stop to think about it, we will realize that many times the reason why we want him caught is because he upset or wronged us, and has little to do with the fact that this wrong thing he did deserves to be punished in this manner. (We may ask ourselves the following question: Would I be as upset if I wouldn't be standing here, and wouldn't have been hurt from what he did? Would I be just as upset if a friend of mine would have done this?) This "indignation" at seeing something wrong is not *leshmah*, but is our personal desire to see someone get what is coming to them. The Ramban is telling us that the Jewish people had no smug feeling after the *Mekallel* was killed.

Rashi explains differently, that the B'nei Yisrael did not leave out any facet of how the Torah commands that an execution be carried out. The *Mekallel* was pushed off of a cliff, was stoned, and his body was then strung up, just before nightfall. Perhaps Rashi is telling us that this was the first time in the B'nei Yisrael's short history that they were carrying out a death penalty, which is something that is not a "natural" part of the nation of רַחֲמָנִים, בַּיְשָׁנִים, וְגוֹמְלֵי חֲסָדִים. Also, how will such an immediate execution make the Torah "look"; already they are putting people to death? Nevertheless, this was a mitzvah that had to be done like any other. B'nei Yisrael did not leave out any requirements of the execution, but completed this mitzvah in all its detail despite its "vicious" nature.

Behar
בְּהַר

> אֶת כַּסְפְּךָ לֹא תִתֵּן לוֹ בְּנֶשֶׁךְ ... אֲנִי ה' אֱלֹקֵיכֶם
> אֲשֶׁר הוֹצֵאתִי אֶתְכֶם מֵאֶרֶץ מִצְרַיִם וכו'
>
> YOU SHALL NOT GIVE HIM YOUR MONEY WITH
> INTEREST... I AM HASHEM, YOUR GOD, WHO
> TOOK YOU OUT OF THE LAND OF MITZRAYIM...
> (VAYIKRA 25:37–38)

When forbidding us to lend money with interest, the Torah mentions that Hashem took us out of Mitzrayim. Rashi explains that the connection between these areas is that during *Makas Bechoros*, Hashem distinguished between the eldest son and the other children in the family, even though the Egyptian women's promiscuity made it that the actual oldest children — firstborn to their mother —were often unknown. So too, He will punish someone who lends another Jew money with interest, and tries to conceal it by making it seem like this interest-laden loan came from a gentile.

This punishment may be further seen in Rashi's comments to *pasuk* 14, where explaining the progression of punishments in the *parashah*, he explains that a person who lends money with interest and does not change his ways will suffer a series of punishments and eventually have to sell himself into slavery due to his dire financial straits. We see from here that the lesson that we must learn from *Yetziyas Mitzrayim* and apply to interest is not just that Hashem is *aware* of hidden sins of which no one else knows about, but that He publically *reveals* the truth of these sins for all to see. The actual firstborn died, making it clear that his mother had been promiscuous, and seeing a person who suffered this series of punishments makes it clear that the "permitted" interest-laden loan he extended was in fact his own money.

וְכִי יָמוּךְ אָחִיךָ עִמָּךְ וְנִמְכַּר לָךְ לֹא תַעֲבֹד בּוֹ עֲבֹדַת עָבֶד:

AND IF YOUR BROTHER BECOMES DESTITUTE WITH YOU, AND IS SOLD TO YOU, DO NOT WORK HIM WITH SLAVE LABOR. (VAYIKRA 25:39)

Why does the Torah say "וְכִי יָמוּךְ אָחִיךָ" — if *your brother* becomes destitute," instead of "when *a person* becomes destitute"? Also, why is this *pasuk* phrased in the passive "וְנִמְכַּר לָךְ" — and is sold to you," instead of the more natural "and you bought him," as the Torah in fact says in *pasuk* 44, when discussing buying an *eved cana'ani*; "מֵאֵת הַגּוֹיִם אֲשֶׁר סְבִיבֹתֵיכֶם מֵהֶם תִּקְנוּ עֶבֶד וְאָמָה" — from (the nations that are around you) you may acquire a slave or a maidservant"?

Rashi implicitly answers both of these questions, when he tells us that the "slave labor" that the Torah is forbidding us is giving an *eved ivri* demeaning labor that makes it clear that he is a slave, for example having him carry the master's clothes to the bathhouse, or putting the master's shoes on his master. These *halachos* reinforce the fact that we are not buying a slave; we are buying our financially down and out brother, who must thus be treated as such. Similarly, the *pasuk's* emphasis is not that you are *buying* him; he is not the object here. Rather, he is the subject, who is being sold *to* you; you are expected to treat him in the right way.

Bechukosai
בְּחֻקֹּתַי

אִם בְּחֻקֹּתַי תֵּלֵכוּ וְאֶת מִצְוֹתַי תִּשְׁמְרוּ
וַעֲשִׂיתֶם אֹתָם:

IF YOU FOLLOW MY STATUTES AND OBSERVE
MY COMMANDMENTS AND PERFORM THEM…
(VAYIKRA 26:3)

The *Baal Haturim* points out that the *roshei teivos* of the words אִם בְּחֻקֹּתַי תֵּלֵכוּ are א-ב-ת, which, spelled backwards, are the *roshei teivos* of תֵּלְכוּ בְּדַרְכֵי אָבוֹת, walk in the forefathers' ways. And, the word אתם also spells the word אמת, truth, if you switch the letters מ and ת.

We may add that the *roshei teivos* of the words (וְ)אֶת מִצְוֹתַי תִּשְׁמְרוּ also spell א-מ-ת. This tells us that besides for being truthful in business and daily life, we must also be truthful in our *avodas Hashem*, as well.

My Rosh Yeshiva, Rav Chaim Kreiswirth, *zatzal*, once told us a very telling example of being truthful in *avodas Hashem*. He said if he could, he would *daven beyechidus* on the *Yamim Nora'im*. With no one watching him, he would know that all of his *shukeling* would be *leshmah*.

וְנָתַתִּי גִשְׁמֵיכֶם בְּעִתָּם וְנָתְנָה הָאָרֶץ יְבוּלָהּ וְעֵץ הַשָּׂדֶה יִתֵּן פִּרְיוֹ:

I WILL GIVE YOUR RAINS IN THEIR PROPER TIME, THE LAND WILL YIELD ITS PRODUCE, AND THE TREE OF THE FIELD WILL GIVE FORTH ITS FRUIT. (VAYIKRA 26:4)

Rashi explains that the *berachah* of "גִשְׁמֵיכֶם בְּעִתָּם — your rains *in their proper time*" is that rains will only fall at times that people are generally not out of the house, such as Friday nights. How do we know this? Perhaps בְּעִתָּם simply means during the winter season! Also, Rashi explains that the next phrase in the *pasuk*, "וְעֵץ הַשָּׂדֶה יִתֵּן פִּרְיוֹ — and the tree of the field will give forth its fruit," means that trees that are normally barren will bear fruit. Here too, how do we know this?

The answer is that in the natural world rain during the rainy season, and fruit-bearing trees bearing fruit, are something to be expected. Rashi therefore understood that the extraordinary *berachos* that are discussed in our *parashah* are something deeper and more special.

אִם בְּחֻקֹּתַי תֵּלֵכוּ וְאֶת מִצְוֹתַי תִּשְׁמְרוּ וַעֲשִׂיתֶם אֹתָם ... וְאִם לֹא תִשְׁמְעוּ לִי וְלֹא תַעֲשׂוּ אֵת כָּל הַמִּצְוֹת הָאֵלֶּה:

IF YOU FOLLOW MY STATUTES AND OBSERVE MY COMMANDMENTS AND PERFORM THEM... BUT IF YOU DO NOT LISTEN TO ME AND DO NOT PERFORM ALL THESE COMMANDMENTS...
(VAYIKRA 26:3,14)

The Torah's discussion of the *berachos* which we will receive for keeping the Torah is several *pesukim*. The description of the terrible things that will happen if we do not listen to Hashem is almost three times longer. What does this mean?

Studying the *berachos* shows us something interesting: that most of them are extraordinary miracles, which are beyond the laws of nature. The *kelallos*, on the other hand, are the loss of the more "natural" blessings that Hashem gives us on a regular basis, such as health, *parnassah*, tranquility, and the like. This contrast shows us Hashem's great *chessed*; that there is simply so much more for Him to take away from us than to give us, for He already gives us so much on a regular basis.

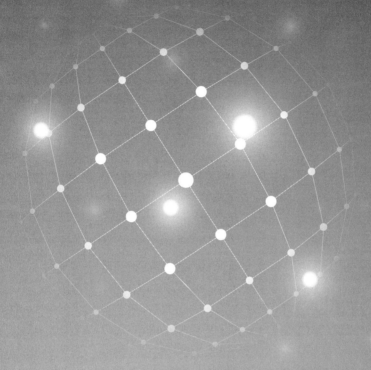

Bamidbar
בְּמִדְבַּר

BAMIDBAR

בְּמִדְבַּר

> שְׂאוּ אֶת רֹאשׁ כָּל עֲדַת בְּנֵי יִשְׂרָאֵל לְמִשְׁפְּחֹתָם
> לְבֵית אֲבֹתָם בְּמִסְפַּר שֵׁמוֹת כָּל זָכָר לְגֻלְגְּלֹתָם:
>
> TAKE THE SUM OF ALL THE CONGREGATION OF
> THE B'NEI YISRAEL, BY FAMILIES FOLLOWING
> THEIR FATHERS' HOUSES; A HEAD COUNT OF
> EVERY MALE ACCORDING TO THE NUMBER OF
> THEIR NAMES. (BAMIDBAR 1:2)

Why was it necessary for Hashem to ask Moshe to count the B'nei Yisrael, which is a project that naturally took time and effort; Hashem of course knows how many Jews there were! Also, if Hashem's objective was to know how many people the Jewish Nation contained, why did He command Moshe to ascertain by a *shevet*-by-*shevet* itemization, instead of simply ending up with one sum total?

In his comments to the previous *pasuk*, Rashi explains that Hashem continuously counted the Jewish people to show His great love for us. This tells us that Hashem did not just want a cold bottom line of the amount of children that He has, so to speak. Love is shown through involvement; and the greater the efforts that Hashem told Moshe to put into counting them, the greater the love that was demonstrated.

An even greater care is expressed by involvement in details, and not just the dry bottom line. Hashem therefore commanded that Moshe ascertain the nitty-gritty details of the amount of people in each *shevet*, all to better show His care, attachment, and relationship to the Jewish people.

A second reason that Hashem told Moshe to calculate the number of people in each *shevet* is because He was now ready to rest His *Shechinah* on the B'nei Yisrael. We may appreciate this point with an example of a person who buys a complicated toy for his child, with many, many pieces, along with lengthy step by step assembly instructions. Together with the instructions will often be an itemized checklist of the number of different pieces in the box: this many one-inch screws, this many half-inch screws, and this many plastic corner pieces. Simply knowing that the box contains exactly one thousand parts, without itemization, won't help a person know where, or how, each piece fits into the greater whole. The same may be said about the B'nei Yisrael; the only way that Hashem could "know" that we were a nation fit for His *Shechinah* is by working out the "nuts and bolts"; this family has so many members, who combine to form a worthy *shevet*, who, in turn, join together to form an exemplary Jewish people. This is also the reason for the constant repetition of "תּוֹלְדֹתָם לְמִשְׁפְּחֹתָם — their numbers according to their families," over and over again throughout the census. Aside from the sum total, the detailed breakdown of that number is just as important.

> אַךְ אֶת מַטֵּה לֵוִי לֹא תִפְקֹד וְאֶת רֹאשָׁם לֹא תִשָּׂא
> בְּתוֹךְ בְּנֵי יִשְׂרָאֵל:
>
> ONLY THE TRIBE OF LEVI YOU SHALL NOT NUMBER, AND YOU SHALL NOT RECKON THEIR SUM AMONG THE B'NEI YISRAEL. (BAMIDBAR 1:49)

Rashi explains that one reason the *B'nei Levi* were counted in a separate census was because Hashem knew there would be a future *gezeirah* against the men counted from twenty and up. Hashem did not want the *B'nei Levi* to be included in this future decree, so He had them excluded from the count; as they belonged to Him, for they were not involved in the *Cheit Ha'Eigel*.

The *Sifsei Chachamim* asks an obvious question: the *Cheit Hameraglim*, which had not yet taken place, was what caused this future *gezeirah*, not the *Cheit Ha'Eigel*! How does the Levi'im's uninvolvement with the *Eigel* spare them from punishment from a future *aveirah*?

When the *B'nei Levi* distanced themselves from the *Cheit Ha'Eigel*, Hashem rewarded them by recruiting them to be the ones who would serve Him in His Mishkan. In other words, Hashem made them "His own." This gave the Levi'im a special relationship, and like every relationship, a special *shemirah*; when we catch someone whom we love doing something wrong, we are more inclined to look the other way, or give him a second chance. Here too, the *B'nei Levi* may have been involved in the *Cheit Hameraglim*, but they were granted protexia due to their not being involved in the *Cheit Ha'Eigel*. The *Cheit Ha'Eigel* is therefore the reason which protected them from being punished in the future.

וְהַלְוִיִּם יַחֲנוּ סָבִיב לְמִשְׁכַּן הָעֵדָת וְלֹא יִהְיֶה קֶצֶף עַל עֲדַת בְּנֵי יִשְׂרָאֵל וְשָׁמְרוּ הַלְוִיִּם אֶת מִשְׁמֶרֶת מִשְׁכַּן הָעֵדוּת:

THE LEVI'IM SHALL ENCAMP AROUND THE MISHKAN OF THE TESTIMONY, SO THAT THERE BE NO WRATH UPON THE NATION OF THE B'NEI YISRAEL AND THE LEVI'IM SHALL KEEP THE CHARGE OF THE MISHKAN OF THE TESTIMONY. (BAMIDBAR 1:53)

Rashi explains that just as there will be no Divine wrath when the Levi'im encamp around the Mishkan, and properly perform the *avodah* as they are commanded to do, Divine wrath will occur if "זָרִים" — strangers" perform the Levi'im's *avodah*, as we in fact find happened in the saga of Korach.

In his comments to *pasuk* 51, Rashi tells us that the Heavenly death penalty is the punishment for strangers who perform *avodah* that is not appropriate to them. The *Sifsei Chachamim* asks an interesting question. Usually, the word "יוּמָת — he shall be killed" is *chenek*, death by strangulation. How, then, does Rashi know that a "זָר — stranger" who performs *avodah* is punished by Heaven, and is not executed in *Beis Din* by being strangled? The *Sifsei Chachamim* answers by bringing our Rashi. Since the word "קֶצֶף — Divine wrath" is used in our *pasuk*, and is also used by the Torah when discussing Korach (*Bamidbar* 18:5), who was openly killed by Heaven, we may conclude that מִיתָה בִּידֵי שָׁמַיִם, the Heavenly death penalty, is being discussed in our *pasuk*, as well.

Perhaps this is not the only reason why Rashi uses Korach as an example. The source for Korach's contention with Moshe was that he felt he should be a Kohen, and he tried to interfere with the way the Mishkan *avodah* was done (Rashi, *Bamidbar* 16:1). Korach was a "זָר — stranger" trying to do *avodah* in the Mishkan. We thus clearly see from Korach's punishment that this crime is something that is punishable with death from Hashem. This then is why Rashi chose Korach as a model, for his saga is a very close example of the idea that the *pasuk* is discussing.

> וַיַּעֲשׂוּ בְּנֵי יִשְׂרָאֵל כְּכֹל אֲשֶׁר צִוָּה ה' אֶת מֹשֶׁה כֵּן עָשׂוּ:
>
> THE B'NEI YISRAEL DID ACCORDING TO ALL THAT HASHEM HAD COMMANDED MOSHE THUS DID THEY DO. (BAMIDBAR 1:54)

What special praise is the Torah conveying in telling us that the B'nei Yisrael followed Hashem's instructions? Why wouldn't they?

The *Malbim* explains that this *pasuk* refers to the B'nei Yisrael's acceptance of their being camped relatively far from the Mishkan, and everyone's living within their *shevet*, as was discussed in *pasuk* 52. While this may sound trivial, the Jews' agreeing to live where Moshe assigned them is quite a compliment. On a very basic level, people could not just live wherever they wanted; yet, they submitted to Moshe's decision.

We find a very similar praise of the B'nei Yisrael later on in our *parashah*, in 2:34. There too the Torah tells us that they did what Hashem told them, and, there too, the Ibn Ezra explains this refers to the way that the Jews encamped, as well as the way that they traveled through the desert. Imagine never having the freedom to choose your community... ever. Yet, the Jewish people lived peacefully among themselves in this fashion for forty years.

In addition, we may also see a deeper praise of the B'nei Yisrael, which is, that the Levi'im separated between the places where the rest of the Jews lived, and the Mishkan. *Ruchniyus*, and, in very practical terms, the distance between the house I am looking to buy and the closest *shul* or *yeshiva*, is the first thing on a Jew's mind when he is looking for a place to live. Wouldn't everyone want to be as close to the Mishkan as possible? Also, settling some distance from the Mishkan is accepting that the Levi'im would be closer to the Mishkan and to its *avodah* than the rest of the *shevatim*. Nevertheless, the B'nei Yisrael accepted Moshe's assignment, without a word of complaint.

וַיִּפְקֹד אֹתָם מֹשֶׁה עַל פִּי ה' כַּאֲשֶׁר צֻוָּה:

SO MOSHE COUNTED THEM BY HASHEM'S WORD, JUST AS HE WAS COMMANDED. (BAMIDBAR 3:16)

Rashi explains that Moshe's "counting the Jewish people *by Hashem's Word*" is literal, for, when told to take a census of the B'nei Yisrael, Moshe questioned how he was able to enter the tents of nursing mothers, to count their children. In response, Hashem told him to do whatever he could, and I, Hashem, will take care of the rest. Moshe walked up to the door of each tent, and a *bas kol* came out, telling him how many young children lived in this house.

Rashi is teaching us a great insight: that not only does Hashem not expect us to do something that is physically impossible, He does not expect us to do something that we are not spiritually able to do either. Moshe was of course physically able to enter the mothers' tents and count their nursing children. However, he felt that entering a tent where a mother may be nursing her child was a lack of modesty. Moshe had a spiritual inability to comply with Hashem's request. And, Hashem agreed with Moshe, and told him that Moshe should do what he could, and He, Hashem, would take care of what Moshe could not.

Hashem is not freehanded with miracles. They are reserved for special situations, where a miracle is absolutely necessary. Why then was a miracle necessary here? Even without a miracle, Moshe could have knocked on the front door of the tent, and the mother inside could call out how many children lived inside. Perhaps Hashem rewarded Moshe's *tznius* with this *nes* simply to make his job easier. Or, perhaps the need for this miracle is to give us a message, that Moshe was justified in his request; and to teach us this lesson that those areas which we see as spiritually wrong and "beyond our pale," need not play a part in our necessary *hishtadlus*.

NASSO
נָשֹׂא

נָשֹׂא אֶת רֹאשׁ בְּנֵי גֵרְשׁוֹן גַּם הֵם לְבֵית אֲבֹתָם לְמִשְׁפְּחֹתָם:

TAKE A CENSUS OF THE SONS OF GERSHON, THEM AS WELL, FOLLOWING THEIR FATHERS' HOUSES, ACCORDING TO THEIR FAMILIES. (BAMIDBAR 2:20)

When discussing the census of the family of Gershon, why does the Torah say "גַּם הֵם — them as well"?

Gershon was the eldest of Levi's three sons: Gershon, Kehas, and Merari. Now the family of Kehas, chosen with carrying the *Aron* and other *klei hamishkan*, was the first of the Levi families to be counted at the end of *Parashas Bamidbar*. It would appear that Gershon was passed over and disrespected. In response to this apparent slight, Hashem commanded Moshe to count Gershon, "them as well," to totally equate the importance of the family of Gershon with the other two Levi families.

We find a similar terminology in *Parashas Vayechi* (*Bereishis* 48:14). When blessing his grandchildren Efraim and Menashe, Yaacov placed his right hand on the head of Efraim, who was Yosef's younger son, instead of upon his older brother Menashe. Yosef became upset when he saw this show of favoritism, and tried to correct his father's "mistake." In response, Yaacov said, "יָדַעְתִּי בְנִי יָדַעְתִּי גַּם הוּא יִהְיֶה לְּעָם וְגַם הוּא יִגְדָּל וְאוּלָם אָחִיו"

A Deeper Dimension

הַקָּטֹן יִגְדַּל מִמֶּנּוּ וְזַרְעוֹ יִהְיֶה מְלֹא הַגּוֹיִם — I know, my son, I know; he too (גַם הוּא) will become a people, and he too will be great. But his younger brother will be greater than he, and his children's fame will fill the nations" (48:19). I know what I am doing, Yaacov told Yosef; my choosing Efraim was not meant to denigrate Menashe. He — "גַם הוּא" — will be great. At the same time, Efraim has an advantage over his brother, for Yehoshua, who will apportion Eretz Yisrael and teach Torah to Klal Yisrael, will descend from him.

The same is true in our *pasuk*. The family of Gershon is called "גַם הֵם" to tell us that they too were important, like the first two Levi families. Yet like Efraim, Kehas was nevertheless written first, not because of the other brothers' flaw, but rather because of a dimension of added greatness, that his family carried the *Aron* and other *klei hamishkan*.

> וַיַּעֲשׂוּ כֵן בְּנֵי יִשְׂרָאֵל וַיְשַׁלְּחוּ אוֹתָם אֶל מִחוּץ לַמַּחֲנֶה כַּאֲשֶׁר דִּבֶּר ה' אֶל מֹשֶׁה כֵּן עָשׂוּ בְּנֵי יִשְׂרָאֵל:
>
> THE B'NEI YISRAEL DID SO: THEY SENT THEM OUTSIDE THE CAMP; AS HASHEM HAD SPOKEN TO MOSHE, SO DID THE B'NEI YISRAEL DO. (BAMIDBAR 5:4)

Why is it so noteworthy that the B'nei Yisrael sent all *tamei* people out of the Camp, as Hashem instructed, that the Torah feels the need to mention it? In fact, "the B'nei Yisrael did so" is even mentioned twice! Why?

The *Sefer Oznayim LaTorah* explains that sending out *tamei* people was an issue of *kavod Shamayaim*, for, the previous *pasuk* says "מִזָּכָר עַד נְקֵבָה תְּשַׁלֵּחוּ אֶל מִחוּץ לַמַּחֲנֶה תְּשַׁלְּחוּם וְלֹא יְטַמְּאוּ אֶת מַחֲנֵיהֶם אֲשֶׁר אֲנִי שֹׁכֵן בְּתוֹכָם — both male and female you shall banish; you shall send them outside the camp, and they not defile their camps, *in which I dwell among them*." Hashem wants to be involved with Jewish people. Yet, He will only dwell His *Shechinah* upon a Jewish camp which is pure. The Torah is telling us that the B'nei Yisrael did not look away when they knew that a spouse, child, or other close relative had become *tamei*, but forced them out of the camp to the place outside where they would stay for the duration of their state of *tumah*. Forcing people to "rat" on a family member for the sake of *taharas hamachaneh* forced people to make the decision between their loyalty to family and their loyalty to Hashem, which can be an incredibly difficult *nisayon*. The Torah attests that nevertheless, the B'nei Yisrael made the right decision.

The *Sifri* says that "כֵּן עָשׂוּ בְּנֵי יִשְׂרָאֵל — so did the B'nei Yisrael do" refers to the people who were *tamei*, that they left the camp willingly, and did not need to be forced out. According to this, the Torah is testifying that *tamei* people accepted Hashem's instruction, and left their homes on their own.

דַּבֵּר אֶל בְּנֵי יִשְׂרָאֵל וְאָמַרְתָּ אֲלֵהֶם אִישׁ אִישׁ כִּי תִשְׂטֶה אִשְׁתּוֹ וּמָעֲלָה בוֹ מָעַל:

SPEAK TO THE B'NEI YISRAEL AND SAY TO THEM, "SHOULD ANY MAN'S WIFE GO ASTRAY AND DEAL TREACHEROUSLY WITH HIM…" (BAMIDBAR 5:12)

Rashi notes that the *parashah* of *sotah* immediately follows discussion of *terumah* and other gifts that are given to the Kohen. This tells us that a person who does not give the Kohen the parts of the animals and crops which are due to him will eventually come to the Kohen for a different reason, to verify his wife's fidelity. What is the Torah telling us in assigning this particular punishment?

A person who "stiffs" a Kohen of his *matnos kehunah* thinks that it's a private issue between himself and the Kohen. Hashem is warning him that he is wrong, that the affairs that he thought were private will become a huge public spectacle.

224 A Deeper Dimension

וַיַּקְרִיבוּ הַנְּשִׂאִים אֵת חֲנֻכַּת הַמִּזְבֵּחַ בְּיוֹם הִמָּשַׁח
אֹתוֹ וַיַּקְרִיבוּ הַנְּשִׂיאִם אֶת קָרְבָּנָם לִפְנֵי הַמִּזְבֵּחַ:

THE NESI'IM BROUGHT OFFERINGS FOR
THE DEDICATION OF THE MIZBEYACH ON
THE DAY IT WAS ANOINTED; THE NESI'IM
PRESENTED THEIR OFFERINGS IN FRONT OF THE
MIZBEYACH. (BAMIDBAR 7:10)

Rashi tells us that Moshe did not accept the *Nesi'im's korbanos* until Hashem told him that he may do so. Why did Moshe hesitate?

The *Nesi'im's* gift included *ketores*. In his comments to *pasuk* 14, Rashi tells that we never find that an individual had ever offered *ketores* as part of their *korban*, nor do we find that *ketores* was ever offered on the Outer Mizbeyach; the gifts of the *Nesi'im* were a one-time exception in both of these areas. This explains Moshe's hesitation, and his need to wait for Hashem's approval before allowing them to offer their gifts.[31]

---

31 I later saw this approach in the *Nachalas Yaacov*.

BEHA'ALOSCHA
בְּהַעֲלֹתְךָ

דַּבֵּר אֶל אַהֲרֹן וְאָמַרְתָּ אֵלָיו בְּהַעֲלֹתְךָ אֶת הַנֵּרֹת אֶל מוּל פְּנֵי הַמְּנוֹרָה יָאִירוּ שִׁבְעַת הַנֵּרוֹת:

SPEAK TO AHARON AND SAY TO HIM, "WHEN YOU LIGHT THE LAMPS, THE SEVEN LAMPS SHALL CAST THEIR LIGHT TOWARD THE FACE OF THE MENORAH." (BAMIDBAR 8:2)

Rashi explains that the Torah's employing the word בְּהַעֲלֹתְךָ, which literally means "when you ascend," instead of saying "when you light the Menorah," teaches us that the Menorah had several steps in front of it that the Kohen would step up upon when cleaning or lighting the Menorah. This halachah applied even when a taller Kohen, who could have technically done without these steps, was doing these *mitzvos*.

The Menorah is compared to the Torah. We may thus understand that the symbolism of these steps is that a person cannot become greater in Torah when "standing where he is," but must always "go up," to encounter something that is bigger than he.

Perhaps this is the reason why we find that, in many *shuls* and *batei medrashos*, the *Aron Kodesh* is several steps above ground level. This too reminds us that in order to take out the Torah, we must always "climb up" the stairs. The only way to be *koneh Torah* is to continuously elevate one's self spiritually. Similarly, one cannot hope to hold on to the Torah he has learned, and remain the same person as before.

> דַּבֵּר אֶל אַהֲרֹן וְאָמַרְתָּ אֵלָיו בְּהַעֲלֹתְךָ אֶת הַנֵּרֹת אֶל מוּל פְּנֵי הַמְּנוֹרָה יָאִירוּ שִׁבְעַת הַנֵּרוֹת:
>
> SPEAK TO AHARON AND SAY TO HIM, "WHEN YOU LIGHT THE LAMPS, THE SEVEN LAMPS SHALL CAST THEIR LIGHT TOWARD THE FACE OF THE MENORAH." (BAMIDBAR 8:2)

The *Sefer Oznayim LaTorah* points out that the primary *avodah* of the Menorah wasn't actually lighting it. Rather, the central mitzvah is הֲטָבַת הַנֵּרוֹת, *arranging* the lights, which was cleaning and preparing the Menorah to be lit. For example, a non-Kohen was not allowed to clean or prepare the Menorah, but he was allowed to kindle the lights.

We know that the Menorah symbolizes the Torah. We may thus understand the *Oznayim LaTorah* to be telling us that the focus of learning Torah is not the "glow" that it inevitably brings, but is the *hachanah* and *ameilus* that we put into our learning.

> דַּבֵּר אֶל אַהֲרֹן וְאָמַרְתָּ אֵלָיו בְּהַעֲלֹתְךָ אֶת הַנֵּרֹת אֶל מוּל פְּנֵי הַמְּנוֹרָה יָאִירוּ שִׁבְעַת הַנֵּרוֹת: וַיַּעַשׂ כֵּן אַהֲרֹן אֶל מוּל פְּנֵי הַמְּנוֹרָה הֶעֱלָה נֵרֹתֶיהָ כַּאֲשֶׁר צִוָּה ה' אֶת מֹשֶׁה:
>
> SPEAK TO AHARON AND SAY TO HIM, "WHEN YOU LIGHT THE LAMPS, THE SEVEN LAMPS SHALL CAST THEIR LIGHT TOWARD THE FACE OF THE MENORAH." AHARON DID SO; HE LIT THE LAMPS TOWARD THE FACE OF THE

Menorah, as Hashem had commanded Moshe. (Bamidbar 8:2-3)

Rashi explains that "וַיַּעַשׂ כֵּן אַהֲרֹן — Aharon did so," is praise of Aharon, that "שֶׁלֹּא שִׁינָה — he did not change"; he did not change the way that Hashem had instructed Moshe that the Menorah was to be lit, but followed Moshe's instructions to the letter. What noteworthy idea is the Torah telling us? Why would we have thought that Aharon would have lit the Menorah differently than how Hashem instructed?

In his comments to *pasuk* 2, Rashi tells us that the Menorah had steps in front of it, which the Kohen would stand upon to clean, or light, the Menorah. Now, the Menorah was three *amos* tall, which is eighteen *tefachim*, or, in contemporary measurements, somewhere between just under five to just under six feet tall. We know that Moshe was ten *amos* tall, and the Midrash (*Yalkut Shimoni Va'eira* 3:181) tells us that Aharon was of similar height. Aharon was thus around seven *amos* — between eleven and fourteen feet — *taller* than the Menorah! Aharon could have easily justified that the steps in front of the Menorah were meant for a Kohen of shorter height, and lit the Menorah without the "help" of climbing these stairs. Yet, Rashi is telling us, Aharon submitted himself to Hashem's commandment entirely, even when it appeared to be counterintuitive.[32]

The *Sefas Emes* explains the Torah's praise of Aharon differently, that lighting the Menorah never became something that Aharon did by rote. It appears that he understands Rashi, in praising Aharon by stating that he never changed, to be telling us that he never changed from the first time that he lit the Menorah. Rather, every time that he walked towards the Menorah to perform this *avodah*, he approached it with a sense of freshness and excitement of a mitzvah that he had never done before.

Based on this *Sefas Emes*, perhaps we can understand Rashi's praise of Aharon, שֶׁלֹּא שִׁינָה, to mean that Aharon did not "do it twice," with the word שִׁינָה being related to "שְׁנֵי — two." Aharon never lit the Menorah "again," but every time that he lit it was like the first time.

---

32   I later saw this approach in the *Maskil LeDavid*.

וְאַחֲרֵי כֵן בָּאוּ הַלְוִיִּם לַעֲבֹד אֶת עֲבֹדָתָם בְּאֹהֶל
מוֹעֵד לִפְנֵי אַהֲרֹן וְלִפְנֵי בָנָיו כַּאֲשֶׁר צִוָּה ה' אֶת
מֹשֶׁה עַל הַלְוִיִּם כֵּן עָשׂוּ לָהֶם:

AFTER THAT, THE LEVI'IM CAME TO PERFORM
THE SERVICE IN THE TENT OF MEETING BEFORE
AHARON AND BEFORE HIS SONS; THEY DID TO
THEM JUST AS HASHEM HAD COMMANDED
MOSHE REGARDING THE LEVI'IM. (BAMIDBAR 8:22)

Rashi explains that the Torah's statement that the Levi'im served Hashem "just as Hashem had commanded Moshe" tells us that no one — neither the Levi'im, nor the B'nei Yisrael — resisted in doing any task that was assigned to them. What is so noteworthy about the fact that everyone followed Hashem's instructions?

The Maharal explains that the rest of the Jewish people did not resent the fact that they were not chosen to be Levi'im. On the contrary, they did whatever was required of them. And the Levi'im accepted the responsibilities of their new jobs, and were not scared off by the very real consequence of the death penalty, if they performed their *avodah* incorrectly.

The Maskil LeDavid suggests a different reason as to why the Levi'im would have not wanted to take on this new job. Becoming inaugurated as a Levi required one to shave the hair on his head and entire body, which is understandably a requirement that may scare some people off. The Torah testifies that they did not concern themselves with these trivial matters and accepted their new jobs in Klal Yisrael without reservation.

וַיַּעֲשׂוּ אֶת הַפֶּסַח בָּרִאשׁוֹן בְּאַרְבָּעָה עָשָׂר יוֹם
לַחֹדֶשׁ בֵּין הָעַרְבַּיִם בְּמִדְבַּר סִינָי כְּכֹל אֲשֶׁר צִוָּה ה'
אֶת מֹשֶׁה כֵּן עָשׂוּ בְּנֵי יִשְׂרָאֵל:

SO THEY DID THE PESACH OFFERING IN THE
FIRST MONTH, ON THE AFTERNOON OF THE

Beha'aloscha

FOURTEENTH DAY OF THE MONTH IN THE SINAI DESERT; ACCORDING TO ALL THAT HASHEM HAD COMMANDED MOSHE, SO DID THE B'NEI YISRAEL DO. (BAMIDBAR 9:5)

Also, what is so noteworthy about the fact that everyone followed Hashem's instructions, to do the mitzvah of *korban Pesach*? Why wouldn't they have done what Hashem commanded?

The Yom Tov of Pesach of course relives our leaving Mitzrayim. At the Seder we are not only commanded to speak about all that happened to the B'nei Yisrael when we left, but חַיָּב אָדָם לִרְאוֹת אֶת עַצְמוֹ כְּאִלּוּ הוּא יָצָא מִשִּׁעְבּוּד מִצְרַיִם, a person must view himself that he personally left Mitzrayim. Most of the Seder is built around this theme. We eat *karpas*, *marror*, and *charoses*, and discuss the *Maggid*, all to get us into the mindset of experiencing leaving Mitzrayim.

The *Dor Hamidbar* had just left Mitzrayim one year earlier. The one year in the desert did not cause them to forget their many decades of slavery. They did not need to reenact their bondage and subsequent freedom to make them appreciate where they are right now. Why, the Jews could have reasoned, should we have to for example eat *marror* to jog our memories? Yet, they followed "כְּכֹל אֲשֶׁר צִוָּה ה' אֶת מֹשֶׁה — according to *all* that Hashem had commanded Moshe"; the *korban Pesach* with all of the accompanying *mitzvos*.

וַיֹּאמֶר מֹשֶׁה לְחֹבָב בֶּן רְעוּאֵל הַמִּדְיָנִי חֹתֵן מֹשֶׁה נֹסְעִים אֲנַחְנוּ אֶל הַמָּקוֹם אֲשֶׁר אָמַר ה' אֹתוֹ אֶתֵּן לָכֶם לְכָה אִתָּנוּ וְהֵטַבְנוּ לָךְ כִּי ה' דִּבֶּר טוֹב עַל יִשְׂרָאֵל:

THEN MOSHE SAID TO CHOVAV BEN REUEL THE MIDYANITE, MOSHE'S FATHER-IN-LAW, "WE ARE TRAVELING TO THE PLACE ABOUT WHICH HASHEM SAID, 'I SHALL GIVE IT TO YOU.' COME

WITH US AND WE WILL BE GOOD TO YOU, FOR
HASHEM HAS SPOKEN OF GOOD FORTUNE FOR
YISRAEL." (BAMIDBAR 10:29)

Rashi tells us that Chovav is Yisro. Why, then, does the Torah use the name "Chovav" specifically here? Also, why is Chovav called "חֹבָב בֶּן רְעוּאֵל הַמִּדְיָנִי — Chovav ben Reuel the Midyanite," instead of the *pasuk* simply saying, "וַיֹּאמֶר מֹשֶׁה לְחֹבָב — Moshe said to Chovav"?

The Sifri (§78) explains that Yisro was called "חוֹבָב — Chovav" because "חִבֵּב אֶת הַתּוֹרָה — he loved the Torah." And he was called "רְעוּאֵל — Reuel" because he was "רֵיעַ שֶׁל אֵל — a 'friend' of Hashem." Our *pasuk* refers to Yisro by these names to tell us the arguments that Moshe used in his efforts to convince him to stay with the Jewish people. Moshe asked Yisro, how could he, someone who loves the Torah, and is Hashem's "friend" leave? Another line of reasoning that Moshe used was that he told Yisro that you are the father-in-law of Moshe, the King. How could you leave us? Moshe tried every angle possible to get Yisro to stay. But it wasn't enough.

The *Oznayim LaTorah* has a slightly different approach. The reason why Moshe enumerated several of Yisro's qualities when trying to convince him to stay was to show him that his leaving the Jewish people at this time would create a very big *chillul Hashem* in the eyes of the nations of the world. Calling him "Chovav" reminded Yisro that his love for the Torah drove him to learn Torah for a very long time at Har Sinai. "Ben Reuel" stressed that he was close to Hashem. "הַמִּדְיָנִי — the Midyanite," made the point that as the former Priest of Midyan, you searched out many different gods, and ultimately realized Hashem's Truth. As "חֹתֵן מֹשֶׁה — Moshe's father-in-law," you would not lack anything if you remain with us. If the rest of the world sees you leave us although you have attained all of these advantages, they will conclude that the reason you left is because these things are meaningless to you, for they did not give you the *seepuk hanefesh* that you were originally seeking. For this reason alone, it is appropriate that you remain.

זָכַרְנוּ אֶת הַדָּגָה אֲשֶׁר נֹאכַל בְּמִצְרַיִם חִנָּם אֵת הַקִּשֻּׁאִים וְאֵת הָאֲבַטִּחִים וְאֶת הֶחָצִיר וְאֶת הַבְּצָלִים וְאֶת הַשּׁוּמִים:

WE REMEMBER THE FISH THAT WE ATE IN MITZRAYIM FOR FREE, THE CUCUMBERS, THE WATERMELONS, THE LEEKS, THE ONIONS, AND THE GARLIC. (BAMIDBAR 11:5)

Rashi explains that the Mitzrim didn't even give the Jews straw to make bricks. They certainly did not give them free fish! Rather, the B'nei Yisrael longed for being able to eat their food in a manner that was "free from *mitzvos*."

What does doing the *mitzvos* have to do with the food that the Jews ate? Where do we find that Hashem withheld food from the B'nei Yisrael because they were not careful about doing a mitzvah?

Perhaps the B'nei Yisrael were referring to the *Mahn*. We know that although every Jew received the same amount of *Mahn* each day, it fell for different people in different places. A *tzadik* got his *Mahn* at his doorstep, a *rasha* had walk to outside the Camp, and other people found their *Mahn* somewhere in the middle. This setup put pressure on a person to do *mitzvos*, for if they did not, their *Mahn* would fall farther away from their homes, making their somewhat lower spiritual standing clear to all of their neighbors.

זָכַרְנוּ אֶת הַדָּגָה אֲשֶׁר נֹאכַל בְּמִצְרַיִם חִנָּם אֵת הַקִּשֻּׁאִים וְאֵת הָאֲבַטִּחִים וְאֶת הֶחָצִיר וְאֶת הַבְּצָלִים וְאֶת הַשּׁוּמִים:

WE REMEMBER THE FISH THAT WE ATE IN MITZRAYIM FOR FREE, THE CUCUMBERS, THE WATERMELONS, THE LEEKS, THE ONIONS, AND THE GARLIC. (BAMIDBAR 11:5)

Rashi explains that the *Mahn* did not taste like the five foods mentioned in this *pasuk* — cucumber, watermelon, leek, onion, and garlic — because these foods are not good for a nursing baby, who would taste these foods in their mother's milk. Why is this information about the *Mahn* told to us here, instead of in *Parashas HaMahn* in *Parashas Beshalach*?

In his previous comment, Rashi explained that the Jews were complaining to Moshe, that they longed for the days that they could eat "חִנָּם מִן הַמִּצְוֹת — free from the *mitzvos*," that is, without restriction. This then, is a similar complaint about being restricted in how they ate and lived. In Mitzrayim we could eat whatever we wanted, complained the B'nei Yisrael. But now, in the Wilderness, we are encumbered to Hashem in many areas.

[As an aside, it is interesting to note, that once these vegetables were off-limits to nursing mothers, no one — men, other women, or children — could wish their *Mahn* to taste like them.]

וְהָאִישׁ מֹשֶׁה עָנָיו מְאֹד מִכֹּל הָאָדָם אֲשֶׁר עַל פְּנֵי הָאֲדָמָה:

NOW THIS MAN MOSHE WAS EXCEEDINGLY HUMBLE, MORE SO THAN ANY PERSON ON THE FACE OF THE EARTH. (BAMIDBAR 12:3)

Why are we told of Moshe's humility within the context of the *lashon hara* that Miriam and Aharon discussed about him?

The Torah is telling us that speaking about someone else because "he doesn't mind" is not an excuse. If anyone didn't mind that he was being spoken about, it was Moshe. And yet, we see very clearly that the discussion about him was still considered absolute *lashon hara*.

Another answer is that true humility is not seen by how a person acts in public, but how he acts with the members of his home. This episode demonstrates Moshe's humility more than any other event in the Torah. Even when his own brother and sister spoke badly about him, Moshe Rabbeinu didn't take any offense.

וְהָאִישׁ מֹשֶׁה עָנָו מְאֹד מִכֹּל הָאָדָם אֲשֶׁר עַל פְּנֵי הָאֲדָמָה:

NOW THIS MAN MOSHE WAS EXCEEDINGLY HUMBLE, MORE SO THAN ANY PERSON ON THE FACE OF THE EARTH. (BAMIDBAR 12:3)

When written in a *Sefer Torah*, the word עָנָיו, which means a humble person, is written עָנָו, without the letter י. Why?

The Torah is giving us a picture of humility. The letter י is the smallest letter in the *Alef-Beis*. And even that is missing. Yet the word is still read, and understood. This tells us that one does not have to stand out to be big and effective. Moshe as well was incredibly self-effacing, despite the important role that he played in Klal Yisrael.

SHELACH
שְׁלַח

שְׁלַח לְךָ אֲנָשִׁים ...

"SEND OUT FOR YOURSELF MEN..." (BAMIDBAR 13:2)

Rashi explains that the episode of the *Meraglim* is written next to the episode of Miriam. The reason for this juxtaposition is because the *Meraglim*, who saw how Miriam was punished for speaking *lashon hara*, should have "taken *mussar*" — learned something and changed — from what they saw, and not spoken *lashon hara* about Eretz Yisrael.

The fact that Rashi sees this juxtaposition as a noteworthy part of the *Meraglim's* story shows us the sheer importance about learning something from any situation in which we find ourselves.

לְמַטֵּה אֶפְרַיִם הוֹשֵׁעַ בִּן נוּן ... לְמַטֵּה יוֹסֵף לְמַטֵּה מְנַשֶּׁה גַּדִּי בֶּן סוּסִי ...

FOR THE SHEVET OF EFRAIM, HOSHEA BIN NUN... FOR THE SHEVET OF YOSEF, THE TRIBE OF MENASHE, GADI BEN SUSI... (BAMIDBAR 13:8,11)

Why doesn't the Torah mention Yosef next to Efraim's name, as it does next to Menashe? After all, both of these *Shevatim* came from Yosef!

Yehoshua distinguished himself by separating himself from the rest of the *Meraglim* by not speaking *lashon hara* about Eretz Yisrael. Unfortunately, Gadi did speak *lashon hara*. In this way, Gadi acted wrongly in the same way as Yosef, who spoke *lashon hara* about his brothers. Since Yehoshua was able to break away from the other *Meraglim*, he is not associated with Yosef like Gadi.[33]

אֵלֶּה שְׁמוֹת הָאֲנָשִׁים אֲשֶׁר שָׁלַח מֹשֶׁה לָתוּר אֶת הָאָרֶץ וַיִּקְרָא מֹשֶׁה לְהוֹשֵׁעַ בִּן נוּן יְהוֹשֻׁעַ:

THESE ARE THE NAMES OF THE MEN MOSHE SENT TO SCOUT THE LAND, AND MOSHE CALLED HOSHEA BIN NUN, YEHOSHUA. (BAMIDBAR 13:16)

Rashi explains that Moshe changed Yehoshua's name as a way of *davening* for him, that Hashem save him from the *Meraglim's* plans. Why didn't Moshe *daven* for Kalev, as well?

This *pasuk* teaches us the value of building a relationship with, and being *meshamesh*, a *rebbi*. Moshe Rabbeinu certainly *davened* for all of the people whom he was sending to scout out Eretz Yisrael. But since the relationship that Moshe had with Yehoshua was deeper than his relationship with the other *Meraglim*, he understood his *techunos hanefesh*, and was able to *daven* for a specific *yeshu'ah* for him, in a way that was impossible to do for the others. A person who is close to a *rebbi* will naturally get extra attention and *shemirah*. Although the *rebbi* undoubtedly wants to help other people as well, it is much harder to *daven* precisely for a person whom you really don't know.

וַיַּהַס כָּלֵב אֶת הָעָם אֶל מֹשֶׁה וַיֹּאמֶר עָלֹה נַעֲלֶה וְיָרַשְׁנוּ אֹתָהּ כִּי יָכוֹל נוּכַל לָהּ:

KALEV SILENCED THE PEOPLE TO HEAR ABOUT MOSHE, AND HE SAID, "WE CAN SURELY GO

---

33 I later saw this idea in the *Mosif Rashi*, and in the *Chizkuni*.

> UP AND TAKE POSSESSION OF IT, FOR WE CAN
> INDEED OVERCOME IT." (BAMIDBAR 13:30)

Why did specifically Kalev try to quiet the *Meraglim* from speaking more *lashon hara* about Eretz Yisrael? After all, it was Yehoshua whom Moshe had *davened* for!

Perhaps an answer to this question is the following. As we learned, the *Meraglim* were punished for seeing Miriam being stricken with *tzaraas* for speaking *lashon hara*, yet they did not learn their lesson. Kalev, on the other hand, was Miriam's husband. He, if anybody, *did* internalize the lesson of what happened to his wife! It was therefore specifically he, more than Yehoshua, who was sensitive to the dangers of *lashon hara*, and thus did whatever he could to try to put a stop to it.

> וַיֹּאמְרוּ אִישׁ אֶל אָחִיו נִתְּנָה רֹאשׁ וְנָשׁוּבָה מִצְרָיְמָה:
>
> THEY SAID TO EACH OTHER, "LET US APPOINT
> A LEADER AND RETURN TO MITZRAYIM!"
> (BAMIDBAR 14:4)

If the B'nei Yisrael were so afraid to go to Eretz Yisrael because of the terrible things that they heard about it, why didn't they just return to Mitzrayim on their own? Why were they insistent that a leader must be appointed to take them back?

A country needs a leader in order to rule effectively. And in order for a revolt to be effective, it must show more organization than the country or system that it is revolting against. While not everyone was happy with the status quo and with Moshe's leadership, they knew that the only way that they would be able to return to Mitzrayim is by appointing a leader to organize it.

Shelach

וַיִּפֹּל מֹשֶׁה וְאַהֲרֹן עַל פְּנֵיהֶם לִפְנֵי כָּל קְהַל עֲדַת
בְּנֵי יִשְׂרָאֵל: וִיהוֹשֻׁעַ בִּן נוּן וְכָלֵב בֶּן יְפֻנֶּה מִן
הַתָּרִים אֶת הָאָרֶץ קָרְעוּ בִּגְדֵיהֶם:

MOSHE AND AHARON FELL ON THEIR FACES
BEFORE THE ENTIRE CONGREGATION OF THE
B'NEI YISRAEL. YEHOSHUA BIN NUN AND KALEV
BEN YEFUNEH, WHO WERE AMONG THOSE
WHO HAD SCOUTED THE LAND, TORE THEIR
CLOTHES. (BAMIDBAR 14:5–6)

Why was Yehoshua and Kalev's reaction to hearing the Jewish people's complaining so different than that of Moshe and Aharon? Also, why does the Torah mention that Yehoshua and Kalev were "מִן הַתָּרִים אֶת הָאָרֶץ — among those who had scouted the Land," when telling us that they tore their clothes?

The Torah mentions that Yehoshua and Kalev were among those who had scouted the Land to explain why their reaction was more severe than that of Moshe and Aharon. Moshe and Aharon appreciated the calamity that had just taken place, and literally fell on their faces in shock and grief. Yehoshua and Kalev, however, had actually been in Eretz Yisrael and seen the Land's beauty. They knew that the other *Meraglim* were lying, and had seen what the B'nei Yisrael were losing by believing this story. More than anyone, they tangibly *felt* the tragedy, of the damage that the other *Meraglim* had caused. Yehoshua and Kalev's instinctive reaction was thus to rip their clothing to show mourning in a way which someone who had not witnessed the beauty of Eretz Yisrael firsthand may not understand.

וְעַתָּה יִגְדַּל נָא כֹּחַ אֲדֹנָי כַּאֲשֶׁר דִּבַּרְתָּ לֵאמֹר: ה'
אֶרֶךְ אַפַּיִם וְרַב חֶסֶד נֹשֵׂא עָוֹן וָפָשַׁע וְנַקֵּה לֹא יְנַקֶּה
פֹּקֵד עֲוֹן אָבוֹת עַל בָּנִים עַל שִׁלֵּשִׁים וְעַל רִבֵּעִים:

NOW, PLEASE, LET THE STRENGTH OF HASHEM BE INCREASED, AS YOU SPOKE, SAYING, "HASHEM IS SLOW TO ANGER AND ABUNDANTLY KIND, FORGIVING INIQUITY AND TRANSGRESSION, WHO CLEANSES SOME, AND DOES NOT CLEANSE OTHERS, WHO VISITS THE INIQUITIES OF PARENTS ON CHILDREN, EVEN TO THE THIRD AND FOURTH GENERATIONS." (BAMIDBAR 14:17–18)

When written in a *Sefer Torah*, the word יִגְדַּל is written with a large letter י. Why?

Moshe is pleading with Hashem to spare the B'nei Yisrael, after the *Meraglim* returned with a disparaging report about Eretz Yisrael. Moshe begged Hashem that He employ His *Middos* of *chessed*, and *erech apayim*, being slow to become angry. Now, the best way to appreciate something small is to put it under a microscope and magnify it. We can then study it and appreciate its qualities that are literally there in front of us, but we wouldn't have otherwise noticed. Similarly, Moshe was asking Hashem to focus on, or "magnify," these *Middos* that were necessary to spare Klal Yisrael. The *pasuk* is creating an image of Moshe's request, by magnifying the smallest letter in the *Alef-Beis*, until it too is large and plays a large role.

Additionally, the letter י in particular is the first letter of Hashem's ineffable Name, which is the Name symbolizing *Middas Harachamim*. Enlarging this letter shows that Moshe was asking that this *middah* in particular be employed and focused upon.

וְעַבְדִּי כָלֵב עֵקֶב הָיְתָה רוּחַ אַחֶרֶת עִמּוֹ ...

But as for My servant Kalev, since he had another spirit... (Bamidbar 14:24)

The Torah describes Kalev as having "רוּחַ אַחֶרֶת — another spirit." Rashi explains that Kalev had "שְׁתֵּי רוּחוֹת, אַחַת בַּפֶּה וְאַחַת בַּלֵּב — two 'spirits,' one with his mouth, and one in his heart." One approach was how he spoke to the other *Meraglim* — telling them that he was with them — and the other the way that he really felt, that he knew the truth about Eretz Yisrael.

It appears that Rashi is praising Kalev's intuitiveness in his dealing with the *Meraglim*, despite the fact that his mouth and heart were not the same. Yet, in his comments to *Bereishis* 37:4, Rashi explains that the *Shevatim* were wrong for hating Yosef. However, they are to be praised that, once in this situation, they did not speak to him peacefully, for "שֶׁלֹּא דִבְּרוּ אַחַת בַּפֶּה וְאַחַת בַּלֵּב — they did not speak one way with their mouths, and one in their hearts." On one hand Rashi praises Kalev for dealing with the *Meraglim* in a way that was not consistent to how he felt in his heart, and on the other, he praises the *Shevatim* for *not* acting in this manner!

Perhaps the answer is that it all depends on the situation. Kalev knew that there was no way that he could get everyone's attention had they thought that he agreed with Yehoshua, who had already been drowned out by the chaos. He realized that only by pretending to agree with the other *Meraglim* would he be given the chance to speak; where he would present the true story and restore order. And for this, he is praised. However, the *Shevatim*, in their total honesty, could not pretend to speak peacefully to Yosef when they in truth hated him. This was *sheker*.

The word "*middos*" literally means "measurements." We must gauge, or measure, each situation in which we find ourselves. Is how I am acting consistent with who I am? In this way, we can use even the *middos* which are normally considered to be negative for an action that elicits praise from the Torah.

Korach
קֹרַח

> וַיִּקַּח קֹרַח בֶּן יִצְהָר בֶּן קְהָת בֶּן לֵוִי וְדָתָן וַאֲבִירָם
> בְּנֵי אֱלִיאָב וְאוֹן בֶּן פֶּלֶת בְּנֵי רְאוּבֵן:
>
> KORACH THE SON OF YITZHAR, THE SON OF
> KEHAS, THE SON OF LEVI, TOOK HIMSELF TO
> ONE SIDE ALONG WITH DASAN AND AVIRAM,
> THE SONS OF ELIAV, AND ON THE SON OF PELES,
> DESCENDANTS OF REUVEN. (BAMIDBAR 16:1)

Rashi explains that the reason that Dasan, Aviram, and the many other people from *Shevet Reuven* were influenced by Korach was because the area where they lived was adjacent to that of *Shevet Levi*, and thus of Korach and his sons; "אוֹי לָרָשָׁע וְאוֹי לִשְׁכֵנוֹ — woe is to a *rasha*, and woe is to his neighbor!" Even so, it still seems difficult to understand. Why did these people join Korach's rebellion against Moshe? What did they have to gain?

The people of *Shevet Reuven* had something else in common with Korach aside from their joint location: they too were skipped over for an important position. Korach's argument was that his father Yitzhar was Kehas' older son, and it was not fair that he was passed up for the leadership position in favor of Elitzafan, who was the son of Uziel, Kehas' younger son. And we know that Reuven, who was Yaacov's first-born, had lost the *Bechorah*, and the accompanying privileges of *Kehunah* and royalty. As a result, the people of Reuven were very sympathetic to Korach's cause, and supported his rebellion, even though it did not benefit them in any way.[34]

This approach allows us another insight into our *pasuk*. The Torah provides us with Korach's lineage generation to generation, all the way back to Levi. Yet, by Dasan, Aviram, and On, were are just told that they came from *Shevet Reuven*. Why the difference?

The answer is as we have just explained; the common denominator between Korach and the other people in his rebellion was that each one felt wronged for being "passed over." So the Torah gives the background that is necessary in each case to allow us to understand their "argument." We are told that Korach was "בֶּן יִצְהָר בֶּן קְהָת בֶּן לֵוִי" — the son of Yitzhar, the son of Kehas, the son of Levi," for Korach's argument came from his feelings that as the son of Yitzhar, Kehas' eldest, he should have been the heir of the special privileges of *Shevet Levi*. Dasan, Aviram, and On, on the other hand, felt wronged simply because of what had happened to their ancestor Reuven. Telling us that they were "בְּנֵי רְאוּבֵן — descendants of Reuven" is therefore enough to provide clarity to their involvement.

וַיֹּאמֶר ה' אֶל מֹשֶׁה הָשֵׁב אֶת מַטֵּה אַהֲרֹן לִפְנֵי הָעֵדוּת לְמִשְׁמֶרֶת לְאוֹת לִבְנֵי מֶרִי וּתְכַל תְּלוּנֹּתָם מֵעָלַי וְלֹא יָמֻתוּ: וַיַּעַשׂ מֹשֶׁה כַּאֲשֶׁר צִוָּה ה' אֹתוֹ כֵּן עָשָׂה:

HASHEM SAID TO MOSHE, "PUT AHARON'S STAFF BACK IN FRONT OF THE TESTIMONY AS A KEEPSAKE, A SIGN FOR REBELLIOUS ONES. THEN THEIR COMPLAINTS AGAINST ME WILL

---

34   I later saw this idea in the *Kli Yakar*.

END AND THEY WILL NOT DIE." MOSHE DID SO; HE DID JUST AS HASHEM HAD COMMANDED HIM. (BAMIDBAR 17:25–26)

Why is it so noteworthy that Moshe did as Hashem told him, that the Torah feels the need to mention it? Also, points out the *Ohr Hachaim*, the Torah twice says that Moshe did as Hashem instructed; "וַיַּעַשׂ מֹשֶׁה כַּאֲשֶׁר צִוָּה ה' אֹתוֹ כֵּן עָשָׂה" — Moshe did so; he did just as Hashem had commanded him." Why the repetition?

Hashem told Moshe to take Aharon's staff, which was full with miraculously blossomed almonds, and to keep it as a sign. He was to show this rod as a sign to anyone who was considering rebelling against Hashem, so they would remember what had happened to Korach. Now, Moshe was the humblest of all men. And Hashem was telling him to use this staff as a way to remind people of his own greatness and total trust that Hashem had in him! Nevertheless Moshe followed Hashem's instruction to the letter, as much as this mission of reminding people about Hashem's choosing him and Aharon went against his natural grain.

Chukas
חֻקַּת

וַיָּבֹאוּ בְנֵי יִשְׂרָאֵל כָּל הָעֵדָה מִדְבַּר צִן בַּחֹדֶשׁ הָרִאשׁוֹן וַיֵּשֶׁב הָעָם בְּקָדֵשׁ וַתָּמָת שָׁם מִרְיָם וַתִּקָּבֵר שָׁם:

THE ENTIRE CONGREGATION OF THE B'NEI YISRAEL ARRIVED AT THE DESERT OF ZIN IN THE FIRST MONTH, AND THE PEOPLE SETTLED IN KADESH. MIRIAM DIED THERE AND WAS BURIED THERE. (BAMIDBAR 20:1)

Rashi explains that the reason for the juxtaposition between Miriam's death and the *parashah* of *Parah Adumah* is to tell us that just as *korbanos* are *mechaper*, so too, a *tzadik's* death is *mechaper* for Klal Yisrael.

The commentaries ask a question when discussing this Rashi. Why then, isn't Miriam's death placed around *Parshios Vayikra* and *Tzav*, for example, where most of the other *korbanos* are discussed? Why specifically next to *Parah Adumah*?

The *kapparah* of most *korbanos* is achieved by substituting an animal for the person who really deserves punishment.[35] The animal is killed

---

35   See the Ramban to *Vayikra* 1:9, for discussion.

in this person's place. The *kapparah* of *Parah Adumah* also includes a different type of "substitution": that the person who is *tamei* becomes *tahor* after being sprinkled with the *Parah Adumah* ashes, and the Kohen sprinkling him, who was previously *tahor*, now becomes *tamei* instead. This "substitution" is not person to animal, like most *korbanos*, but is "person to person," instead. In this sense, *Parah Adumah* is most similar to the *kapparah* that a *tzadik's* death provides for the *klal*, in the sense that one person, who has quite possibly done nothing wrong, achieves the *kapparah* for someone else.

We may understand another reason for the specific comparison of a *tzadik's* death to *Parah Adumah*, from the Midrash which explains that the *Parah Adumah* was *mechaper* for the Jews' worshipping the *Eigel Hazahav* (Rashi 19:22). The relationship between the Red Cow and the Golden Calf may be understood with a *mashal* of the child of a maid who dirtied the floor of the king's palace. The king then called for the mother to clean up the mess which her son had made. Similarly, a cow is used to repair the *aveirah* that was done with the calf.

Perhaps the same is true in regard to the death of a *tzadik*, who like a mother, guides the *klal* and thus takes responsibility for its actions. Miriam's death serves as a *kaparah* for the B'nei Yisrael, for she was acting as the proverbial mother, just like the *Parah* is for its *Eigel*.

וְהוֹצֵאתָ לָהֶם מַיִם מִן הַסֶּלַע וְהִשְׁקִיתָ אֶת הָעֵדָה וְאֶת בְּעִירָם:

YOU SHALL BRING FORTH WATER FOR THEM FROM THE ROCK AND GIVE THE CONGREGATION AND THEIR LIVESTOCK TO DRINK." (BAMIDBAR 20:8)

The halachah is that a person must feed his animals before eating, himself. And, some opinions maintain that a person must give his animals water before he drinks as well. Why then, did Hashem tell Moshe that "וְהוֹצֵאתָ לָהֶם מַיִם מִן הַסֶּלַע וְהִשְׁקִיתָ אֶת הָעֵדָה וְאֶת בְּעִירָם" — You shall bring forth water for them from the rock and give the congregation and their livestock to drink"; first the people and only then the animals?

Perhaps this halachah of feeding our animals before we eat only applies to a situation of actual hunger or thirst. Nowhere in this episode, however, does the Torah say that the Jewish people were actually thirsty, as it does in a similar story in *Shemos* 15:22–24. For example, when grumbling to Moshe and Aharon, the Jews said "וְלָמָה הֶעֱלִיתָנוּ מִמִּצְרַיִם לְהָבִיא אֹתָנוּ אֶל הַמָּקוֹם הָרָע הַזֶּה לֹא מְקוֹם זֶרַע וּתְאֵנָה וְגֶפֶן וְרִמּוֹן וּמַיִם אַיִן לִשְׁתּוֹת — Why have you taken us out of Mitzrayim to bring us to this evil place; it is not a place for seeds, or for fig trees, grapevines, or pomegranate trees, and there is no water to drink," (*Bamidbar* 20:5), first complaining about the lack of seeds and trees, and only afterwards mentioning that this place has no water to drink. Rather, the Jewish people suffered from "fast-day syndrome," where they got thirsty as soon as drinking became prohibited or impossible. Since the water they were demanding was not yet pressing, for both they and their animals were not yet thirsty, there is no reason why the people could not drink before tending to their animals.

וַיֹּאמֶר ה' אֶל מֹשֶׁה וְאֶל אַהֲרֹן יַעַן לֹא הֶאֱמַנְתֶּם בִּי לְהַקְדִּישֵׁנִי לְעֵינֵי בְּנֵי יִשְׂרָאֵל לָכֵן לֹא תָבִיאוּ אֶת הַקָּהָל הַזֶּה אֶל הָאָרֶץ אֲשֶׁר נָתַתִּי לָהֶם:

HASHEM SAID TO MOSHE AND AHARON, "SINCE YOU DID NOT HAVE FAITH IN ME TO SANCTIFY ME IN THE EYES OF THE B'NEI YISRAEL, THEREFORE YOU SHALL NOT BRING THIS ASSEMBLY TO THE LAND WHICH I HAVE GIVEN THEM." (BAMIDBAR 20:12)

What did Aharon do wrong that he was also punished in not being allowed to enter Eretz Yisrael? Moshe hit the rock, not Aharon!

Perhaps we can compare this episode to the story of the *Meraglim*, who were sent to scout the Land and give a report to the B'nei Yisrael.

Imagine the tremendous *kiddush Hashem* that would have happened had they come back and given the Jews a good report, that Eretz Yisrael is indeed the wonderful place that Hashem promised us, and that just as He protected us from the Land's inhabitants as we traveled through it, He will also take care of us when we enter to conquer it. The punishment that they ultimately received was not only for the *lashon hara* that they had spoken. It was for creating a tremendous *chillul Hashem* instead. Yehoshua and Kalev, on the other hand, fought this *chillul Hashem* as best as they could. They were therefore allowed into Eretz Yisrael.

Aharon had a chance to act like Yehoshua and Kalev and fight the tremendous *chillul Hashem* that had just taken place, either by convincing Moshe not to hit the rock before he did so, or by saying or doing something afterwards. Unfortunately, he did neither. In this way he somewhat participated in the *chillul Hashem* that had taken place, and was punished together with Moshe.

וַיַּעַשׂ מֹשֶׁה כַּאֲשֶׁר צִוָּה ה' וַיַּעֲלוּ אֶל הֹר הָהָר לְעֵינֵי כָּל הָעֵדָה:

MOSHE DID AS HASHEM COMMANDED HIM. THEY ASCENDED MOUNT HOR IN THE PRESENCE OF THE ENTIRE CONGREGATION. (BAMIDBAR 20:27)

Rashi explains that the Torah is praising Moshe that although it was incredibly difficult for him to take his older brother to his demise, he did not hesitate to follow Hashem's instructions and do so.

We often procrastinate relaying bad news to someone who needs to hear what happened. We think of all sorts of ways how to tell him, or sometimes even avoid telling them altogether. Moshe carried out this very difficult instruction from Hashem with the same promptness that he did anything else that Hashem asked of him. It was Hashem's Will, which cannot be postponed for any personal biases.

Balak
בָּלָק

וְעַתָּה לְכָה נָּא אָרָה לִּי אֶת הָעָם הַזֶּה...

So now, please come and slightly curse this people for me... (Bamidbar 22:6)

וַיֹּאמֶר בִּלְעָם אֶל הָאֱלֹקִים בָּלָק בֶּן צִפֹּר מֶלֶךְ מוֹאָב שָׁלַח אֵלָי: הִנֵּה הָעָם... אוּלַי אוּכַל לְהִלָּחֶם בּוֹ וְגֵרַשְׁתִּיו: וַיֹּאמֶר אֱלֹקִים אֶל בִּלְעָם לֹא תֵלֵךְ עִמָּהֶם לֹא תָאֹר אֶת הָעָם כִּי בָרוּךְ הוּא:

Bilaam said to Hashem, "Balak the son of Tzippor the king of Moav has sent them to me, saying, "Behold the people... come and curse them for me, perhaps I will be able to fight against them and drive them out." Hashem said to Bilaam, "You shall not go with them! You shall not curse the nation because they are blessed."
(Bamidbar 22:10–13)

Lashon Hakodesh includes several words for "curse." אָרָה is the word used for a lower-level curse, and קָבָה, explains Rashi, means a stronger curse. In *pasuk* 6, Balak invites Bilaam by asking him to "וְעַתָּה לְכָה נָּא אָרָה לִּי אֶת הָעָם הַזֶּה — please come and 'slightly' curse (אָרָה) this people for me." Yet, in *pasuk* 11, when Bilaam recounts the story to Hashem, he tells him that Balak asked him to "עַתָּה לְכָה קָבָה לִּי אֹתוֹ — come and 'strongly' curse them (קָבָה) for me." Why did Bilaam use a different expression? Also, when Hashem warns Bilaam that he must not go with Balak, He tells him, "לֹא תָאֹר אֶת הָעָם — you shall not 'slightly' curse (אָרָה) the nation." Again, why the change?

Bilaam, in his arrogance, could not tell Hashem that he had only been hired to deliver a lower-level curse upon the B'nei Yisrael. He had to show Hashem how important he was, and so he raised the level of the job which he had been asked to do.

In response, Hashem told Bilaam that he could not fool Him, and so answered him using the exact phrase of the lower-level אָרָה, with which Balak had originally delivered his invitation.

> וַיֹּאמֶר אֲלֵיהֶם לִינוּ פֹה הַלַּיְלָה וַהֲשִׁבֹתִי אֶתְכֶם דָּבָר כַּאֲשֶׁר יְדַבֵּר ה' אֵלָי וַיֵּשְׁבוּ שָׂרֵי מוֹאָב עִם בִּלְעָם:
>
> HE SAID TO THEM, "LODGE HERE FOR THE NIGHT, AND I WILL GIVE YOU AN ANSWER WHEN HASHEM SPEAKS TO ME." SO THE NOBLES OF MOAV STAYED WITH BILAAM. (BAMIDBAR 22:8)

> וְעַתָּה שְׁבוּ נָא בָזֶה גַּם אַתֶּם הַלָּיְלָה וְאֵדְעָה מַה יֹּסֵף ה' דַּבֵּר עִמִּי:
>
> NOW, YOU TOO, PLEASE REMAIN HERE OVERNIGHT, AND I WILL KNOW WHAT HASHEM WILL CONTINUE TO SPEAK WITH ME. (BAMIDBAR 22:19)

Why does Bilaam extend an offer to the first group of nobles to "lodge here for the night," yet the second group he just tells to remain — sit tight — until the morning?

We know that the first group of nobles was of lower ranking than the second. And, Bilaam, who was the peak of human arrogance, wanted to assert his authority over both of them. So for the lower class group, he offered them a place to sleep, so they would feel dependent on him. And when dealing with the more important delegation, he wanted to give them the message that he is very important and worth waiting for. Bilaam told them to just sit and wait for him to return.

וַיָּבֹא אֱלֹקִים אֶל בִּלְעָם לַיְלָה וַיֹּאמֶר לוֹ אִם לִקְרֹא לְךָ בָּאוּ הָאֲנָשִׁים קוּם לֵךְ אִתָּם וְאַךְ אֶת הַדָּבָר אֲשֶׁר אֲדַבֵּר אֵלֶיךָ אֹתוֹ תַעֲשֶׂה: וַיָּקָם בִּלְעָם בַּבֹּקֶר וַיַּחֲבֹשׁ אֶת אֲתֹנוֹ וַיֵּלֶךְ עִם שָׂרֵי מוֹאָב: וַיִּחַר אַף אֱלֹקִים כִּי הוֹלֵךְ הוּא וַיִּתְיַצֵּב מַלְאַךְ ה' בַּדֶּרֶךְ לְשָׂטָן לוֹ ...

HASHEM CAME TO BILAAM AT NIGHT AND SAID TO HIM, "IF THESE MEN HAVE COME TO CALL FOR YOU, ARISE AND GO WITH THEM, BUT THE WORD I SPEAK TO YOU, THAT YOU SHALL DO." IN THE MORNING BILAAM AROSE, SADDLED HIS SHE-DONKEY AND WENT WITH THE MOAVI DIGNITARIES. HASHEM'S WRATH FLARED BECAUSE HE WAS GOING, AND AN ANGEL OF HASHEM STATIONED HIMSELF ON THE ROAD TO THWART HIM... (BAMIDBAR 22:20-22)

Hashem just gave Bilaam permission to go with Balak's officers as long as he did not try to curse the B'nei Yisrael. Yet, in *pasuk* 22, He became angry with Bilaam as soon as he left, before Bilaam even said anything. What changed?

A closer look at *pasuk* 21 will answer our question. The Torah tells us that Bilaam saddled his donkey upon waking up in the morning. Rashi notes that this behavior was unusual for a distinguished person like Bilaam, whose servants generally took care of this menial task. However, "הַשִּׂנְאָה מְקַלְקֶלֶת אֶת הַשּׁוּרָה" — hate causes one to ignore the standards of normal conduct." Bilaam's zeal, brought about by his passionate hatred for the B'nei Yisrael, caused him to saddle his donkey himself.

Hashem saw this and got upset with Bilaam before he had a chance to do anything. Since Bilaam had already showed his true intentions, his actually disobeying Hashem was only a matter of time, for it was already clear what the ending would be.

וַיָּקָם בִּלְעָם בַּבֹּקֶר וַיַּחֲבֹשׁ אֶת אֲתֹנוֹ וַיֵּלֶךְ עִם שָׂרֵי מוֹאָב: וַיִּחַר אַף אֱלֹקִים כִּי הוֹלֵךְ הוּא וַיִּתְיַצֵּב מַלְאַךְ ה' בַּדֶּרֶךְ לְשָׂטָן לוֹ וְהוּא רֹכֵב עַל אֲתֹנוֹ וּשְׁנֵי נְעָרָיו עִמּוֹ:

IN THE MORNING BILAAM AROSE, SADDLED HIS SHE-DONKEY AND WENT WITH THE MOAVI DIGNITARIES. HASHEM'S WRATH FLARED BECAUSE HE WAS GOING, AND AN ANGEL OF HASHEM STATIONED HIMSELF ON THE ROAD TO THWART HIM. HE WAS RIDING ON HIS SHE-DONKEY, AND HIS TWO ATTENDANTS WERE WITH HIM. (BAMIDBAR 22:21–22)

These two *pesukim* are the only occasions that Bilaam's donkey is called "אֲתֹנוֹ — *his* she-donkey." The following *pesukim* all refer to it as "הָאָתוֹן — the she-donkey," without being identified as belonging to Bilaam. Why the change?

The shift happens in *pasuk* 23, which says "וַתֵּרֶא הָאָתוֹן אֶת מַלְאַךְ ה' נִצָּב בַּדֶּרֶךְ וְחַרְבּוֹ שְׁלוּפָה בְּיָדוֹ — the she-donkey saw Hashem's angel standing on the road, with an outstretched sword in its hand." When the donkey saw Hashem's angel, it began acting on its own, and Bilaam no longer had any control over it. No longer "his," the Torah now calls it "הָאָתוֹן" — the she-donkey."

Alternatively, when the donkey saw the angel and began to speak, it became the donkey created *bein hashmashos* that is discussed in the Mishnah in *Pirkei Avos* (5:6). This donkey was created by Hashem especially for this purpose. It is therefore called "הָאָתוֹן" — the she-donkey," with a definitive letter ה.

וַיִּפְתַּח ה' אֶת פִּי הָאָתוֹן וַתֹּאמֶר לְבִלְעָם מֶה עָשִׂיתִי לְךָ כִּי הִכִּיתַנִי זֶה שָׁלֹשׁ רְגָלִים:

HASHEM OPENED THE MOUTH OF THE SHE-DONKEY, AND SHE SAID TO BILAAM, "WHAT HAVE I DONE TO YOU THAT YOU HAVE STRUCK ME THESE THREE TIMES?" (BAMIDBAR 22:28)

We usually find that when Hashem changes nature with an open miracle, He later does something proactive, to bring nature back to its normal state. For example, after each of the *Makos* in Mitzrayim, we find the Torah states that the conditions brought about by the *makah* ceased; and after *Krias Yam Suf*, the Torah makes a point of saying that the Sea went back to normal. We nowhere find, however, that Hashem did anything to "undo" the talking mouth of Bilaam's donkey. Why not?

In his comments to *pasuk* 33, Rashi explains that Hashem killed the donkey after it finished speaking to Bilaam, in order to spare Bilaam the embarrassment of other people mocking him whenever they saw the donkey. There was therefore no need for a "second miracle" to take away the donkey's power of speech.

מֶה עָשִׂיתִי לְךָ כִּי הִכִּיתַנִי זֶה שָׁלֹשׁ רְגָלִים ...

WHAT HAVE I DONE TO YOU THAT YOU HAVE STRUCK ME THESE THREE TIMES? (BAMIDBAR 22:28)

Rashi explains that this phrase is hinting that Bilaam wanted to "לַעֲקוֹר אוּמָה הַחוֹגֶגֶת שָׁלשׁ רְגָלִים בַּשָּׁנָה — uproot a nation which celebrates three festivals (שָׁלשׁ רְגָלִים) each year."

Understanding this gives us insight into the *Haggadah shel Pesach*, where we say that "וְלָבָן בִּקֵּשׁ לַעֲקוֹר אֶת הַכֹּל — Lavan wanted to *uproot* the entire Jewish people." Chazal (Gemara *Sanhedrin* 105a, and *Targum Yonason*) tell us that Lavan and Bilaam were the same person. We now understand where Lavan wanted to *uproot* the Jewish Nation: in our *parashah*, where he tried, with his curse, to "לַעֲקוֹר אוּמָה הַחוֹגֶגֶת שָׁלשׁ רְגָלִים בַּשָּׁנָה — uproot a nation which celebrates three festivals (שָׁלשׁ רְגָלִים) each year."

Another similarity which we find between Bilaam and Lavan is their love for money. When Bilaam first refused Balak's offer when Hashem told him that he may not go, he said "אִם יִתֶּן לִי בָלָק מְלֹא בֵיתוֹ כֶּסֶף וְזָהָב לֹא אוּכַל לַעֲבֹר אֶת פִּי ה' — Even if Balak gives me a house full of silver and gold, I cannot do anything small or great that would transgress the word of Hashem" (22:18). Rashi notes that this reply shows us what was always on Bilaam's mind: other people's money. And in *Parashas Vayeitzei* we find than when Lavan first saw Yaacov, he ran towards him, hugged him, and kissed him (*Bereishis* 29:13). Rashi explains that warmly greeting his long-lost cousin wasn't what was on Lavan's mind. Rather, he ran towards Yaacov eagerly expecting to see him laden with wads of money and other valuables; hugged him to search for the gold that Yaacov may have concealed under his shirt; and kissed him on the chance that Yaacov hid some pearls in his mouth. This is Bilaam and Lavan, whom we again see are indeed one and the same.

וַיַּעַן בִּלְעָם וַיֹּאמֶר אֶל עַבְדֵי בָלָק אִם יִתֶּן לִי בָלָק
מְלֹא בֵיתוֹ כֶּסֶף וְזָהָב לֹא אוּכַל לַעֲבֹר אֶת פִּי ה'
אֱלֹקָי לַעֲשׂוֹת קְטַנָּה אוֹ גְדוֹלָה:

BILAAM ANSWERED AND SAID TO BALAK'S
SERVANTS, "EVEN IF BALAK GIVES ME A HOUSE

FULL OF SILVER AND GOLD, I CANNOT DO
ANYTHING SMALL OR GREAT THAT WOULD
TRANSGRESS THE WORD OF HASHEM, MY GOD."
(BAMIDBAR 22:18)

וַיֹּאמֶר בִּלְעָם אֶל בָּלָק הֲלֹא גַּם אֶל מַלְאָכֶיךָ אֲשֶׁר שָׁלַחְתָּ אֵלַי דִּבַּרְתִּי לֵאמֹר: אִם יִתֶּן לִי בָלָק מְלֹא בֵיתוֹ כֶּסֶף וְזָהָב לֹא אוּכַל לַעֲבֹר אֶת פִּי ה' לַעֲשׂוֹת טוֹבָה אוֹ רָעָה מִלִּבִּי אֲשֶׁר יְדַבֵּר ה' אֹתוֹ אֲדַבֵּר:

BALAAM SAID TO BALAK, "BUT I EVEN TOLD THE
MESSENGERS YOU SENT TO ME, SAYING, 'IF BALAK
GIVES ME HIS HOUSE FULL OF SILVER AND GOLD,
I CANNOT TRANSGRESS THE WORD OF HASHEM
TO DO EITHER GOOD OR EVIL ON MY OWN;
ONLY WHAT HASHEM SPEAKS CAN I SPEAK.'"
(BAMIDBAR 24:13)

When Balak's messengers came to Bilaam, Hashem told Bilaam that he may not curse the Jewish people. So in the morning, Bilaam told these people that "Even if Balak gives me a house full of silver and gold, I cannot do anything small or great that would transgress the word of Hashem, my God" (22:18).

Bilaam went along with them anyways, and tried his best to curse the Jews. Hashem did not allow him to do so, and changed his curses into blessings. After several tries, a frustrated Balak turned to Bilaam and told him that he had failed at the mission for which he had been brought. Bilaam retorted that he told your messengers this at the outset, that "I cannot transgress the word of Hashem to do either good or evil on my own." (24:13) In the original conversation with Balak's messengers Bilaam said that he could not do anything "קְטַנָּה אוֹ גְדוֹלָה — small or great" against Hashem. Yet, while speaking to Balak, he told him he had said that he could do neither "טוֹבָה אוֹ רָעָה — good or evil." Why the shift?

Originally, Bilaam wanted to let Balak's messengers know that he was under Hashem's auspices, that he enjoyed direct communication with Hashem, and had happened to have a conversation with Him just last night. He therefore told them that he could not do anything, whether large or small, without Hashem's approval. And, despite that, he went to curse the B'nei Yisrael.

When *berachos* came out of his mouth instead of curses, Bilaam, who Chazal tell us was in fact the same person as Lavan, was reminded of something that Hashem had told him many, many years earlier (Gemara *Sanhedrin* 105a, and *Targum Yonason*). When Lavan was chasing after Yaacov at the end of *Parashas Vayeitzei*, Hashem appeared to him and told him "הִשָּׁמֶר לְךָ פֶּן תְּדַבֵּר עִם יַעֲקֹב מִטּוֹב עַד רָע — Watch out, lest you speak with Yaacov either *good or evil*" (*Bereishis* 31:24). Now, when Bilaam tried to harm Klal Yisrael and simply could not do so, he was forced to admit that Hashem had previously told him that he would not be able to do so.

PINCHAS
פִּינְחָס

וְשֵׁם אִישׁ יִשְׂרָאֵל הַמֻּכֶּה אֲשֶׁר הֻכָּה אֶת הַמִּדְיָנִית
זִמְרִי בֶּן סָלוּא נְשִׂיא בֵית אָב לַשִּׁמְעֹנִי:

THE NAME OF THE YISRAEL MAN WHO WAS KILLED, WHO WAS SLAIN WITH THE MIDYANITE WOMAN WAS ZIMRI BEN SALU, THE NASI OF SHEVET SHIMON. (BAMIDBAR 25:14)

The actual story of Pinchas killing Zimri and Kozbi occurred at the end of last week's *parashah*. Why does the Torah only tell us their names now, instead of giving us this information when discussing what happened?

In waiting until now to mention the names of the people who were killed, the Torah is telling us a very important lesson. The Torah described Pinchas' actions as "וַיַּרְא פִּינְחָס ... וַיָּקָם ... וַיִּקַּח רֹמַח בְּיָדוֹ ... וַיִּדְקֹר אֶת שְׁנֵיהֶם — Pinchas saw... arose... took a spear in his hand... and drove it through both of them" (25:7–8). Pinchas saw a tremendous *chillul Hashem* happening and understood that it was correct to act to stop it, and to make sure the halachah was followed. The fact that the man was the *Nasi* of *Shevet Shimon* and the woman was the daughter of the King of Midyan was not the point, one way or the other. Had the

Torah mentioned the people's names as part of the story, we would have focused on the politics and publicity; we would have missed the point about the basic halachah that was being violated, and the appropriate response.

A story is told that about a year after Yitzchak Rabin was killed, someone asked a Torah Jew the following question: if the Torah community agrees that what had taken place is indeed so terrible, why hasn't the Torah community built any monument, or done any other form of commemorative *zikaron*? The person answered that as religious Jews, we don't differentiate between the murder of a public figure, and the murder of an "ordinary person." Killing any human being is a tragedy. If there should be a monument for Rabin, there should also be a monument for every Jew who has been killed.

This story brings out the lesson that the Torah is teaching us. A public *aveirah* is a public *aveirah*, and murder is murder. Getting caught up in peripheral details, such as the specific personalities involved will only distract us from feeling the depths of the tragedy that has just taken place.

וַיְהִי אַחֲרֵי הַמַּגֵּפָה וַיֹּאמֶר ה' ... שְׂאוּ אֶת רֹאשׁ כָּל עֲדַת בְּנֵי יִשְׂרָאֵל ...

IT WAS AFTER THE PLAGUE, THAT HASHEM SAID...
"COUNT THE ENTIRE CONGREGATION OF THE
B'NEI YISRAEL..." (BAMIDBAR 26:1–2)

Rashi explains the need for this census with an example of a shepherd, who counted his sheep after the flock was attacked by wolves. Similarly, Hashem ordered that the Jewish people be counted after the plague, following their sin with Midyan.

This approach is very similar to how Rashi explains the census discussed in *Parashas Ki Sisa* (*Shemos* 30:16), where Hashem counted the B'nei Yisrael following the plague that erupted after the *Cheit Ha'Eigel*. However, we find a slight difference between the two examples that

Rashi provides. In *Ki Sisa*, the example given is not of a flock attacked by wolves, but is instead an epidemic that struck a beloved flock of sheep. Why does Rashi change the example that he uses?

The plague that the Jews suffered in our *parashah* came as a punishment for their promiscuous behavior with the women of Midyan; a downfall that came about from Bilaam's suggestion to Balak that they send Midyanite women to tempt the Jewish people. So, Rashi's example is a wolf attack, which is a danger from the outside. In contrast, the plague suffered in *Parashas Ki Sisa* was a punishment for worshipping the *Eigel HaZahav*. Since this sin came from *within* the Jewish Camp, the example that Rashi chooses is an epidemic, which cannot be blamed on an outside source.

וְשֵׁם אֵשֶׁת עַמְרָם יוֹכֶבֶד בַּת לֵוִי אֲשֶׁר יָלְדָה אֹתָהּ לְלֵוִי בְּמִצְרָיִם וַתֵּלֶד לְעַמְרָם אֶת אַהֲרֹן וְאֶת מֹשֶׁה וְאֵת מִרְיָם אֲחֹתָם:

THE NAME OF AMRAM'S WIFE WAS YOCHEVED THE DAUGHTER OF LEVI, WHOM HER MOTHER HAD BORNE TO LEVI IN MITZRAYIM. SHE BORE TO AMRAM, AHARON, MOSHE, AND THEIR SISTER MIRIAM. (BAMIDBAR 26:59)

Why aren't Amram's children listed in the order of their birth? Also, why is Miriam called "אֲחֹתָם — their sister" in the context of our *pasuk*?

Later on in our *parashah*, Rashi explains that the names of the five *B'nos Tzelafchad* are written in varying orders in the different times the Torah mentions them, to show us that they were all of equal righteousness (27:1).[36]

Perhaps this reason also applies to Amram's children, who were also equal in many respects. For example, all three died with a *misas neshikah*. The Torah thus wrote them in different orders, to show that they all had similar levels of spiritual greatness. This approach would also

---

36 See also *Rashi* to *Shemos* 6:26.

explain why Miriam is called "אֲחֹתָם — their sister." אֲחוֹתָה, (for example, see *Shemos* 26:3) is sometimes used to mean "peer." The Torah is saying that Miriam was on the spiritual level of Moshe and Aharon.

וַיַּקְרֵב מֹשֶׁה אֶת מִשְׁפָּטָן לִפְנֵי ה':

SO MOSHE BROUGHT THEIR CASE BEFORE HASHEM. (BAMIDBAR 27:5)

When written in a *Sefer Torah*, the letter ן that appears at the end of the word מִשְׁפָּטָן is written larger than usual. Why?

Rashi explains that the reason why Moshe had to bring the *B'nos Tzelafchad's* question to Hashem was because he forgot the halachah. This happened because Moshe told the judges whom he appointed "וְהַדָּבָר אֲשֶׁר יִקְשֶׁה מִכֶּם תַּקְרִבוּן אֵלַי וּשְׁמַעְתִּיו — the case that is too difficult for you, bring to me, and I will hear it" (*Devarim* 1:17). Because Moshe was relying on his own intellect he was punished by forgetting a simple halachah.

The *pasuk* in *Mishlei* tells us "בְּטַח אֶל ה' בְּכָל לִבֶּךָ וְאֶל בִּינָתְךָ אַל תִּשָּׁעֵן — Rely on Hashem with all your heart, and on your own intellect do not lean" (3:5). The Vilna Gaon explains that this means a person should not even say that he will trust in Hashem, but really rely on his own knowledge. We must depend on Hashem completely. The large letter ן, whose *gematria* is fifty, represents the fifty *shaarei binah* [referred to in this *pasuk*, וְאֶל בִּינָתְךָ אַל תִּשָּׁעֵן] that were closed to Moshe in this relatively simple halachah of inheritance, for having relied on himself to adjudicate the difficult cases.

וַיֹּאמֶר ה' אֶל מֹשֶׁה קַח לְךָ אֶת יְהוֹשֻׁעַ בִּן נוּן אִישׁ אֲשֶׁר רוּחַ בּוֹ וְסָמַכְתָּ אֶת יָדְךָ עָלָיו:

HASHEM SAID TO MOSHE, "TAKE FOR YOURSELF YEHOSHUA BIN NUN, A MAN OF SPIRIT, AND YOU SHALL LAY YOUR HAND UPON HIM." (BAMIDBAR 27:18)

Rashi explains that the phrase "קַח לְךָ — take *for yourself*," means that the new Jewish leader whom Moshe was to choose in fulfillment of his request in the previous *pesukim* should be "someone whom *you* have verified, someone with whom *you* are familiar."

The *Meforshei Rashi* explain that our *pasuk* does not use the word "לְךָ — for yourself" in the way that it is generally used, which is "for your benefit," because Moshe would have wanted one of his sons to succeed him as the Jewish leader, as we see from Rashi's comments to *Vayikra* 20:25. Rashi therefore explains "לְךָ — for yourself" differently, that *you* are the one who will take him as a leader, "someone whom *you* have verified, someone with whom *you* are familiar."

We may suggest differently, that even though the next leader would indeed not be Moshe's ideal choice, Rashi is still telling us how selecting Yehoshua is to Moshe's benefit. It is a source of great comfort knowing that the person into whom you have expended great energies molding will be the one to succeed you, and is indeed someone with whom Moshe could entrust his life's work of leading Klal Yisrael. Since Yehoshua is "someone whom *you* have verified, someone with whom *you* are familiar," his appointment is to Moshe's benefit, for his leadership will be a direct outgrowth of Moshe's efforts.

Additionally, Chazal famously tell us, "הַתַּלְמִידִים קְרוּיִים בָּנִים — the *talmidim* are called sons." Moshe's biological children would not succeed him as king. But Yehoshua, his spiritual child, would. This too is "לְךָ — for yourself," for Moshe.

וְנָתַתָּה מֵהוֹדְךָ עָלָיו לְמַעַן יִשְׁמְעוּ כָּל עֲדַת בְּנֵי יִשְׂרָאֵל:

YOU SHALL BESTOW SOME OF YOUR MAJESTY
UPON HIM SO THAT ALL THE CONGREGATION
OF THE B'NEI YISRAEL WILL TAKE
HEED. (BAMIDBAR 27:20)

Rashi explains that "so that all the congregation of the B'nei Yisrael will take heed," means "that they will respect and revere Yehoshua, in the way that they have acted towards you." Why wouldn't the B'nei Yisrael have revered and respected Yehoshua, had Moshe not bestowed some of his "הוֹד — majesty" upon him?

The B'nei Yisrael would have certainly acted with honor towards Yehoshua for who he was. But it would not have been the same level of respect given to Moshe. Only someone who is a real *talmid* of a *rebbi*, and literally and figuratively exudes and radiates the *rebbi's* words, thoughts, and actions, will be accorded the respect given to the *rebbi* himself. Hashem wanted Yehoshua to receive the respect and reverence that was paid to Moshe, as Rashi says "כְּדֶרֶךְ שֶׁנּוֹהֲגִין בָּךְ — in the way that they have acted towards you." He thus commanded Moshe to give over some of himself, so the Jewish people would see Moshe in Yehoshua, and honor him as they did Moshe.

Matos
מַטּוֹת

וַיְדַבֵּר ה' אֶל מֹשֶׁה לֵּאמֹר: נְקֹם נִקְמַת בְּנֵי יִשְׂרָאֵל
מֵאֵת הַמִּדְיָנִים אַחַר תֵּאָסֵף אֶל עַמֶּיךָ:

HASHEM SPOKE TO MOSHE SAYING, "TAKE
REVENGE FOR THE B'NEI YISRAEL AGAINST
THE MIDYANITES; AFTERWARDS YOU WILL BE
GATHERED TO YOUR PEOPLE." (BAMIDBAR 31:1–2)

Midyan caused the B'nei Yisrael to sin towards the end of *Parashas Chukas*. Why does Hashem only instruct Moshe to take revenge now, several *perakim* later?

Hashem is teaching us a crucial life lesson, that despite the general prohibition against reacting to another person in a way that will cause harm, these actions are sometimes necessary. However, our actions must never be something that comes from the impulse to get even or out of anger. To drive this lesson home, the Torah discusses many different subjects — *B'nos Tzelafchad*, choosing Yehoshua as the next Jewish leader, *korbanos*, *nedarim* — before instructing Moshe to wage war on Midyan. Now, and only now, the war would be conducted with strategy and *sechel*, instead of anger, impulse, and wounded pride.

אִישׁ כִּי יִדֹּר נֶדֶר לַה' אוֹ הִשָּׁבַע שְׁבֻעָה לֶאְסֹר אִסָּר עַל נַפְשׁוֹ לֹא יַחֵל דְּבָרוֹ כְּכָל הַיֹּצֵא מִפִּיו יַעֲשֶׂה:

If a man makes a vow to Hashem or makes an oath to prohibit himself, he shall not violate his word; according to whatever came out of his mouth, he shall do. (Bamidbar 30:3)

נְקֹם נִקְמַת בְּנֵי יִשְׂרָאֵל מֵאֵת הַמִּדְיָנִים אַחַר תֵּאָסֵף אֶל עַמֶּיךָ:

Take revenge for the B'nei Yisrael against the Midyanites; afterwards you will be gathered to your people. (Bamidbar 31:2)

Why does the *parashah* of waging war against Midyan follow the *parashah* of *nedarim*?

Midyan was a nation that was infamously known for its promiscuity, as we see from the way they enticed the B'nei Yisrael. Waging war with them was spiritually dangerous. How could Jewish soldiers fight them in good conscience?

In preceding *Milchemes Midyan* with *nedarim*, the Torah is teaching us that the way to prepare for war against Midyan is by making a *neder*, a vow of being careful with our eyes, bodies, and souls. Only after this precaution will we be prepared to fight such a battle.

MATOS

וַהֲרֵמֹתָ מֶכֶס לַה' מֵאֵת אַנְשֵׁי הַמִּלְחָמָה הַיֹּצְאִים לַצָּבָא אֶחָד נֶפֶשׁ מֵחֲמֵשׁ הַמֵּאוֹת מִן הָאָדָם וּמִן הַבָּקָר וּמִן הַחֲמֹרִים וּמִן הַצֹּאן ... וּמִמַּחֲצִת בְּנֵי יִשְׂרָאֵל תִּקַּח אֶחָד אָחֻז מִן הַחֲמִשִּׁים מִן הָאָדָם מִן הַבָּקָר מִן הַחֲמֹרִים וּמִן הַצֹּאן מִכָּל הַבְּהֵמָה וְנָתַתָּה אֹתָם לַלְוִיִּם שֹׁמְרֵי מִשְׁמֶרֶת מִשְׁכַּן ה': וַיַּעַשׂ מֹשֶׁה וְאֶלְעָזָר הַכֹּהֵן כַּאֲשֶׁר צִוָּה ה' אֶת מֹשֶׁה:

AND YOU SHALL LEVY A TAX FOR HASHEM FROM THE SOLDIERS WHO WENT OUT TO BATTLE: ONE SOUL OUT OF EVERY FIVE HUNDRED, FROM THE PEOPLE, FROM THE CATTLE, FROM THE DONKEYS, AND FROM THE SHEEP... FROM THE HALF BELONGING TO THE B'NEI YISRAEL YOU SHALL TAKE ONE PART OUT OF FIFTY OF THE PEOPLE, OF THE CATTLE, OF THE DONKEYS, OF THE SHEEP, AND OF ALL ANIMALS, AND YOU SHALL GIVE THEM TO THE LEVI'IM, THE GUARDIANS OF THE MISHKAN OF HASHEM. MOSHE AND ELAZAR THE KOHEN DID AS HASHEM HAD COMMANDED MOSHE. (BAMIDBAR 31:28,30–31)

After commanding that part of the booty be given to Hashem, and part to the Levi'im, the Torah tells us that this in fact happened; "וַיַּעַשׂ מֹשֶׁה וְאֶלְעָזָר הַכֹּהֵן כַּאֲשֶׁר צִוָּה ה' אֶת מֹשֶׁה — Moshe and Elazar the Kohen did as Hashem had commanded Moshe." Why then, does the Torah spend the next eight *pesukim* detailing exactly what was captured, the quantities of each item, and exactly how much was given to Hashem?

When a person speaks about how he will split the proceeds of the lottery that he will soon win, he is usually quite generous with "his" money; this much to *tzedakos*, this much to *yeshivos*, this much to help relatives, and so on. After he actually wins it however, he begins to justify and reason that these people and organizations really don't need all that much. They would be fine, happy, and highly appreciative with a far lesser amount.

The Torah is telling us that the soldiers actually came through with what Hashem wanted, despite the great difficulty in dividing this money among the rest of the B'nei Yisrael whom did not fight, and to *hekdesh*. Before they conquered the booty they were commanded to give it to these recipients and after they received it, they did exactly as they were instructed. Spending so many *pesukim* detailing exactly what was given really illustrates this point.

וַיַּעַשׂ מֹשֶׁה וְאֶלְעָזָר הַכֹּהֵן כַּאֲשֶׁר צִוָּה ה' אֶת מֹשֶׁה:

MOSHE AND ELAZAR THE KOHEN
DID AS HASHEM HAD COMMANDED
MOSHE. (BAMIDBAR 31:31)

What special praise is the Torah telling us, that Moshe and Elazar followed Hashem's direction in distributing part of the soldier's booty to *hekdesh* and to the Levi'im?

Moshe and Elazar were in the uncomfortable position of having to take some of the booty away from the soldiers who had fought in the battle, and redistribute it equally among the soldiers and the regular people. Who wants to tell the soldiers they must divide the spoils of war with those who did not risk their lives? Furthermore, even part of the booty that the soldiers kept was taxed, and was given to Elazar as tribute. This could certainly be understood by people as self-serving and convenient for Elazar. Moshe too, could have been accused of funneling off money to his nephew, the Kohen Gadol. Despite these very real fears that Moshe and Elazar could have had, of being accused of looking after their own interests and enriching themselves at the expense of the rest of the B'nei Yisrael, they nevertheless did exactly what Hashem commanded of them.

> עֲטָרוֹת וְדִיבֹן וְיַעְזֵר וְנִמְרָה וְחֶשְׁבּוֹן וְאֶלְעָלֵה וּשְׂבָם וּנְבוֹ וּבְעֹן:
>
> ATAROS, DIBON, YAZER, AND NIMRAH, CHESHBON, ELEALEH, SEBAM, NEVO, AND BE'ON. (BAMIDBAR 32:3)

> וְאֶת נְבוֹ וְאֶת בַּעַל מְעוֹן מוּסַבֹּת שֵׁם וְאֶת שִׂבְמָה וַיִּקְרְאוּ בְשֵׁמֹת אֶת שְׁמוֹת הֶעָרִים אֲשֶׁר בָּנוּ:
>
> AND NEVO AND BAAL MEON, THEIR NAMES HAVING BEEN CHANGED, AND SIVMAH. AND THEY WERE CALLED WITH NAMES OF THE NAMES OF THE CITIES THEY BUILT. (BAMIDBAR 32:38)

In *pasuk 3, Targum Onkelous* translates the name of the city of Nevo as "בֵּית קְבוּרְתָּא דְמֹשֶׁה" — the area of Moshe's *kever*." Yet, in *pasuk* 38, he simply writes "נְבוֹ — Nevo." Why?

Perhaps this is a *limud zechus* for *B'nei Gad* and *B'nei Reuven*, that they didn't only want these cities because the surrounding lands were spacious for their animals. They wanted to be near the place where Moshe would by then be buried.[37]

When Moshe actually gives those areas to *B'nei Gad* and *B'nei Reuven* in *pasuk* 38, he didn't have to go into detail as to *why* they wanted them, but just mentions the cities' names.

---

37   See also *Sefas Emes*, year 5640.

Maasei

מָסְעֵי

אֵלֶּה מַסְעֵי בְנֵי יִשְׂרָאֵל אֲשֶׁר יָצְאוּ מֵאֶרֶץ מִצְרַיִם לְצִבְאֹתָם בְּיַד מֹשֶׁה וְאַהֲרֹן:

THESE ARE THE JOURNEYS OF THE B'NEI YISRAEL WHO LEFT THE LAND OF MITZRAYIM IN THEIR LEGIONS, UNDER THE CHARGE OF MOSHE AND AHARON. (BAMIDBAR 33:1)

Rashi gives us an example to illustrate why each of the forty-two places that the B'nei Yisrael encamped in the *Midbar* are mentioned. A king took his sick son to a faraway land, where he was treated for his illness and cured. On the way back, continues Rashi, the father recounted all of the places that they had visited on their journey there. This is where we slept one night, said the father in one place. This is where we were cold, he said in another. And, here you had a headache, the father said in a third. Similarly, at the end of their travels through the *Midbar*, Hashem recounted the past forty years of B'nei Yisrael's experiences.

Why does Rashi's story begin with a "king," and end with a "father"?

One of the interesting things about human nature is that people who go through traumatic events together almost naturally form a strong bond with one another, even when they did not even know one another before the episode happened. Perhaps one of the things that Rashi is telling us in his example is that the king and his son grew closer through their experiences of traveling from place to place to reach a faraway city to be cured from a serious illness. It is for this reason that he is called a "king" at the journey's beginning, and a "father" towards its end.

With this approach, the *mashal's* message is describing how the B'nei Yisrael's relationship to Hashem changed over the forty years in the *Midbar*. When Hashem took us out of Mitzrayim, we knew Him as our *Melech*, our King. But, the forty year relationship of feeling His Presence among us in the *Midbar* took what was once a more formal relationship of a king to his subjects, and changed it to a warmer and closer relationship of father and son.

> וַיִּסְעוּ מֵרַעְמְסֵס בַּחֹדֶשׁ הָרִאשׁוֹן בַּחֲמִשָּׁה עָשָׂר יוֹם לַחֹדֶשׁ הָרִאשׁוֹן מִמָּחֳרַת הַפֶּסַח יָצְאוּ בְנֵי יִשְׂרָאֵל בְּיָד רָמָה לְעֵינֵי כָּל מִצְרָיִם:

THEY JOURNEYED FROM RAMSES IN THE FIRST MONTH, ON THE FIFTEENTH DAY OF THE FIRST MONTH; ON THE DAY FOLLOWING THE PASSOVER SACRIFICE, THE B'NEI YISRAEL LEFT WITH A HIGH HAND BEFORE THE EYES OF ALL OF MITZRAYIM. (BAMIDBAR 33:3)

The Torah tells us that "יָצְאוּ בְנֵי יִשְׂרָאֵל בְּיָד רָמָה לְעֵינֵי כָּל מִצְרָיִם — the B'nei Yisrael left with a high hand before the eyes of all of Mitzrayim." What is "יָד רָמָה — a high hand"?

We would have supposed that when it was time for the B'nei Yisrael to leave Mitzrayim, they all left their homes, walked to the city's or country's outskirts, and left. However, our *pasuk* implies that they did not just leave. First, they gathered in Ramses and only then left from there. This sent the Mitzrim a message, that they were no longer slaves, yet were not yet leaving; they preferred to remain for a few minutes longer, to flaunt to the Mitzrim that they were now free. [Imagine an employee coming in to work on his day off, just to walk around the cubicles filled with other employees, and "feel his freedom"!] In this way the B'nei Yisrael did not run away as soon as they were able to do so, but walked out slowly and calmly, with their heads held high.

Similarly, *Targum Onkelous* does not translate בְּיָד רָמָה literally, as "with a high hand," rather, בְּרֵישׁ גְּלֵי, which literally means "with a revealed head." The B'nei Yisrael left Mitzrayim in a way that openly showed that they were proud to leave at the Mitzrim's expense.

> וַיַּעַל אַהֲרֹן הַכֹּהֵן אֶל הֹר הָהָר עַל פִּי ה' וַיָּמָת שָׁם בִּשְׁנַת הָאַרְבָּעִים לְצֵאת בְּנֵי יִשְׂרָאֵל מֵאֶרֶץ מִצְרַיִם בַּחֹדֶשׁ הַחֲמִישִׁי בְּאֶחָד לַחֹדֶשׁ:

AHARON THE KOHEN ASCENDED MOUNT HOR AT HASHEM'S BIDDING AND DIED THERE ON THE FIRST DAY OF THE FIFTH MONTH IN THE FORTIETH YEAR AFTER THE B'NEI YISRAEL'S EXODUS FROM MITZRAYIM. (BAMIDBAR 33:38)

Why does the Torah interrupt the flow of the review of the places that the B'nei Yisrael stopped in the desert, with Aharon's death?

The first *pasuk* in the *parashah* tells us "אֵלֶּה מַסְעֵי בְנֵי יִשְׂרָאֵל ... בְּיַד מֹשֶׁה וְאַהֲרֹן — these are the journeys of the B'nei Yisrael ... under the charge of Moshe *and Aharon*." Aharon played a large role in taking the Jewish people out of Mitzrayim, directing and leading them throughout their years in the *Midbar*. For example, the *Ohr Hachaim* explains that Aharon was the one who blew the trumpets, signaling when the B'nei Yisrael were to begin traveling, and when they were to encamp. It is therefore important to know when and where Aharon died, for at this point the way that the Jews traveled through the *Midbar* changed, for now they were led only by Moshe.

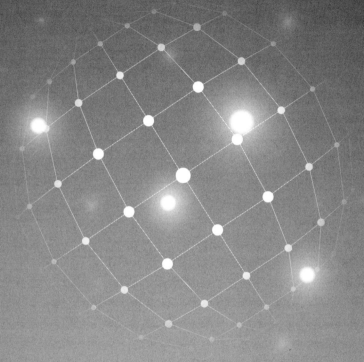

Devarim
דְּבָרִים

Devarim
דְּבָרִים

> אֵלֶּה הַדְּבָרִים אֲשֶׁר דִּבֶּר מֹשֶׁה אֶל כָּל יִשְׂרָאֵל
> בְּעֵבֶר הַיַּרְדֵּן בַּמִּדְבָּר בָּעֲרָבָה מוֹל סוּף בֵּין פָּארָן
> וּבֵין תֹּפֶל וְלָבָן וַחֲצֵרֹת וְדִי זָהָב:
>
> THESE ARE THE WORDS WHICH MOSHE SPOKE
> TO ALL THE JEWISH PEOPLE ON THAT SIDE OF
> THE YARDEN, IN THE DESERT, IN THE PLAIN
> OPPOSITE THE YAM SUF, BETWEEN PARAN
> AND TOFEL, AND LAVAN AND CHAZEROS AND
> DI-ZAHAV. (DEVARIM 1:1)

Rashi explains that *Sefer Devarim* is a book of *tochachah*, and that the places mentioned in this *pasuk* are references to the occasions that the B'nei Yisrael angered Hashem throughout their years in the Desert.

With this background, we may understand a *remez* from *Hoshea*, "קְחוּ עִמָּכֶם דְּבָרִים וְשׁוּבוּ אֶל ה' — take words (דְּבָרִים) for yourselves, and return to Hashem" (14:3). The end of *Sefer Devarim* is always read during the month of Elul, and around Rosh Hashanah and Yom Kippur. But, the *teshuvah* process begins long before that. We must *come into* Elul with the appropriate mindset! Thus, the way to be שׁוּבוּ אֶל ה', to return to Hashem in *teshuvah*, is through קְחוּ עִמָּכֶם דְּבָרִים, by internalizing the messages and discussions of *Sefer Devarim*.

> וַיְהִי בְּאַרְבָּעִים שָׁנָה בְּעַשְׁתֵּי עָשָׂר חֹדֶשׁ בְּאֶחָד
> לַחֹדֶשׁ דִּבֶּר מֹשֶׁה אֶל בְּנֵי יִשְׂרָאֵל כְּכֹל אֲשֶׁר צִוָּה
> ה' אֹתוֹ אֲלֵהֶם:
>
> IT CAME TO PASS IN THE FORTIETH YEAR, IN THE ELEVENTH MONTH, ON THE FIRST OF THE MONTH, THAT MOSHE SPOKE TO THE B'NEI YISRAEL ACCORDING TO ALL THAT HASHEM HAD COMMANDED HIM REGARDING THEM. (DEVARIM 1:3)

Sefer Devarim is a book of *tochachah*, filled with the words of rebuke that Moshe delivered to the B'nei Yisrael. Rashi notes that although the Jews had acted wrongly for many years — indeed, most of the events that Moshe discussed had happened almost forty years earlier — Moshe waited to rebuke the Jewish people until close to his death. He learned this from Yaacov, who also waited between forty and fifty years to tell Reuven that he had acted hastily. The reason for this, explains Rashi, is because Yaacov was fearful that had he spoken to Reuven prematurely, at a time that was not right for *tochachah*, Reuven would have left and turned to Esav.

This shows us an important point, that it is preferable to let someone continue to err in the way he is acting, rather than "give him *mussar*" at the wrong time. If Yaacov was afraid of his *bechor* Reuven following Esav because of *tochachah* given at the wrong time, imagine how careful we must be when deciding if and when to correct someone else's mistakes!

> בְּעֵבֶר הַיַּרְדֵּן בְּאֶרֶץ מוֹאָב הוֹאִיל מֹשֶׁה בֵּאֵר אֶת
> הַתּוֹרָה הַזֹּאת לֵאמֹר:
>
> ON THAT SIDE OF THE YARDEN, IN THE LAND OF MOAV, MOSHE COMMENCED, AND EXPLAINED THIS LAW, SAYING … (DEVARIM 1:5)

Rashi explains that Moshe explained the Torah in each one of the seventy languages. Why? Why did Moshe have to explain the Torah in so many languages, when all that the Jews spoke was *lashon hakodesh*, and maybe Egyptian?

Moshe's explaining the Torah in all seventy languages gives us the ability to learn Torah in each of these languages. Since these languages were now used for Torah, their *kedushah* was elevated, allowing Torah to be studied in these languages in the future. Moshe's seventy-fold *derashah* is what allows the B'nei Yisrael throughout the generations and throughout the world to teach and spread the Torah in whichever language they are speaking, and not just in the original *lashon hakodesh* in which it was written and given.[38]

אַל תִּתְגָּרוּ בָם כִּי לֹא אֶתֵּן לָכֶם מֵאַרְצָם עַד מִדְרַךְ
כַּף רָגֶל כִּי יְרֻשָּׁה לְעֵשָׂו נָתַתִּי אֶת הַר שֵׂעִיר:

YOU SHALL NOT PROVOKE THEM, FOR I WILL NOT GIVE YOU ANY OF THEIR LAND NOT SO MUCH AS A FOOTSTEP, BECAUSE I HAVE GIVEN MOUNT SEIR TO ESAV FOR AN INHERITANCE. (DEVARIM 2:5)

Rashi explains that the lands of ten nations were given to Avraham. The B'nei Yisrael received seven — the lands of the Seven Nations in Eretz Canaan — Esav received one — discussed in our *pasuk* — and the children of Lot, who were Amon and Moav, received the other two. [In the times of Mashiach, all ten lands will be given to the B'nei Yisrael.] Lot received these lands, continues Rashi, because he remained quiet when Avraham told Pharaoh that Sarah was his sister.

The *Sefas Emes* asks the following question. We know that Lot was a *baal chessed*, and *machnis orei'ach*, even in Sedom. Why didn't his keeping these *mitzvos* give his offspring the *zechus* of inheriting Avraham? After all, these were *mitzvos* that were part of his life on

---

38   See also the *Sefas Emes*.

274 A Deeper Dimension

an ongoing basis, while remaining silent in Mitzrayim only happened once!

The *Sefas Emes* answers that Lot's *chessed* — even great *chessed* — was something that he learned from Avraham. His remaining silent before Pharaoh, on the other hand was an achievement that he reached on his own. It is therefore specifically this mitzvah that allowed him the great *sechar* of inheriting Avraham.

Realizing the greatness of an achievement that a person reaches on their own allows us to better understand our *perek*. In *pasuk* 9, Hashem told Moshe that he was not to wage war with Moav. However, explains Rashi, the B'nei Yisrael were permitted to disturb them in ways short of open battle. Yet in *pasuk* 19, Hashem forbade the Jews from causing any distress to the nation of Amon. What is the difference between Amon and Moav?

In his comments to *pasuk* 9, Rashi answers this question, explaining that although both of Lot's daughters sinned with their father in the same way, the second daughter named her son that came from this union in a more modest fashion than did her older sister. For this reason, the nation that descended from her merited Hashem's protection against the Jews. This act of "modesty" pales in comparison to the incestuous act that she committed. However, no one had taught her to be modest; her achievement came from within. For this, she was incredibly rewarded.

Seeing the great reward that Lot's daughter received for how she named her son also tells us something else: the great value and reward that is given for acts of modesty in regard to how we speak.

לֹא תֹסִפוּ עַל הַדָּבָר אֲשֶׁר אָנֹכִי מְצַוֶּה אֶתְכֶם וְלֹא תִגְרְעוּ מִמֶּנּוּ לִשְׁמֹר אֶת מִצְוֹת ה' אֱלֹקֵיכֶם אֲשֶׁר אָנֹכִי מְצַוֶּה אֶתְכֶם: עֵינֵיכֶם הָרֹאוֹת אֵת אֲשֶׁר עָשָׂה ה' בְּבַעַל פְּעוֹר כִּי כָל הָאִישׁ אֲשֶׁר הָלַךְ אַחֲרֵי בַעַל פְּעוֹר הִשְׁמִידוֹ ה' אֱלֹקֶיךָ מִקִּרְבֶּךָ:

DO NOT ADD TO THE WORD WHICH I
COMMAND YOU, NOR DIMINISH FROM IT, TO

OBSERVE THE COMMANDMENTS OF HASHEM
YOUR GOD WHICH I COMMAND YOU. YOUR EYES
HAVE SEEN WHAT HASHEM DID AT BAAL PEOR,
FOR EVERY MAN WHO WENT AFTER BAAL PEOR,
THE HASHEM, YOUR GOD HAS EXTERMINATED
FROM YOUR MIDST. (DEVARIM 4:2–3)

Why is a reminder of the fate of the people who followed Baal Peor said right after the prohibition of *baal tosif*, which is adding to Hashem's *mitzvos*? (A similar juxtaposition is also found in *Parashas Re'eh*, 12:31 and 13:1.)

The Torah and its *halachos* are of course perfect, and a person who carries out these *mitzvos* because Hashem instructed him to do them is serving Hashem. Someone who does these same actions slightly differently clearly isn't doing them because Hashem commanded, for if he was only thinking about Hashem, why would he tweak the details? The Torah is bringing out this point by juxtaposing *baal tosif* to *avodah zarah*. A mitzvah done in a different way isn't a service of Hashem. Like *avodah zarah*, it is a "religious" action done to serve either another cause or one's self.

VA'ESCHANAN
וָאֶתְחַנַּן

שְׁמַע יִשְׂרָאֵל ה' אֱלֹקֵינוּ ה' אֶחָד:

LISTEN, YISRAEL, HASHEM IS OUR LORD; HASHEM IS ONE. (DEVARIM 6:4)

When written in a *Sefer Torah*, the letter ע in the word שְׁמַע is written larger than usual. Why?

The *Shema* is and always has been the way that we — the B'nei Yisrael — proclaim our belief in Hashem and His Omnipotence. We proclaim "Listen, Jewish people! Hashem is our Lord, Hashem is One!" However, this proclamation is not enough. The letter ע is spelled עַיִן, which also means "eye." Not only is it crucial to *hear* that Hashem is the One and Only, but *seeing* that Hashem is One is also an important part of proclaiming Hashem's total rule. Seeing Hashem as One means observing our day, and watching how He is part of every moment of our day. This understanding adds another dimension to the way that we say *Shema* on a daily and nightly basis.

שְׁמַע יִשְׂרָאֵל ה' אֱלֹקֵינוּ ה' אֶחָד:

LISTEN, YISRAEL, HASHEM IS OUR LORD; HASHEM IS ONE. (DEVARIM 6:4)

When written in a *Sefer Torah*, the letter ד in the word אֶחָד is written larger than usual. Why?

The *Baal Haturim* answers this question, telling us that the letter ד is larger so we that we don't mistake the ד for a ר. We may better appreciate what he is telling us based on the Midrash that discusses a *pasuk* in *Parashas Ki Sisa* "כִּי לֹא תִשְׁתַּחֲוֶה לְאֵל אַחֵר — for you shall not prostrate yourself before another god" (*Shemos* 34:14), in which the letter ר at the end of the word אַחֵר is also written larger than usual (*Vayikra Rabbah* 19:2). The Midrash explains that if someone would even mistakenly change the letter ר of אַחֵר to a ד, perhaps by adding a bit too much ink to the letter's top right corner, he is essentially destroying the world, for he has entirely changed its meaning. Altering the letter ר to a ד changes the *pasuk*'s translation from "you shall not prostrate yourself before another god," to "you shall not bow down to the G-d Who is One," *chas veshalom*.

Our *pasuk* is a similar issue, but in reverse. In *Shema*, we proclaim that "ה' אֶחָד — Hashem is One." Even slightly altering the letter ד to a ר will turn this statement of Hashem's ultimate unity to a statement of absolute heresy, that Hashem is "Another," *chas veshalom*. Perhaps this is the message the Torah is telling us in enlarging the letter ד, to emphasize this letter's sheer importance.

EIKEV
עֵקֶב

> וְהֵסִיר ה' מִמְּךָ כָּל חֹלִי וְכָל מַדְוֵי מִצְרַיִם הָרָעִים אֲשֶׁר יָדַעְתָּ לֹא יְשִׂימָם בָּךְ וּנְתָנָם בְּכָל שֹׂנְאֶיךָ:
>
> AND HASHEM WILL REMOVE FROM YOU ALL ILLNESS, AND ALL OF THE EVIL DISEASES OF MITZRAYIM WHICH YOU KNEW, HE WILL NOT SET UPON YOU, BUT HE WILL LAY THEM UPON ALL YOUR ENEMIES. (DEVARIM 7:15)

Why does the Torah promise us that Hashem will remove "all illness, and all of the evil diseases *of Mitzrayim*"? What do illnesses and evil diseases, that the Torah is promising that we will not have, have to do with Mitzrayim?

We know that Yaacov Avinu was the first person to become sick before he died. Yaacov asked Hashem for this "wake-up call," in order to allow a person to prepare for death by setting his affairs in order and reckoning with his past. It would thus appear that Mitzrayim was then the birthplace for physical sickness and ailment.

Perhaps another type of malady also began in Mitzrayim. Before the *Makos*, famine is the only "epidemic" mentioned in the Torah; there is no mention of any widespread sickness. Perhaps we can conclude that the *Makos* introduced epidemics to the world; therefore, when discussing "illness and disease," the Torah refers to them as "מַדְוֵי מִצְרַיִם" — the evil diseases of Mitzrayim."

> וְזָכַרְתָּ אֶת כָּל הַדֶּרֶךְ אֲשֶׁר הוֹלִיכְךָ ה' אֱלֹקֶיךָ זֶה אַרְבָּעִים שָׁנָה בַּמִּדְבָּר לְמַעַן עַנֹּתְךָ לְנַסֹּתְךָ לָדַעַת אֶת אֲשֶׁר בִּלְבָבְךָ הֲתִשְׁמֹר מִצְוֹתָיו אִם לֹא: וַיְעַנְּךָ וַיַּרְעִבֶךָ וַיַּאֲכִלְךָ אֶת הַמָּן אֲשֶׁר לֹא יָדַעְתָּ וְלֹא יָדְעוּן אֲבֹתֶיךָ לְמַעַן הוֹדִיעֲךָ כִּי לֹא עַל הַלֶּחֶם לְבַדּוֹ יִחְיֶה הָאָדָם כִּי עַל כָּל מוֹצָא פִי ה' יִחְיֶה הָאָדָם: שִׂמְלָתְךָ לֹא בָלְתָה מֵעָלֶיךָ וְרַגְלְךָ לֹא בָצֵקָה זֶה אַרְבָּעִים שָׁנָה:

AND YOU SHALL REMEMBER THE ENTIRE WAY ON WHICH HASHEM, YOUR GOD, LED YOU THESE FORTY YEARS IN THE DESERT, IN ORDER TO AFFLICT YOU TO TEST YOU, TO KNOW WHAT IS IN YOUR HEART, WHETHER YOU WOULD KEEP HIS COMMANDMENTS OR NOT. AND HE AFFLICTED YOU AND LET YOU GO HUNGRY, AND THEN FED YOU WITH MAHN, WHICH YOU DID NOT KNOW, NOR DID YOUR FOREFATHERS KNOW, SO THAT HE WOULD MAKE YOU KNOW THAT MAN DOES NOT LIVE BY BREAD ALONE, BUT RATHER BY, WHATEVER COMES FORTH FROM THE MOUTH OF HASHEM DOES MAN LIVE. YOUR CLOTHING DID NOT WEAR OUT UPON YOU, NOR DID YOUR FOOT SWELL THESE FORTY YEARS. (DEVARIM 8:2–4)

In *pasuk* 2, the Torah tells us that life in the Desert was a test for the B'nei Yisrael, to see whether we would properly keep Hashem's *mitzvos*. *Pasuk* 3 discusses the *Mahn*, which tested the B'nei Yisrael, to see if they could learn to live on anything that Hashem prepared for them. Then, in *pasuk* 4, the Torah continues to describe the Jews' life in the Desert.

Rashi explains that their clothing was always freshly laundered and grew with them, and their feet never became sore despite the fact that they were always walking barefoot. How does reminding us about these miracles follow the discussion of Hashem's testing the B'nei Yisrael? How is it challenging to always have freshly laundered clothing and healthy feet?

Sometimes the biggest test is when we have everything we need, but not everything we want. Hashem gave us food, clothing, and health. What more, we may think, could a person possibly ask for. Yet people aren't built like that; we "need" variety, change, and excitement. Although the *Mahn* could taste like anything, it gets boring to eat *Mahn* day in, day out, for years on end! [For example, although soy can be made to taste like a steak, it still looks like soy.] The same is true in regard to clothing. True, we never had to worry about holes, fraying, stains, and their becoming a bit too tight. But, wearing the same suit, tie, or outfit every single day can start to get boring. Or, how can women go forty years without going shopping? The *nisayon* in the Desert wasn't a *nisayon* of following Hashem despite lack. It was a *nisayon* of plenty and perfection. When everything — our food, our clothing, our physical needs, and even our health — is perfect, what will the B'nei Yisrael do then? Do we get bored, and look for new ways to give us excitement? Or now undistracted by physical needs, do we put our total focus on becoming closer to Hashem?

וְרָם לְבָבֶךָ וְשָׁכַחְתָּ אֶת ה' אֱלֹקֶיךָ הַמּוֹצִיאֲךָ מֵאֶרֶץ מִצְרַיִם מִבֵּית עֲבָדִים:

YOUR HEART GROWS HAUGHTY, AND YOU FORGET HASHEM, YOUR GOD, WHO HAS BROUGHT YOU OUT OF THE LAND OF MITZRAYIM, OUT OF THE HOUSE OF BONDAGE. (DEVARIM 8:14)

The Torah predicts that we will get haughty and forget Hashem, Who took us out of Mitzrayim. Appreciating that Hashem is the One Who took us out of Mitzrayim is one of the basic foundations of Judaism, mentioned in the first one of the *Aseres Hadibros*, and is the theme upon which Pesach and the rest of the *Yamim Tovim* are based. Why, however, do we not find any recollection of Who brought us down to Mitzrayim, which was of course Hashem, as well?

The Jewish people were supposed to be in Mitzrayim for four hundred years. Hashem, in His mercy, saved us after two hundred and ten. If not for this *chessed*, we would have sunk to an incredibly low spiritual level, from the depths of which we would have never been able to escape, and leave Mitzrayim. Perhaps this is the praise to which we constantly refer. Indeed, Hashem sent us to Mitzrayim, because this was the way that the Jewish Nation was to be built. But He did not allow the four hundred year period to naturally run its course. He intervened, and, in His great love for us, took us out of Mitzrayim many years before we were supposed to be ready to leave. Our great *hakaras hatov* for *Yetzias Mitzrayim* is thus not only that we are no longer slaves. It is gratitude to Hashem that He took us out in a way that allowed Klal Yisrael to get off the ground, in a way that we were still able to become His people. In this way our leaving Mitzrayim will always be the beginning point of reference for the Jewish Nation.

מַמְרִים הֱיִיתֶם עִם ה' מִיּוֹם דַּעְתִּי אֶתְכֶם:

YOU HAVE BEEN REBELLING AGAINST HASHEM SINCE THE DAY I BECAME ACQUAINTED WITH YOU. (DEVARIM 9:24)

When written in a *Sefer Torah*, the first letter מ in the word מַמְרִים is written smaller than usual. Why?

The next *pasuk* says "וָאֶתְנַפַּל לִפְנֵי ה' אֵת אַרְבָּעִים הַיּוֹם וְאֶת אַרְבָּעִים הַלַּיְלָה אֲשֶׁר הִתְנַפָּלְתִּי כִּי אָמַר ה' לְהַשְׁמִיד אֶתְכֶם — so I fell down before Hashem the forty days and the forty nights that I had fallen down; because Hashem had said to destroy you." Moshe was reproaching the B'nei Yisrael for the episode of the *Eigel Hazahav*; and their incessant rebelling against

Hashem; and stressed the forty days and forty nights of his interceding on their behalf. Perhaps this is what the small letter מ is alluding to. The letter מ is spelled מֵם, whose *gematria* is 80: 40 for מ, and 40 for ם. Maybe the open מ represents the forty days that Moshe *davened* because they were "מַמְרִים," and the closed ם the forty nights.

RE'EH
רְאֵה

כִּי יִהְיֶה בְךָ אֶבְיוֹן מֵאַחַד אַחֶיךָ בְּאַחַד שְׁעָרֶיךָ בְּאַרְצְךָ אֲשֶׁר ה' אֱלֹקֶיךָ נֹתֵן לָךְ לֹא תְאַמֵּץ אֶת לְבָבְךָ וְלֹא תִקְפֹּץ אֶת יָדְךָ מֵאָחִיךָ הָאֶבְיוֹן: כִּי פָתֹחַ תִּפְתַּח אֶת יָדְךָ לוֹ וְהַעֲבֵט תַּעֲבִיטֶנּוּ דֵּי מַחְסֹרוֹ אֲשֶׁר יֶחְסַר לוֹ:

IF THERE WILL BE AMONG YOU A NEEDY PERSON, FROM ONE OF YOUR BROTHERS IN ONE OF YOUR CITIES, IN YOUR LAND HASHEM, YOUR GOD, IS GIVING YOU, YOU SHALL NOT HARDEN YOUR HEART, AND YOU SHALL NOT CLOSE YOUR HAND FROM YOUR NEEDY BROTHER. RATHER, YOU SHALL OPEN YOUR HAND TO HIM, AND YOU SHALL LEND HIM SUFFICIENT FOR HIS NEEDS, WHICH HE IS LACKING. (DEVARIM 15:7–8)

Why does the *pasuk* begin with the prohibition of closing your heart and hand to your brother in need, instead of first saying the *mitzvas esei* of opening your hand to help him?

The Torah is speaking in the way that a person often reacts when being solicited for tzedakah by a needy person. A common gut reaction is to close your heart and hand, while thinking, "Why should I give away my hard-earned money?" The Torah is telling us that we must overcome this instant reflex, and replace it with a generous and open hand.

We may also suggest another insight into the sequence of these *pesukim*. The Torah tells us that we may not close our hearts and hands, but rather open our hands. What about opening our hearts? The answer is that indeed, in the ideal world, we must open our hearts as well. But if we are not prepared to do that, opening our hands — our wallets — will suffice, to help the person who needs our assistance.

לֹא יִקְשֶׁה בְעֵינֶךָ בְּשַׁלֵּחֲךָ אֹתוֹ חָפְשִׁי מֵעִמָּךְ כִּי מִשְׁנֶה שְׂכַר שָׂכִיר עֲבָדְךָ שֵׁשׁ שָׁנִים וּבֵרַכְךָ ה' אֱלֹקֶיךָ בְּכֹל אֲשֶׁר תַּעֲשֶׂה:

YOU SHALL NOT BE TROUBLED WHEN YOU SEND HIM FREE FROM YOU, FOR TWICE AS MUCH AS A HIRED SERVANT, HE HAS SERVED YOU SIX YEARS, AND HASHEM, YOUR GOD, WILL BLESS YOU IN ALL THAT YOU SHALL DO. (DEVARIM 15:18)

This *pasuk*, which discusses a master sending away his *eved ivri* after having completed his six year term of service, seems like it would have been better positioned after *pasuk* 14, "הַעֲנֵיק תַּעֲנִיק לוֹ מִצֹּאנְךָ וּמִגָּרְנְךָ וּמִיִּקְבֶךָ אֲשֶׁר בֵּרַכְךָ ה' אֱלֹקֶיךָ תִּתֶּן לוֹ — you shall surely provide him from your flock, from your threshing floor, and from your vat, you shall give him from what Hashem, your God, has blessed you"; that tells us to be generous with the severance package that we give the *eved*. Why is it said after *pasuk* 17, which speaks about an *eved nirtza*, who is an *eved ivri* who chose to remain until *Yovel*?[39]

Perhaps the Torah is directing this blessing to a master whose *eved* wants to stay beyond his term, until *Yovel*. The master is probably overjoyed when he hears that the *eved* wants to stay and work for him,

---

39   I heard this question from R' Tzvi Thaler.

without demanding any pay beyond room and board. The Torah is telling the master that an *eved* remaining in bondage is not ideal, and the master should try to convince him to leave and return to his family. This is the *berachah* of "You shall not be troubled when you send him free from you... Hashem, your God, will bless you in all that you shall do"; although the master may not think that setting his *eved* free is in his best interests, Hashem is assuring him that it is indeed so.

וְזָכַרְתָּ כִּי עֶבֶד הָיִיתָ בְּמִצְרָיִם וְשָׁמַרְתָּ וְעָשִׂיתָ אֶת הַחֻקִּים הָאֵלֶּה:

AND YOU SHALL REMEMBER THAT YOU WERE A SLAVE IN MITZRAYIM, AND YOU SHALL KEEP AND PERFORM THESE STATUTES. (DEVARIM 16:12)

Rashi explains that the second part of this *pasuk* is the condition for the first; the reason why Hashem took us out of Mitzrayim is only to keep and perform these statutes.

This relationship between *Yetziyas Mitzrayim* and performing the *mitzvos* is said within the context of the discussion of the *Yom Tov* of Shavuos. Perhaps the reason for this is because Shavuos, of course, celebrates our receiving the Torah. So Rashi gives the background, that *kabbalas haTorah* was in fact the original plan, from the beginning of *Yetziyas Mitzrayim*. It is only because of Shavuos that we have Pesach and Succos.

Shoftim
שׁוֹפְטִים

שֹׁפְטִים וְשֹׁטְרִים תִּתֶּן לְךָ בְּכָל שְׁעָרֶיךָ ...
YOU SHALL GIVE JUDGES AND LAW ENFORCEMENT OFFICIALS FOR YOURSELF IN ALL YOUR CITIES... (DEVARIM 16:18)

The phrase תִּתֶּן לְךָ literally means "you shall give yourself." Wouldn't תָּשִׂים לְךָ, which means "you will place upon yourself," be more appropriate for establishing a judiciary system with enforcement powers, as the Torah in fact says later on in the *parashah* "שׂוֹם תָּשִׂים עָלֶיךָ מֶלֶךְ — you shall place a king over yourself" (17:15)?

My Rosh Yeshiva, Rav Aryeh Rottman *shlita*, would tell the *bochurim* the following message before he would leave the Yeshiva to travel overseas. Now that I am leaving, he would say, your job as *bochurim* will be harder. When I am here, I can be your *mashgiach*, and watch over you. When I am not here, however, you must be your own *mashgiach*, and watch over yourselves.

This vignette gives us insight in our *pasuk*. Appointing a person to watch over us, to make sure that we do the right thing, is the greatest gift that we can give ourselves, even if the system is a policeman with a stick, for it is so much harder to be our own policeman. The Torah *gave* us this system to keep us in line, and to tell us this message, refers to the judges and law enforcement officials as "תִּתֶּן לְךָ — you shall give yourself."

> לֹא תַטֶּה מִשְׁפָּט לֹא תַכִּיר פָּנִים
> וְלֹא תִקַּח שֹׁחַד... צֶדֶק צֶדֶק תִּרְדֹּף ...
>
> YOU SHALL NOT PERVERT JUSTICE; YOU SHALL NOT SHOW FAVORITISM, AND YOU SHALL NOT TAKE A BRIBE... JUSTICE, JUSTICE, YOU SHALL PURSUE... (DEVARIM 16:19–20)

Why does the Torah need to tell us that bribery is forbidden, as well as mentioning that we must pursue justice and the truth? Isn't it clear that if we may not pervert justice, show favoritism and take bribes, we must judge correctly?

Indeed, we would know that we must judge correctly. But *seeking out* the truth, "צֶדֶק צֶדֶק תִּרְדֹּף — justice, justice, you shall pursue," is an altogether different level.

> רַק לֹא יַרְבֶּה לּוֹ סוּסִים ... וְלֹא יַרְבֶּה לּוֹ נָשִׁים...
> וְכֶסֶף וְזָהָב לֹא יַרְבֶּה לּוֹ מְאֹד:
>
> ONLY, HE MAY NOT ACQUIRE MANY HORSES FOR HIMSELF... AND HE SHALL NOT TAKE MANY WIVES FOR HIMSELF... AND HE SHALL NOT ACQUIRE MUCH SILVER AND GOLD FOR HIMSELF. (DEVARIM 17:16–17)

The Torah enumerates the three overindulgences in which a Jewish king is forbidden; horses, wives, and money. What do these three have in common?

My Rosh Yeshiva, Rav Aryeh Rottman *shlita*, would often talk of man's three base desires, *taavas nashim*, money, and *kavod*. He explained that the lust for women is strongest when a person is young and healthy. The lust for money follows as a person grows a bit older, as he settles down and the need for money becomes more apparent. Finally, the drive for honor comes at a later stage in life, after a person has already tired of pursuing women and money. These — horses being the symbol of pomp, ceremony, and might — are the three areas that a king may not be drawn towards. The Torah is giving him a set of restrictions, which bind him and keep him focused on Hashem, throughout every step of his life.

> וְדִבְּרוּ הַשֹּׁטְרִים אֶל הָעָם לֵאמֹר מִי הָאִישׁ אֲשֶׁר בָּנָה בַיִת חָדָשׁ וְלֹא חֲנָכוֹ יֵלֵךְ וְיָשֹׁב לְבֵיתוֹ פֶּן יָמוּת בַּמִּלְחָמָה וְאִישׁ אַחֵר יַחְנְכֶנּוּ: וּמִי הָאִישׁ אֲשֶׁר נָטַע כֶּרֶם וְלֹא חִלְּלוֹ יֵלֵךְ וְיָשֹׁב לְבֵיתוֹ פֶּן יָמוּת בַּמִּלְחָמָה וְאִישׁ אַחֵר יְחַלְּלֶנּוּ: וּמִי הָאִישׁ אֲשֶׁר אֵרַשׂ אִשָּׁה וְלֹא לְקָחָהּ יֵלֵךְ וְיָשֹׁב לְבֵיתוֹ פֶּן יָמוּת בַּמִּלְחָמָה וְאִישׁ אַחֵר יִקָּחֶנָּה:

> AND THE OFFICERS SHALL SPEAK TO THE PEOPLE, SAYING, "WHAT MAN IS THERE WHO HAS BUILT A NEW HOUSE AND HAS NOT YET INAUGURATED IT? LET HIM GO AND RETURN TO HIS HOUSE, LEST HE DIE IN THE WAR, AND ANOTHER MAN INAUGURATE IT. AND WHAT MAN IS THERE WHO HAS PLANTED A VINEYARD, AND HAS NOT YET REDEEMED IT? LET HIM GO AND RETURN TO HIS HOUSE, LEST HE DIE IN THE WAR, AND ANOTHER MAN REDEEM IT. AND WHAT MAN IS THERE WHO HAS BETROTHED A WOMAN AND HAS NOT YET TAKEN HER? LET HIM GO AND RETURN TO HIS HOUSE, LEST HE DIE IN THE WAR, AND ANOTHER MAN TAKE HER." (DEVARIM 20:5–7)

The Torah tells us that three types of people were exempt from participating in battle, and would return home before the fighting began. These are the following people: a person who built a new house but has not yet inaugurated it; someone who planted a vineyard but has not yet redeemed it; and a *chassan* who has begun to marry a woman, but has not yet completed the marriage with *nesu'in*. What do these three types of people have in common?

The end of our *parashah* discusses the mitzvah of *eglah arufah*, which is done when a dead body is found in the countryside. As part of this mitzvah, *Beis Din* takes a young calf which has never been used for work, and decapitates it in a plot of land that has never been cultivated. My Rosh Yeshiva, Rav Aryeh Rottman *shlita*, said the following idea in the name of his *rebbi*, Rav Mordechai Rolgoff *zatzal*: what is the significance of these *halachos*, that neither the calf nor the place where it is killed may be worked?

Rav Rolgoff answers that using an unworked calf and a barren piece of land symbolizes a loss of *peiros*, which literally means "fruit" or "offspring," but in its broader sense includes all actualized potential that something or someone achieves. *Eglah arufah* is done because a person's life was lost. And, included in this is anything that he may have produced over the future decades that he would have lived, such as children, grandchildren, and great-grandchildren, *chessed*, tzedakah and other *mitzvos*, and a lifetime of learning Torah. To better drive home the message that part of the tragedy of murder is that the victim will never realize any of these *peiros*, *eglah arufah* is done using an animal and plot of land which are also devoid of *peiros*.

Perhaps this void of *peiros* is also what connects the three people who do not go to war, who are someone who builds a new home, plants a vineyard, or is in the middle of getting married. All three have begun to sow seeds that have yet to ripen, and compelling them to go to war raises a real possibility that they will never return home to see the fruits of their efforts. The eternal loss of *peiros* is too great of a price to pay, and these people are absolved from the battle.

We see another example of Rav Rolgoff's idea in the mitzvah that precedes *eglah arufah*, and is several *pesukim* after the list of people who do not go to war; the prohibition of *baal tashchis*, of cutting down fruit-bearing trees (20:19). Although this tree of course has no *neshomah* and feels no pain, the Torah is telling us the important of sustaining something that has the opportunity to give or produce. In one *parashah* after another, the Torah reminds us of the greatness of potential, and the literally incomparable disaster of wasted *peiros*.

Ki Seitzei
כִּי תֵצֵא

וְרָאִיתָ בַּשִּׁבְיָה אֵשֶׁת יְפַת תֹּאַר וְחָשַׁקְתָּ בָה וְלָקַחְתָּ לְךָ לְאִשָּׁה:

AND YOU SEE AMONG THE CAPTIVES A BEAUTIFUL WOMAN AND YOU DESIRE HER, YOU MAY TAKE HER FOR YOURSELF AS A WIFE. (DEVARIM 21:11)

Rashi famously explains that in permitting this union, — "לֹא דִּבְּרָה תוֹרָה אֶלָּא כְּנֶגֶד יֵצֶר הָרָע — the Torah is only speaking against the *Yetzer Hara*." Hashem would not have permitted this union, but He understood that a soldier in the heat of battle would act in this way, regardless. Hashem therefore permitted a soldier to marry a captive enemy woman after a set of criteria have been fulfilled.

Rashi's source in the *pasuk* that tells us that *yefas to'ar* is less than ideal appears to be "וְלָקַחְתָּ לְךָ — you may take her *for yourself*," as a wife. And the Midrash Tanchuma explains part of the tragedy that will come out of taking a *yefas to'ar*. The next *parashah* discussed in the Torah is *ben sorer u'moreh*. This tells us that a Jewish soldier who ignores Hashem's "warning" that this isn't a good idea and marries a *yefas to'ar* will eventually come to hate her, and their offspring will be a *ben sorer u'moreh*.

We find that "לְךָ — for yourself" connotes a less than ideal acquiescence of "you may do this only because you asked for it, but it's not in your best interests" in another place as well, in the beginning of *Parashas Shelach* (*Bamidbar* 13:2), where Hashem told Moshe, "שְׁלַח לְךָ אֲנָשִׁים — send out for yourself men," to scout out Eretz Yisrael. There too, Rashi explains that Hashem told Moshe that you may send out *meraglim* if you choose to do so, but at the same time, I am not commanding, nor encouraging this plan of action.

The lesson of these two *parshios* is a very powerful one, that Hashem allows us to make a decision for ourselves, despite His clear awareness of the tragic outcome. Interestingly, this message gives us a powerful example of how we must act as parents. In the same way Hashem allows us freedom of choice to make decisions, even when they will harm us, we, as parents, must allow our children this space as well. Even when we "know" that their decision is a wrong one, we must rein in our naturally overprotective parental instincts, and give our children the freedom if necessary to learn from their own mistakes.

> וְהֵסִירָה אֶת שִׂמְלַת שִׁבְיָהּ מֵעָלֶיהָ וְיָשְׁבָה בְּבֵיתֶךָ וּבָכְתָה אֶת אָבִיהָ וְאֶת אִמָּהּ יֶרַח יָמִים וְאַחַר כֵּן תָּבוֹא אֵלֶיהָ וּבְעַלְתָּהּ וְהָיְתָה לְךָ לְאִשָּׁה:
>
> AND SHE SHALL REMOVE THE GARMENT OF HER CAPTIVITY FROM UPON HERSELF, AND STAY IN YOUR HOUSE, AND WEEP FOR HER FATHER AND HER MOTHER FOR A FULL MONTH OF DAYS. AFTER THAT, YOU MAY BE INTIMATE WITH HER AND POSSESS HER, AND SHE WILL BE A WIFE FOR YOU. (DEVARIM 21:13)

Before a soldier may marry a *yefas to'ar* whom he captured, he must wait a month, during which she removes her beautiful clothing, doesn't care for her personal appearance, and longs for her father and mother. If he still desires her after this period of time, he may then marry her.

When discussing this month, the Torah uses the unusual phrase "יֶרַח יָמִים," which is literally translated "a moon's period of days," instead of the more familiar word "חֹדֶשׁ — month." The *Baal Haturim* explains that this tells us that just as the light of the moon is clearly inferior when it is compared to the light of the sun, so too, marrying a non-Jewish woman is simply no comparison to a home and relationship formed together with a *bas Yisrael*.

We may understand another reason for this terminology. The Torah specifies that she is to spend this month weeping and despondent, in order to, explains Rashi, better highlight the difference between this woman and a *bas Yisrael*. Perhaps the Torah is telling us that it is not enough to make her miserable for thirty days, rather, this entire time should be "a moon's period," that is, "a month filled with nights." When a person has a tough day, he generally looks forward to the next morning to freshly begin again. This hope was not to be given to the *yefas to'ar*; she was to experience "a month of nights"; thirty days of unrelenting darkness and gloom.

> כִּי יִהְיֶה לְאִישׁ בֵּן סוֹרֵר וּמוֹרֶה אֵינֶנּוּ שֹׁמֵעַ בְּקוֹל אָבִיו וּבְקוֹל אִמּוֹ וְיִסְּרוּ אֹתוֹ וְלֹא יִשְׁמַע אֲלֵיהֶם:
>
> IF A MAN HAS A WAYWARD AND REBELLIOUS SON, HE DOES NOT LISTEN TO THE VOICE OF HIS FATHER AND THE VOICE OF HIS MOTHER, AND THEY CHASTEN HIM, AND HE STILL DOES NOT LISTEN TO THEM. (DEVARIM 21:18)

Why does the Torah say "אֵינֶנּוּ שֹׁמֵעַ בְּקוֹל אָבִיו וּבְקוֹל אִמּוֹ — he does not listen to the voice of his father and the voice of his mother," instead of simply writing "אֵינֶנּוּ שֹׁמֵעַ בְּקוֹל אָבִיו וְאִמּוֹ — he does not listen to the voice of his father and mother"?

Chazal say several *derashos* in explanation of these words. Perhaps we can also suggest the following. The Gemara in *Kiddushin* (31a) notes that, in the mitzvah of *yiras av v'eim*, revering one's parents (*Vayikra* 19:3), the mother is mentioned before the father; "אִישׁ אִמּוֹ

וְאָבִיו תִּירָאוּ — a person shall fear their mother and father." And, when commanding us to honor our parents, "כַּבֵּד אֶת אָבִיךָ וְאֶת אִמֶּךָ — honor your father and mother" (*Shemos* 20:12), the father is said first. The reason for this shift is that in both places, the Torah is speaking against the natural instinct. A father is generally stricter with his children than the mother, so there is more of a need for the child to work on fearing his mother. And since the relationship between mother and child is one which naturally brings honor and respect, the father is mentioned first when discussing the mitzvah of honoring one's parent.

This Gemara shows us that the קוֹל אָבִיו, the voice of the father, is an altogether different relationship to the child than is the קוֹל אִמּוֹ, the voice of the mother. Each parent reaches out to the child with a different approach. The Torah is thus telling us that in order to qualify as a *ben sorer u'moreh*, the child is one who has rebelled against several very different approaches in parenting, and despite their great variety, all have failed to reach him.

> לֹא יָבֹא עַמּוֹנִי וּמוֹאָבִי בִּקְהַל ה' גַּם דּוֹר עֲשִׂירִי
> לֹא יָבֹא לָהֶם בִּקְהַל ה' עַד עוֹלָם: עַל דְּבַר אֲשֶׁר
> לֹא קִדְּמוּ אֶתְכֶם בַּלֶּחֶם וּבַמַּיִם בַּדֶּרֶךְ בְּצֵאתְכֶם
> מִמִּצְרָיִם וַאֲשֶׁר שָׂכַר עָלֶיךָ אֶת בִּלְעָם בֶּן בְּעוֹר
> מִפְּתוֹר אֲרַם נַהֲרַיִם לְקַלְלֶךָ:

> AN AMONITE OR MOABITE SHALL NOT ENTER THE ASSEMBLY OF HASHEM; EVEN THE TENTH GENERATION SHALL NEVER ENTER THE ASSEMBLY OF HASHEM. BECAUSE THEY DID NOT GREET YOU WITH BREAD AND WATER ON THE WAY, WHEN YOU LEFT MITZRAYIM, AND BECAUSE THEY HIRED BILAAM THE SON OF BEOR FROM PESOR IN ARAM NAHARAIM AGAINST YOU, TO CURSE YOU. (DEVARIM 23:4–5)

The Torah's restriction against forever marrying someone from

Amon and Moav seems to be unnecessarily strict. What is so terrible about not greeting B'nei Yisrael with bread and water when they were traveling in the desert, that this warrants a literally eternal punishment? Moreover, it would seem that their hiring Bilaam to curse the Jews would be an even stronger reason to keep them away. Yet, the Torah mentions this second, almost as an afterthought.

The Gemara (*Yevamos* 79a) famously tells us that the B'nei Yisrael have three traits which the Avos made a part of our essence, that we are "רַחֲמָנִים בַּיְישָׁנִין וְגוֹמְלֵי חֲסָדִים — people filled with mercy, unpretentious simplicity, who always do *chessed*." A nation that can hear of another nation in need in the desert and simply ignore them is missing at least two out of three of these *middos*. Simply put, this indicates that they are not Klal Yisrael material. A person or nation who can hear of such a *chessed* opportunity and just squander it has no place in a nation built on mercy and doing good for others.

Ki Savo
כִּי תָבוֹא

וְעָנִיתָ וְאָמַרְתָּ לִפְנֵי ה' אֱלֹקֶיךָ אֲרַמִּי אֹבֵד אָבִי וַיֵּרֶד מִצְרַיְמָה וַיָּגָר שָׁם בִּמְתֵי מְעָט וַיְהִי שָׁם לְגוֹי גָּדוֹל עָצוּם וָרָב:

AND YOU SHALL CALL OUT AND SAY BEFORE HASHEM, YOUR GOD, "AN ARAMI SOUGHT TO DESTROY MY FOREFATHER, AND HE WENT DOWN TO MITZRAYIM AND SOJOURNED THERE WITH A SMALL NUMBER OF PEOPLE, AND THERE, HE BECAME A GREAT, MIGHTY, AND NUMEROUS NATION." (DEVARIM 26:5)

Rashi explains that "אֲרַמִּי אֹבֵד אָבִי — an *Arami* sought to destroy my forefather" refers to Lavan. Why do we only mention Lavan's wanting to destroy Yaacov in these *pesukim*? How about Esav? Didn't he also want to destroy Yaacov?

Perhaps Esav is also alluded to in this passage. The *sofei teivos* of the three words "אֲרַמִּי אֹבֵד אָבִי" spells the word "ידי". This may be a reference to Esav, about whom Yitzchak said, "וְהַיָּדַיִם יְדֵי עֵשָׂו — the hands are the hands of Esav." Our *pasuk* thus does not only refer to Lavan, but refers to Esav as well.

Nitzavim
נִצָּבִים

> וַיִּתְּשֵׁם ה' מֵעַל אַדְמָתָם בְּאַף וּבְחֵמָה וּבְקֶצֶף
> גָּדוֹל וַיַּשְׁלִכֵם אֶל אֶרֶץ אַחֶרֶת כַּיּוֹם הַזֶּה:
>
> AND HASHEM UPROOTED THEM FROM UPON THEIR LAND, WITH FURY, ANGER, AND GREAT WRATH, AND HE THREW THEM TO ANOTHER LAND, AS IT IS THIS DAY.
>
> (DEVARIM 29:27)

When written in a *Sefer Torah*, the letter ל in the word "וַיַּשְׁלִכֵם" is written larger than usual. Why?

This *pasuk* is telling us that if the B'nei Yisrael worship *avodah zarah*, *chas veshalom*, then Hashem will remove us from our Land with great fury, and throw — exile, explains the *Targum* — us to another land. This is quite a punishment, and is quite an embarrassment to the Jewish people. The larger letter ל serves to separate "וַיַּשְׁלִכֵם — and He threw them," into two words, "וְיֵשׁ לָכֶם — and they will have." This tells us that indeed, Hashem will remove us from our Land with an intense fury. Yet despite the fact that we will be in exile, we will always have another place to go to, where we will be able to live. The *pasuk* is thus showing Hashem's great love for us, even when He is angry with us. We see that He only wants to punish the Jewish people, not destroy them.[40]

> לֹא בַשָּׁמַיִם הִוא לֵאמֹר מִי יַעֲלֶה לָּנוּ הַשָּׁמַיְמָה
> וְיִקָּחֶהָ לָּנוּ וְיַשְׁמִעֵנוּ אֹתָהּ וְנַעֲשֶׂנָּה:
>
> IT IS NOT IN HEAVEN, THAT YOU SHOULD SAY,
> "WHO WILL GO UP TO HEAVEN FOR US AND
> FETCH IT FOR US, TO TELL IT TO US, SO THAT WE
> CAN FULFILL IT?" (DEVARIM 30:12)

The *Baal Haturim* points out that the *roshei teivos* of the words "מִי יַעֲלֶה לָּנוּ הַשָּׁמַיְמָה" spell the word מִילָה, and the *sofei teivos* spell Hashem's ineffable Name. This teaches us that one cannot go to heaven — become closer to Hashem — unless he is circumcised.

We may extend this idea, that the *roshei teivos* of the words "לֹא בַשָּׁמַיִם" spell the word "לֵב — heart." While the Torah cannot be found in the heavens or across the sea, it can be found in our heart, like the Torah tells us several *pesukim* later, in *pasuk* 14, "כִּי קָרוֹב אֵלֶיךָ הַדָּבָר מְאֹד בְּפִיךָ וּבִלְבָבְךָ לַעֲשֹׂתוֹ — rather, this thing is very close to you; it is in your mouth and in your heart, so that you can fulfill it."

> כִּי קָרוֹב אֵלֶיךָ הַדָּבָר מְאֹד בְּפִיךָ וּבִלְבָבְךָ לַעֲשֹׂתוֹ:
>
> RATHER, THIS THING IS VERY CLOSE TO YOU; IT IS
> IN YOUR MOUTH AND IN YOUR HEART, SO THAT
> YOU CAN FULFILL IT. (DEVARIM 30:14)

Rashi explains that "this thing" that is very close to you is the Torah that was partially given in written form, and was partially given orally. Perhaps these two parts of the Torah are hinted to in this *pasuk*. "בְּפִיךָ — in your mouth," refers to the *Torah Shebe'al Peh*. The *Torah Shebechsav* begins with the word "בְּרֵאשִׁית," and ends with

---

40   See also Rav Hirsch and the *Oznayim LaTorah*.

"לְעֵינֵי כָּל יִשְׂרָאֵל." The Torah's first letter, and last letter, therefore spell "לֵב" — heart." Thus, the word "וּבִלְבָבְךָ — and in your heart" in our *pasuk* hints to the *Torah Shebechsav*.

VAYELECH
וַיֵּלֶךְ

וַיֵּלֶךְ מֹשֶׁה וַיְדַבֵּר אֶת הַדְּבָרִים הָאֵלֶּה אֶל כָּל יִשְׂרָאֵל: וַיֹּאמֶר אֲלֵהֶם בֶּן מֵאָה וְעֶשְׂרִים שָׁנָה אָנֹכִי הַיּוֹם לֹא אוּכַל עוֹד לָצֵאת וְלָבוֹא וַה' אָמַר אֵלַי לֹא תַעֲבֹר אֶת הַיַּרְדֵּן הַזֶּה: ה' אֱלֹקֶיךָ הוּא עֹבֵר לְפָנֶיךָ הוּא יַשְׁמִיד אֶת הַגּוֹיִם הָאֵלֶּה מִלְּפָנֶיךָ וִירִשְׁתָּם יְהוֹשֻׁעַ הוּא עֹבֵר לְפָנֶיךָ כַּאֲשֶׁר דִּבֶּר ה':

AND MOSHE WENT, AND HE SPOKE THE FOLLOWING WORDS TO ALL OF THE JEWISH PEOPLE. HE SAID TO THEM, "TODAY I AM ONE HUNDRED AND TWENTY YEARS OLD. I CAN NO LONGER GO OR COME, AND HASHEM SAID TO ME, 'YOU SHALL NOT CROSS THIS YARDEN.' HASHEM, YOUR GOD, HE WILL CROSS BEFORE YOU; HE WILL DESTROY THESE NATIONS FROM BEFORE YOU SO THAT YOU WILL POSSESS THEM. YEHOSHUA; HE WILL CROSS BEFORE YOU, AS HASHEM HAS SPOKEN." (DEVARIM 31:1–3)

VAYELECH

וַיִּקְרָא מֹשֶׁה לִיהוֹשֻׁעַ וַיֹּאמֶר אֵלָיו לְעֵינֵי כָל־יִשְׂרָאֵל חֲזַק וֶאֱמָץ כִּי אַתָּה תָּבוֹא אֶת־הָעָם הַזֶּה אֶל־הָאָרֶץ אֲשֶׁר נִשְׁבַּע ה' לַאֲבֹתָם לָתֵת לָהֶם וְאַתָּה תַּנְחִילֶנָּה אוֹתָם: וַה' הוּא הַהֹלֵךְ לְפָנֶיךָ הוּא יִהְיֶה עִמָּךְ לֹא יַרְפְּךָ וְלֹא יַעַזְבֶךָּ לֹא תִירָא וְלֹא תֵחָת:

And Moshe called Yehoshua and said to him in the presence of all of the Jewish people, "Be strong and courageous! For you shall come with this people to the land which Hashem swore to their forefathers to give them. And you shall apportion it to them as an inheritance. Hashem He is the One Who goes before you; He will be with you; He will neither fail you, nor forsake you. Do not fear, and do not be dismayed." (Devarim 31:7–8)

In *pasuk* 3 Moshe tells the B'nei Yisrael that Hashem will allow them to cross the Yarden River, and Yehoshua will be the one to "cross before you." This of course puts the emphasis on Hashem, and Yehoshua was just the technical person who led the way.

Then, in *pesukim* 7 and 8, the order is reversed. Moshe tells Yehoshua that he should not fear, he will lead the Jewish people into Eretz Yisrael; and he should not fear, for Hashem will be with him. Here it seems that Yehoshua was given a much larger role, and Hashem would support whatever he would do. Why the shift?

The difference between these *pesukim* is who Moshe was speaking to, and which point was most important for them to hear. In *pasuk* 3, Moshe was speaking to the B'nei Yisrael, and had just told the nation that he would not be crossing the Yarden with them to enter Eretz

Yisrael. B'nei Yisrael were naturally despondent; if Moshe cannot lead us in, who can? To this Moshe responded that you do not really need me. Hashem is in truth the One Who is leading you in to Eretz Yisrael, and I am just a technical conduit. It really doesn't make a difference who succeeds me, as long as Hashem is with that person. As part of making this point, Moshe thus stressed Hashem first, and only then Yehoshua.

In *pesukim* 7 and 8, however, Moshe was speaking to Yehoshua, and told him that he would be the one to lead the B'nei Yisrael. However, he should not worry, for Hashem would always be behind him. Yehoshua needed to know that as a leader he would be the one upon whom everyone would rely, but at the same time he was just Hashem's messenger, and would be receiving Hashem's ongoing assistance.

> וַיֹּאמֶר אֲלֵהֶם בֶּן מֵאָה וְעֶשְׂרִים שָׁנָה אָנֹכִי הַיּוֹם לֹא אוּכַל עוֹד לָצֵאת וְלָבוֹא וַה' אָמַר אֵלַי לֹא תַעֲבֹר אֶת הַיַּרְדֵּן הַזֶּה:

> HE SAID TO THEM, "TODAY I AM ONE HUNDRED AND TWENTY YEARS OLD. I CAN NO LONGER GO OR COME, AND HASHEM SAID TO ME, 'YOU SHALL NOT CROSS THIS YARDEN.'" (DEVARIM 31:2)

Moshe told the B'nei Yisrael that today, on my one hundred and twentieth birthday, "לֹא אוּכַל עוֹד לָצֵאת וְלָבוֹא וַה' אָמַר אֵלַי לֹא תַעֲבֹר אֶת הַיַּרְדֵּן הַזֶּה — I can no longer go or come, and Hashem said to me, 'You shall not cross this Yarden.'" Rashi explains that Moshe did not mean that he was physically weak, and thus unable to cross the Yarden. Rather, he could no longer go and come, because the permission to cross the Yarden had been taken from him and given to Yehoshua. Even with Rashi's explanation, the *pasuk* still seems redundant, for Moshe immediately says that Hashem has not allowed me to cross. Why does Moshe say that he is unable to go and come, and then state that Hashem has not allowed him to cross the Yarden, if both statements refer to the same thing?

When Moshe said that he could not cross the Yarden, he explained why: that Hashem did not allow him to do so. And the way that Moshe expressed this lack of permission was not "I am not allowed to," but rather "לֹא אוּכַל — I am not able to," or, in other words, "I can't." Hashem's telling Moshe that he may not do something was a literal brick wall in his way, blocking his physical ability to do it. This point can be illustrated with a story involving Rav Moshe Feinstein *zatzal*. There was a very urgent phone call for Rav Moshe after *davening*. However, Rav Moshe did not move, for there was a person who was still standing and *davening shemoneh esrei* behind him. Rav Moshe later explained he could not take the call, as urgent as it was, because there was a wall there, preventing him from getting to the phone. The halachah that one cannot not move when someone is *davening* behind you was very real to Rav Moshe. So much so, it was tantamount to his being physically unable to perform the task required of him, because he was "chained" to that spot.

Moshe's telling us that he was *unable* to cross the Yarden also tells us something else: an important message about saying "I can't." Moshe said that he was now unable to cross, and explained why there was simply no way for him to do so. Are we the same way? When we tell someone "I am sorry, but I can't do the favor for you," what do we mean? Is it true that we *can't* do it — with an explanation as good as Moshe's — or we mean that we simply don't want to?

> הַקְהֵל אֶת הָעָם הָאֲנָשִׁים וְהַנָּשִׁים וְהַטַּף וְגֵרְךָ
> אֲשֶׁר בִּשְׁעָרֶיךָ לְמַעַן יִשְׁמְעוּ וּלְמַעַן יִלְמְדוּ וְיָרְאוּ
> אֶת ה' אֱלֹקֵיכֶם וְשָׁמְרוּ לַעֲשׂוֹת אֶת כָּל דִּבְרֵי
> הַתּוֹרָה הַזֹּאת:

> ASSEMBLE THE PEOPLE: THE MEN, THE WOMEN, AND THE CHILDREN, AND YOUR STRANGER IN YOUR CITIES, IN ORDER THAT THEY HEAR, AND IN ORDER THAT THEY LEARN AND FEAR HASHEM, YOUR GOD, AND THEY WILL OBSERVE TO DO ALL THE WORDS OF THIS TORAH. (DEVARIM 31:12)

Rashi explains that the men came to *Hakhel* to learn, which is the "וּלְמַעַן יִלְמְדוּ — in order that they learn" mentioned in the *pasuk*. And, the women came to hear, as the *pasuk* says "לְמַעַן יִשְׁמְעוּ — in order that they hear." If this is the case, why doesn't the *pasuk* first write "לְמַעַן יִשְׁמְעוּ — in order that they hear," in a way that is consistent with the order that men and women are written?

Perhaps the Torah reverses the natural order of the *pasuk* to teach us that the obligation for men and women to come to *Hakhel* was equal. We may have supposed that since the women only came to listen, and not to learn, their attendance at *Hakhel* wasn't so important. The Torah therefore switches the order in which the reasons for attendance is said, first writing "לְמַעַן יִשְׁמְעוּ — in order that they hear," to make it clear that the women's coming to hear is of primary value, as well.[41]

The Gemara in *Kiddushin* (31a) notes that in the mitzvah of *yiras av v'eim*, revering one's parents (*Vayikra* 19:3), the mother is mentioned before the father; "אִישׁ אִמּוֹ וְאָבִיו תִּירָאוּ — a person shall fear their mother and father." And when commanding us to honor our parents (*Shemos* 20:12), "כַּבֵּד אֶת אָבִיךָ וְאֶת אִמֶּךָ — honor your father and mother," the father is said first. The reason for this shift is that in both places, the Torah is speaking against the natural instinct. A father is generally stricter with his children than is the mother, so there is more of a need for the child to work on fearing his mother. And, since the relationship between mother and child is one which naturally brings honor and respect, the father is mentioned first when discussing the mitzvah of honoring one's parents.

---

41 This switch is in line with the Gemara *Kiddushin* 31a, which explains that *pesukim* instructing honoring parents and revering parents, are written with the father and mother in different orders, for each *pasuk* is written in a way that tells us the bigger *chiddush* first. See above, page 293.

HA'AZINU
הַאֲזִינוּ

הֲ‍לַה' תִּגְמְלוּ זֹאת עַם נָבָל וְלֹא חָכָם הֲלוֹא הוּא
אָבִיךָ קָּנֶךָ הוּא עָשְׂךָ וַיְכֹנְנֶךָ:

IS THIS HOW YOU REPAY HASHEM, YOU
DISGRACEFUL, UNWISE PEOPLE?! IS HE NOT YOUR
FATHER, YOUR MASTER? HE HAS MADE YOU AND
ESTABLISHED YOU. (DEVARIM 32:6)

When written in a *Sefer Torah*, the letter ה which begins this *pasuk* is written larger than usual. Why?

The *Baal Haturim* answers that this letter ה, whose *gematria* value is five, is a reference to the Torah, which has five *Chumashim*. According to this approach, the *pasuk* is telling us the following: "Is this how you are going to repay Hashem, Who gave us the Torah?! A disgraceful and unwise People; is He not your Father, your Master, Who has created you! He has made you and established you."

We may suggest another approach: that the letter ה may be understood as a reference to Hashem's creating the world; for the Gemara (*Menachos* 29b) explains the word בְּהִבָּרְאָם (*Bereishis* 2:4) may also be read בְּ-הֵ בְּרָאָם — *with the letter* ה *He [Hashem] created them*, telling us that Hashem created this world using the letter ה. This approach would read the *pasuk* slightly differently; "Is this how you are going to repay Hashem; He created the world! A disgraceful and unwise People; is He not your Father, your Master, Who has created you! He has made you and established you."

The second approach raises an interesting question. In *Parashas Bereishis* (2:4), we noted that the word בְּהִבָּרְאָם is written in a *Sefer Torah* with a *small* letter ה. If both appearances of the letter ה are referring to Hashem's creating the world, why is the ה in our *pasuk* written large, and the ה in *Bereishis* small?

Perhaps the answer lies in the message which each letter ה is telling us. *Parashas Bereishis* is being written from Hashem's perspective, so to speak; we explained in *Parashas Bereishis* that the small ה is teaching us of the absolute effortlessness with which Hashem created the world. In our *pasuk*, on the other hand, Moshe is rebuking the B'nei Yisrael, telling them that the One that they are acting against in ingratitude is Hashem, Who has created the utter vastness of the world and everything that it contains. The Torah is thus emphasizing the greatness of what Hashem has done for us, using a specifically large letter ה.

צוּר יְלָדְךָ תֶּשִׁי וַתִּשְׁכַּח אֵל מְחֹלְלֶךָ:

YOU FORGOT THE ROCK WHO BORE YOU;
YOU FORGOT THE GOD WHO DELIVERED
YOU. (DEVARIM 32:18)

When written in a *Sefer Torah*, the letter י in the word תֶּשִׁי is written smaller than usual. Why?

Rashi explains (in his second approach) that the word תֶּשִׁי means "to weaken." Although Hashem wishes to help us, we constantly anger Him, and weaken, so to speak, His ability to help us more.

According to this, we may understand that our sins, so to speak, weaken Hashem's Hand, His יָד. This is thus alluded to in the smaller letter י.

Alternatively, the word "weakened," which Rashi is discussing, is actually תָּשׁ, for example the common phrase "תָּשׁ כֹּחוֹ — his strength was weakened." It is only by making the letter י smaller, effectively minimizing it, that the שִׁי is understood to be תִּשׁ, as Rashi explains.

> וַיָּבֹא מֹשֶׁה וַיְדַבֵּר אֶת כָּל דִּבְרֵי הַשִּׁירָה הַזֹּאת
> בְּאָזְנֵי הָעָם הוּא וְהוֹשֵׁעַ בִּן נוּן:

AND MOSHE CAME AND SPOKE ALL THE WORDS OF THIS SONG INTO THE EARS OF THE PEOPLE, HE AND HOSHEA THE SON OF NUN. (DEVARIM 32:44)

Rashi explains that Yehoshua is suddenly called Hoshea in this *pasuk* to demonstrate that although he was about to succeed his *rebbi* Moshe as the leader of the Jewish people, he humbled himself as he had done in the beginning, when he had just started to learn Torah from Moshe.

Another answer to this question may be as follows. Almost forty years earlier, Moshe had changed Hoshea's name to Yehoshua, in prayer that Hashem save him from the *Meraglim's* plans. The B'nei Yisrael listened to the *lashon hara* said by the other *Meraglim* however, and was punished with forty years of wandering in the Desert. Now, a generation later, the punishment was finally over. The nation was finally about to enter Eretz Yisrael, and the "fallout" of the *Meraglim's aveirah* was finally about to dissipate. We now see that Moshe's *tefillos* for Hoshea were totally successful, for they had protected him from any effects that the *Meraglim*, or the lasting effects of their sin, could have had on him. Yehoshua can now safely return to being Hoshea.

> וַיְדַבֵּר ה' אֶל מֹשֶׁה בְּעֶצֶם הַיּוֹם הַזֶּה לֵאמֹר: עֲלֵה
> אֶל הַר הָעֲבָרִים הַזֶּה הַר נְבוֹ אֲשֶׁר בְּאֶרֶץ מוֹאָב
> אֲשֶׁר עַל פְּנֵי יְרֵחוֹ וּרְאֵה אֶת אֶרֶץ כְּנַעַן אֲשֶׁר אֲנִי
> נֹתֵן לִבְנֵי יִשְׂרָאֵל לַאֲחֻזָּה:

AND HASHEM SPOKE TO MOSHE IN THE MIDDLE OF THAT DAY, SAYING, "GO UP THIS MOUNT

> AVARIM, MOUNT NEVO, WHICH IS IN THE LAND
> OF MOAV, THAT IS FACING YERICHO, AND SEE THE
> LAND OF CANAAN, WHICH I AM GIVING TO THE
> B'NEI YISRAEL AS A POSSESSION." (DEVARIM 32:48-49)

Rashi points out that the Torah says "בְּעֶצֶם הַיּוֹם הַזֶּה" — in the middle of that day," on several occasions. The people of Noach's generation said that they would stop Noach from entering the *Teivah*, and the Mitzrim declared that they would prevent the B'nei Yisrael from leaving Mitzrayim. And finally, when the Jewish people heard that Hashem had told Moshe to ascend Mount Nevo and die, they exclaimed, "Moshe Rabbeinu! The man who brought us out of Mitzrayim, split the Yam Suf for us, brought the *Mahn* down for us, made flocks of quails fly over to us, brought up the Well for us, and gave us the Torah — we will not let him!" And on all three of these occasions, Hashem declared, "I have decided that this is what will happen! I will even do it in the very middle of the day! Whoever wants to try and stop me, let them try!"

We understand how the people around Noach thought they could stop him from entering the *Teivah*: by surrounding it and smashing it to pieces. And we similarly understand how the Mitzrim thought that they could block the gates of Mitzrayim and prevent anyone from leaving. How did the B'nei Yisrael think that they could prevent Moshe from dying?

Perhaps, the B'nei Yisrael did not really think that they could physically stop Moshe from passing away once Hashem had made the decision to take his life. But they thought that they could argue with Hashem before it came to that point. They reasoned that they would point out to Hashem that there was no reason for Moshe to die, as he was an almost perfect *tzadik*, who followed Hashem's instructions almost flawlessly. To which Hashem responded that I have already made a decision, let us see if anyone will be able to stop me.

We in fact find a Midrash (*Yalkut Shimoni* 32:949) who tells us that the *malachei hashareis* had this line of reasoning; for they asked Hashem why Adam was killed. Hashem responded to them because he did not listen to what I told him to do. If so, argued the *Malachim*, why should Moshe die like Adam? He did listen to you! Hashem answered that the decree of death has no exceptions, and Moshe too must die, like everyone else.

> עַל אֲשֶׁר מְעַלְתֶּם בִּי בְּתוֹךְ בְּנֵי יִשְׂרָאֵל בְּמֵי מְרִיבַת קָדֵשׁ מִדְבַּר צִן עַל אֲשֶׁר לֹא קִדַּשְׁתֶּם אוֹתִי בְּתוֹךְ בְּנֵי יִשְׂרָאֵל:

> BECAUSE YOU BETRAYED ME IN THE MIDST OF THE B'NEI YISRAEL AT THE WATERS OF MERIVAS KADESH, IN THE DESERT OF TZIN, BECAUSE YOU DID NOT SANCTIFY ME IN THE MIDST OF THE B'NEI YISRAEL. (DEVARIM 32:51)

Rashi explains that Moshe was punished due to the loss of the potential *kiddush Hashem* that he could have created had he spoken to the rock, instead of hitting it. Looking at the *pesukim* in *Parashas Chukas* discussing this episode (*Bamidbar* 20:7–8) tells us something interesting; there is never any mention that the B'nei Yisrael knew that Moshe was supposed to speak to the rock instead of hitting it. This commandment had been said to Moshe alone. How then was a *kiddush Hashem* lost?

Indeed, the Jewish people did not know that Moshe was supposed to speak to the rock. However, had Moshe spoken to the rock as he had been told to do, the miracle of its giving forth water would have been so open, clear, and obvious to all. Moshe's hitting the rock, on the other hand, somewhat concealed the effects of the *nes*, which could now be partially explained to natural causes. The tremendous lesson that could have been learned was now lost.

Understanding this teaches us a tremendous lesson. We aren't only held responsible for what we did and did not actually do. We are held responsible for all the good that could have come out of something positive had we done it.

Vezos Haberachah
וְזֹאת הַבְּרָכָה

וְלִזְבוּלֻן אָמַר שְׂמַח זְבוּלֻן בְּצֵאתֶךָ וְיִשָּׂשכָר בְּאֹהָלֶיךָ:

And to Zevulun he said: "Rejoice, Zevulun, in your going out, and Yissachar, in your tents." (Devarim 33:18)

Rashi explains that Yissachar and Zevulun made a deal that Zevulun would work and support Yissachar in his learning. *Targum Onkelous* translates "בְּצֵאתֶךָ — in your going out," as "בְּמִפְקָךְ לְאַגָחָא קְרָבָא עַל בַּעֲלֵי דְבָבָךְ — in your going out to war against your enemies." Where was Zevulun going to war?

It would appear that *Targum Onkelous* is in fact explaining the *pasuk* like Rashi, and is equating making a *parnassah* with going out to war. And I am sure that many a bread-winner would agree with this comparison.

Interestingly, the word "לֶחֶם — bread" is also the *shoresh* of "מִלְחָמָה — war"; and "מַצָּה," besides for being what we eat on Pesach, also means "quarrel," in *lashon hakodesh*. These related words also suggest that going to work to earn our daily bread is likened to warring with an enemy.[42]

---

[42] I told this idea to my Rosh Yeshiva, Rav Chaim Kreiswirth *zatzal*, and he agreed.

> וְלִזְבוּלֻן אָמַר שְׂמַח זְבוּלֻן בְּצֵאתֶךָ וְיִשָּׂשכָר בְּאֹהָלֶיךָ:

> AND TO ZEVULUN HE SAID: "REJOICE, ZEVULUN, IN YOUR GOING OUT, AND YISSACHAR, IN YOUR TENTS." (DEVARIM 33:18)

Rashi explains that the names of the five *shevatim* whom Moshe blessed last — Zevulun, Gad, Dan, Naftali, and Asher — are repeated in order to strengthen them, for these were the weakest of the *shevatim*, as we find (*Bereishis* 47:2) that Yosef brought specifically them before Pharaoh. Why, we may ask, is Yissachar mentioned among this group of *shevatim*? The fact that his name is not repeated means that he was from the stronger *shevatim*. Why isn't he mentioned towards the beginning of Moshe's *Berachos*, together with the other more powerful *shevatim*?

It would appear that this question is what Rashi is coming to answer in his famous next comment, that Yissachar and Zevulun arranged a partnership in which Zevulun went out to work and supported Yissachar, allowing him to focus on learning Torah on behalf of both of them. Rashi is telling this to us to explain that this partnership made it that Yissachar and Zevulun are seen as one unit. Thus, Yissachar, although he was more powerful, is mentioned among the weaker *shevatim*, for his place is alongside his partner Zevulun.

> וִיהוֹשֻׁעַ בִּן נוּן מָלֵא רוּחַ חָכְמָה כִּי סָמַךְ מֹשֶׁה אֶת יָדָיו עָלָיו וַיִּשְׁמְעוּ אֵלָיו בְּנֵי יִשְׂרָאֵל וַיַּעֲשׂוּ כַּאֲשֶׁר צִוָּה ה' אֶת מֹשֶׁה:

> AND YEHOSHUA THE SON OF NUN WAS FULL OF THE SPIRIT OF WISDOM, BECAUSE MOSHE HAD LAID HIS HANDS UPON HIM. AND THE B'NEI YISRAEL OBEYED HIM, AND THEY DID AS HASHEM HAD COMMANDED MOSHE. (DEVARIM 34:9)

Why does the Torah say that that the B'nei Yisrael obeyed Yehoshua "כַּאֲשֶׁר צִוָּה ה' אֶת מֹשֶׁה" — as Hashem had commanded Moshe"? Shouldn't the *pasuk* say that they listened to him, and did "as Hashem had commanded Yehoshua," or, "as Hashem had commanded him"?

The Torah is telling us that the B'nei Yisrael continued to do all that Hashem had commanded Moshe even after Moshe's death. Very often when a leader dies people listen to his successor, and are tempted to "forget" some of the things that the previous leader had said, which weren't very convenient to begin with. The Torah is telling us that this was not the case after Moshe passed away. The B'nei Yisrael obeyed Yehoshua, and continued doing all that Hashem had commanded Moshe, as well.

Yet at the same time, although the B'nei Yisrael still had the utmost respect for Moshe even after his death, Yehoshua did not suffer from living in his *rebbi's* shadow, as unfortunately so often happens. Just as they had listened to Moshe, the B'nei Yisrael listened to Yehoshua, as well.

לְכֹל הַיָּד הַחֲזָקָה וּלְכֹל הַמּוֹרָא הַגָּדוֹל אֲשֶׁר עָשָׂה מֹשֶׁה לְעֵינֵי כָּל יִשְׂרָאֵל:

AND ALL THE POWERFUL HAND, AND ALL THE GREAT AWE, WHICH MOSHE PERFORMED BEFORE THE EYES OF ALL OF THE JEWISH PEOPLE. (DEVARIM 34:12)

Rashi explains that the powerful hand and great awe which Moshe performed before the entire Jewish people was that he broke the *Luchos*, and Hashem agreed with his decision. Breaking the *Luchos* hardly seems like an appropriate way to finish off the Torah. For example, *mesechtos* in Gemara try to find a positive note to conclude with. Why does the Torah conclude with one of the B'nei Yisrael's greatest foibles?

A relationship between two people or two parties can have any of several levels. The most basic is where one side does as he is asked or told. A greater bond is when one person anticipates the needs of the other. And the third, deepest relationship is where one person does something for the other, even when the other insists that there is no need to do it, because the person realizes that this is what they *really* want. To use an example of a husband and wife, a husband may take out the garbage at his wife's request. Or he anticipates his wife asking him to take out the garbage and does it before she asks. The greatest level is when the wife insists that there is no need for him to take out the garbage in a howling rainstorm, and the husband does anyway, knowing that it will make his wife happy to be rid of the garbage.

In *pasuk* 10, Hashem praised Moshe, saying that never again will there be a *Navi* like Moshe, who spoke with Me with open revelation. Our *pasuk* is now an example of this elevated relationship. Hashem gave Moshe the *Luchos*, with the implicit instructions to *give* them to the B'nei Yisrael, not to break them. Yet, Moshe understood that breaking them was what Hashem would *really* want him to do. And after he broke them, Hashem told him, "Good job!" This praise that Moshe was able to "read between the lines" of what Hashem told him to understand what He *really* wanted, is not only the ultimate tribute that the Torah can possibly give Moshe. It also shows us of Hashem's deepest desire to relate to the B'nei Yisrael under all circumstances. He didn't disown us and destroy us after we committed the worst *aveirah* possible, but wanted Moshe to break the *Luchos*, so He would then be able to give us a second chance. And this, of course, is the most positive way that the Torah could possibly conclude, with a description of Hashem's great love for us.

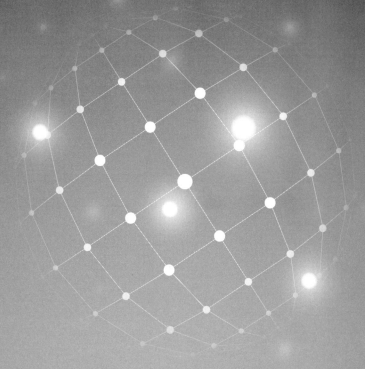

Moadim

מוֹעֲדִים

Rosh Hashanah
רֹאשׁ הַשָּׁנָה

וַיִּשְׁמַע אֱלֹקִים אֶת קוֹל הַנַּעַר וַיִּקְרָא מַלְאַךְ אֱלֹקִים אֶל הָגָר מִן הַשָּׁמַיִם וַיֹּאמֶר לָהּ מַה לָּךְ הָגָר אַל תִּירְאִי כִּי שָׁמַע אֱלֹקִים אֶל קוֹל הַנַּעַר בַּאֲשֶׁר הוּא שָׁם:

AND HASHEM HEARD THE LAD'S VOICE, AND HASHEM'S MALACH CALLED TO HAGAR FROM HEAVEN, AND SAID TO HER, "WHAT IS TROUBLING YOU, HAGAR? FEAR NOT, FOR HASHEM HAS HEARD THE LAD'S VOICE IN THE PLACE WHERE HE IS." (BEREISHIS 21:17)

The main focus of the *krias haTorah* of the first day of Rosh Hashanah appears to be Hashem's remembering Sarah after so many years of childlessness. However, we should not overlook another important point which this *kri'ah* discusses: Hashem spared Yishmael's life, for at the moment he was innocent of wrongdoing, despite what would happen in the future. Let us remember this to better push us to *teshuvah*: at the moment we are doing *teshuvah*, we too can be judged for life.

> אָמַר רַבִּי כְרוּסְפְּדַאי אָמַר רַבִּי יוֹחָנָן: שְׁלשָׁה סְפָרִים נִפְתָּחִין בְּרֹאשׁ הַשָּׁנָה, אֶחָד שֶׁל רְשָׁעִים גְּמוּרִין, וְאֶחָד שֶׁל צַדִּיקִים גְּמוּרִין, וְאֶחָד שֶׁל בֵּינוֹנִיִּים. צַדִּיקִים גְּמוּרִין נִכְתָּבִין וְנֶחְתָּמִין לְאַלְתַּר לְחַיִּים, רְשָׁעִים גְּמוּרִין נִכְתָּבִין וְנֶחְתָּמִין לְאַלְתַּר לְמִיתָה, בֵּינוֹנִיִּים תְּלוּיִין וְעוֹמְדִין מֵרֹאשׁ הַשָּׁנָה וְעַד יוֹם הַכִּפּוּרִים. זָכוּ, נִכְתָּבִין לְחַיִּים, לֹא זָכוּ, נִכְתָּבִין לְמִיתָה.

> RAV KRUSPEDAI SAID IN THE NAME OF RAV YOCHANAN, "THREE BOOKS ARE OPEN ON ROSH HASHANAH. ONE IS OF ABSOLUTE RESHA'IM, ONE IS OF ABSOLUTE TZADIKIM, AND ONE IS OF PEOPLE IN THE MIDDLE. ABSOLUTE TZADIKIM ARE IMMEDIATELY WRITTEN AND SEALED FOR LIFE, ABSOLUTE RESHA'IM ARE IMMEDIATELY WRITTEN AND SEALED FOR DEATH, AND THE PEOPLE IN THE MIDDLE ARE LEFT HANGING FROM ROSH HASHANAH UNTIL YOM KIPPUR. IF THEY MERIT, THEY ARE WRITTEN FOR LIFE, IF THEY DO NOT MERIT, THEY ARE WRITTEN FOR DEATH.
>
> (GEMARA ROSH HASHANAH 16B)

The Rambam explains that the word "זָכוּ — if they merit," means "if they did *teshuvah*."

Many ask the following question: if the scales are perfectly balanced, why not just do another mitzvah, which will tip the scales to the side of life? Why can only *teshuvah* save this person?

The answer is that after Rosh Hashanah the year is over and books are closed. The Court, so to speak, is no longer accepting any more pieces of evidence, and the scales reckoning the previous year will not be tipped, no matter how many new *mitzvos* the person does. *Teshuvah* may be compared to a bribe, in that the person on trial develops a relationship with the judge outside of the details of the case on the table, which will inevitably affect his judgment. Hashem is not doing a recount. However, during the *Aseres Yemei Teshuvah*, Hashem is, so to speak, willing to allow Himself to develop this relationship with people who search it out.

Knowing that the Judge of Judges will allow Himself a closeness with people on trial, makes our doing *teshuvah* during this time all the more important. Continuing our example of bribing the judge, let us imagine a serial killer on trial for his life, who was just told that the judge can be bought. It is clear that he will do whatever he can to put together and raise the amount of money that he needs to be freed, no matter the amount. How would we look at this person if when hearing his prospects of a real trial, or a guaranteed mistrial on a technicality, he yawned and said thank you, but I'm just too tired to start running around. Or he said forget it, it's too much money. We would think, This man is nothing more than a fool! This is the opportunity we have during the *Aseres Yemei Teshuvah*. It is in our hands to take advantage, or foolishly lose out.

We may also suggest a second way to answer this question. A person who does *teshuvah* is not the same person as the one who did all the *aveiros* on the scale. He becomes a new man. *Teshuvah* makes it that Hashem, in His great *chessed*, does not look at the scales, rather He looks at the person, and sees a different person who has no relation to all the previous indiscretions of the past year. Thus, although the scales are still balanced, they have no effect on him. In this way a person who does real *teshuvah* can be judged favorably on Yom Kippur, although based on the whole year he does not merit to be written in the *Sefer Hachaim*.

Yom Kippur
יוֹם הַכִּפּוּרִים

וַה׳ הֵטִיל רוּחַ גְּדוֹלָה אֶל הַיָּם וַיְהִי סַעַר גָּדוֹל בַּיָּם וְהָאֳנִיָּה חִשְּׁבָה לְהִשָּׁבֵר:

NOW HASHEM CAST A MIGHTY WIND INTO THE SEA, AND THERE WAS A MIGHTY STORM ON THE SEA, AND THE SHIP THREATENED TO BE BROKEN UP. (YONAH 1:4)

If Hashem sent the storm to punish Yonah, why did all of the other people on the ship have to suffer?

Perhaps the entire ship suffered in line with the Mishnah (*Negaim* 12:6; see also Gemara *Succah* 56b), "אוֹי לְרָשָׁע אוֹי לִשְׁכֵנוֹ — woe is to a *rasha*, and woe is to his neighbor." Alternatively, perhaps Hashem indeed wanted to shake up everyone on the ship. We see that a lot of good came out of this storm for the people on the ship, for after the storm, "וַיִּירְאוּ הָאֲנָשִׁים יִרְאָה גְדוֹלָה אֶת ה׳ וַיִּזְבְּחוּ זֶבַח לַה׳ וַיִּדְּרוּ נְדָרִים — The men feared Hashem exceedingly, and they made sacrifices to Hashem and made vows." According to Rashi, the people on the boat converted to Judaism.

Yom Kippur

> וַיִּירְאוּ הַמַּלָּחִים וַיִּזְעֲקוּ אִישׁ אֶל אֱלֹהָיו וַיָּטִלוּ אֶת הַכֵּלִים אֲשֶׁר בָּאֳנִיָּה אֶל הַיָּם לְהָקֵל מֵעֲלֵיהֶם וְיוֹנָה יָרַד אֶל יַרְכְּתֵי הַסְּפִינָה וַיִּשְׁכַּב וַיֵּרָדַם:

> AND THE SAILORS WERE FRIGHTENED, AND EACH ONE CRIED OUT TO HIS GOD, AND THEY CAST THE CARGO THAT WAS IN THE SHIP INTO THE SEA TO LIGHTEN IT FOR THEM, AND YONAH WENT DOWN TO THE SHIP'S HOLD, LAY DOWN, AND FELL FAST ASLEEP. (YONAH 1:5)

How could Yonah go to sleep with such pandemonium on the ship, especially when it seemed that the ship would break apart and everyone would drown?

It is certainly hard to imagine falling asleep in the middle of an earthquake or other such cataclysmic event. However, the truth is that we do this every day! People unfortunately do a very good job of ignoring what is going on around them, because they are so absorbed in their own lives. How often do we simply ignore things that can impact us negatively? We too are guilty of falling asleep, when we should be screaming to the Heavens for our own and for our nation's, survival.

> וַיְמַן ה' דָּג גָּדוֹל לִבְלֹעַ אֶת יוֹנָה וַיְהִי יוֹנָה בִּמְעֵי הַדָּג שְׁלֹשָׁה יָמִים וּשְׁלֹשָׁה לֵילוֹת: וַיִּתְפַּלֵּל יוֹנָה אֶל ה' אֱלֹקָיו מִמְּעֵי הַדָּגָה:

> AND HASHEM APPOINTED A HUGE FISH TO SWALLOW UP YONAH, AND YONAH WAS IN THE BELLY OF THE FISH FOR THREE DAYS AND THREE NIGHTS. AND YONAH PRAYED TO THE HASHEM, HIS GOD, FROM THE BELLY OF THE FISH. (YONAH 2:1–2)

Pasuk 1 calls the huge fish a דָּג, and *pasuk* 2, a דָּגָה. Rashi explains that Yonah was first swallowed by a tremendous male fish, where there was room to relax, and to *daven*. Yonah, however, did not take advantage of this opportunity, and Hashem made the male spit him out into a pregnant female, where there was less room in her belly. Only then did Yonah begin to *daven* to Hashem. Why, we may ask, didn't Hashem just put Yonah in the female fish to begin with?

This teaches us a great lesson of how Hashem tries to get our attention. First He sends us a message with a weak signal, which is not so intrusive, in the hopes that we will come back to Him without much pain. If this message is ignored, Hashem may send another message that will be louder and clearer, which may cost time and money, or may involve pain, loss or discomfort. Hashem put Yonah in the more comfortable male fish first, in the hopes he would turn to Hashem in *tefillah* simply by virtue of his being saved in this very miraculous manner. When this did not work, Hashem turned the heat up a bit and made it more uncomfortable for Yonah, who then took the hint and began to *daven*.

Succos
סוכות

Succah

The Gemara in *Avodah Zarah* (3a) famously tells us that when Mashiach comes, the nations of the world will complain to Hashem that they too want a mitzvah. Hashem will give them the mitzvah of *succah*. He will extend the hot summer season until Succos, until the unbearable heat makes it simply impossible to remain in the *succah*, at which point the peoples of the nations will angrily kick the *succah*, and storm out. The Gemara is puzzled as to what is wrong with the way that these people acted. A person does not have to remain in the *succah* in intense and uncomfortable heat! The Gemara answers, indeed these people are *patur* from the mitzvah, but that was no reason to kick the *succah* on the way out.

We may ask the following question. Of all of the weather patterns and natural disasters at Hashem's disposal, why did He specifically choose heat to test the sincerity that the nations of the world professed to have for the mitzvah of *succah*? Why not extreme cold, rain, or snow?

Perhaps this is why the Gemara makes a point of saying דִּמְשַׁכָּא לְהוּ תְקוּפַת תַּמּוּז עַד חַגָּא, that Hashem extended the hot summer season until Succos. Hashem wanted to conduct this test under real conditions, for He did not wish the nations to complain that their test was unfair, that B'nei Yisrael living in Eretz Yisrael under normal circumstances would never be faced with the challenge with which they contended. Rain on Succos in Eretz Yisrael is not a *siman berachah*, and is in fact unseasonable. So is snow and extreme cold. However, it is plausible that, for example, in the year before a leap year, Succos occurs at the end of the summer, and is very, very hot. This shows the nations that although the Jews have the mitzvah of *succah* under the exact same conditions, they do not react to this hardship in the same way as the peoples of the world.

Arba Minim

We all know of the symbolism of the *arba minim*, that each one represents a part of the body. The *lulav* represents the spine, the *esrog* the heart, *hadassim* the eyes, and *aravos* the lips. What is unique about these organs, that from all of the parts of the body, specifically they are the ones represented by the *arba minim*?

Going through the *vidui* of Yom Kippur will show us that most of the *aveiros* which we mention are connected to these four body parts. The spine represents *aveiros* done out of haughtiness, or being stiff-necked. The heart represents those *aveiros* that sully the heart. The eyes represent *aveiros* done by the eyes, for example by looking at forbidden things, or being envious of other people's things which we see. Finally the lips represent the *aveiros* done with the mouth, such as speaking *lashon hara*, *leitzanus*, and eating things of questionable *kashrus*.

We know that the *haddasim* represent our eyes. Why, then, is the halachah that they be in rows of three? Shouldn't a row of two be enough, just like the two eyes?

Perhaps the third *hadas* leaf on each row reminds us of a different eye that is always with us, of the "עַיִן רוֹאָה — the Eye that always sees," mentioned in the mishnah in *Pirkei Avos* (2:1). Perhaps this is why the *halachos* of *hadassim* are so strict. It is not enough to watch our own eyes. We must also always remember that there is another Eye always watching our eyes, and everything that we do.

הֲבֵל הֲבָלִים אָמַר קֹהֶלֶת הֲבֵל הֲבָלִים הַכֹּל הָבֶל:

FUTILITY OF FUTILITIES, SAID KOHELES; FUTILITY
OF FUTILITIES, ALL IS FUTILE. (KOHELES 1:2)

The phrase "הַכֹּל הָבֶל — all is futile," is used six times throughout Koheles. It would seem that these six occurrences refer to the six days of the workweek, which are days of futility and pointlessness. In contrast, the seventh day — Shabbos — is what is really important. These six days serve the seventh, for the type of life that we live on Shabbos justifies running around the entire week to make a living.

Purim
פּוּרִים

בְּהַרְאֹתוֹ אֶת עֹשֶׁר כְּבוֹד מַלְכוּתוֹ וְאֶת יְקָר
תִּפְאֶרֶת גְּדוּלָּתוֹ יָמִים רַבִּים שְׁמוֹנִים וּמְאַת יוֹם:

WHEN HE SHOWED THE RICHES OF HIS GLORIOUS KINGDOM, AND THE SPLENDOR OF HIS EXCELLENT MAJESTY, MANY DAYS, ONE HUNDRED AND EIGHTY DAYS. (ESTHER 1:4)

Why does the Megillah say both that Achashveirosh's party was "יָמִים רַבִּים — many days," as well as "שְׁמוֹנִים וּמְאַת יוֹם — one hundred and eighty days"?

Saying that the party lasted "יָמִים רַבִּים — many days," implies that each day had its own importance, and uniqueness. And "שְׁמוֹנִים וּמְאַת יוֹם — one hundred and eighty days" tells us how long the party in fact lasted.

וּבְהַגִּיעַ תֹּר אֶסְתֵּר בַּת אֲבִיחַיִל דֹּד מָרְדֳּכַי אֲשֶׁר
לָקַח לוֹ לְבַת לָבוֹא אֶל הַמֶּלֶךְ לֹא בִקְשָׁה דָּבָר כִּי
אִם אֶת אֲשֶׁר יֹאמַר הֵגַי סְרִיס הַמֶּלֶךְ שֹׁמֵר הַנָּשִׁים
וַתְּהִי אֶסְתֵּר נֹשֵׂאת חֵן בְּעֵינֵי כָּל רֹאֶיהָ:

NOW WHEN THE TURN OF ESTHER, THE DAUGHTER OF AVICHAYIL, MORDECHAI'S UNCLE,

> WHO HAD TAKEN HER FOR A DAUGHTER,
> CAME TO GO IN TO THE KING, SHE REQUESTED
> NOTHING, EXCEPT WHAT HEGAI THE KING'S
> CHAMBERLAIN, THE GUARD OF THE WOMEN,
> WOULD SAY, AND ESTHER OBTAINED GRACE IN
> THE EYES OF ALL WHO BEHELD HER. (ESTHER 2:15)

The Megillah first mentions Esther in *pasuk* 7, yet does not tell us who her father was until *pasuk* 15, when she was taken in to the king. Why not?

Esther was sequestered for an entire year, in an environment filled with other women who only had one thing on their minds: preparing for their upcoming night with the king. Like Yosef in Mitzrayim, she was alone, with no one around her to see whether or not these negative influences would penetrate, and somewhat affect her, diminishing her *tzidkus*. The Megillah mentions her name when she was called in to Achashveirosh to tell us that she had not at all been changed by the year she had just experienced; she was still Avichayil's daughter, and Mordechai's niece, even as she was about to be sent in to Achashveirosh.

ACHASHVEIROSH

"Achashveirosh" is generally spelled אֲחַשְׁוֵרוֹשׁ, throughout the Megillah. However, we find five places where this name is written *chasser*, without the second letter ו: אֲחַשְׁוֵרֹשׁ. Why?

Let us examine these five occurrences. They are 2:21, which relates Bigsan and Seresh's plan to kill Achashveirosh; 3:12, telling about the messengers that Haman sent out with edicts stamped with the king's ring; 8:7, where Achashveirosh tells Mordechai and Esther that Esther was given Haman's house and Haman was killed; 8:10, discussing the second messengers bearing messages signed by the king, that the Jews may defend themselves; and finally, 10:1, that the king Achashveirosh levied taxes at the end of the Megillah.

It appears that the commonality that these five places share is that each of them relates some sort of deficiency in Achashveirosh, either in his knowledge or his capability. It is for this reason that his name is spelled "deficient" in these places.

With this in mind, let us review these five *pesukim* again. Naturally, Achashveirosh had no knowledge of Bigsan and Seresh's plot to kill him. On the contrary; at this point, his life was incredibly vulnerable. In the second *pasuk* (3:12), which discusses Haman's sending out edicts stamped with the king's ring, Achashveirosh was being used by Haman to achieve his — Haman's — own goal. In fact, the *Malbim* even explains that Haman dictated an edict which was signed using Achashveirosh's ring but without his knowledge.

The *pesukim* leading up to the third *pasuk* (8:7) describe how Esther had asked Achashveirosh to retract the genocidal letter that Haman had sent out. Achashveirosh responded by describing how he had given her Haman's house and killed him. Yet, continues *pasuk* 8, I am unable to directly nullify the letter, "כִּי כְתָב אֲשֶׁר נִכְתָּב בְּשֵׁם הַמֶּלֶךְ וְנַחְתּוֹם בְּטַבַּעַת הַמֶּלֶךְ אֵין לְהָשִׁיב — for a document that is written in the name of the king and sealed with the king's ring cannot be rescinded"; the law simply forbids me from doing so. And, in the fourth *pasuk* (8:10), Mordechai and Esther drafted their own edict and signed it with Achashveirosh's ring, without his knowing what went into the letter.

The fifth and final *pasuk* discusses levying taxes, at the end of the Megillah. The *Malbim* explains that Mordechai, who was now the viceroy, was in fact the one responsible for raising taxes; Achashveirosh's name was used only to give honor to the king. However, Mordechai was the one who was actually running the kingdom, in a manner similar to Yosef, who totally governed for Pharaoh. Again, although Achashveirosh was king, he was not the one actually in charge.

Understanding the *pesukim* in this light brings us to two other observations. Why, we may ask, is the second letter ו of אֲחַשְׁוֵרוֹשׁ, the letter that is specifically omitted from the king's name?

When spelled without its second letter ו, the final part of the word אֲחַשְׁוֵרוֹשׁ spells רָשׁ, which means "pauper." Based on how we explained above, this makes sense, for these *pesukim* are all describing instances where Achashveirosh was not in full control.

Additionally, it is noteworthy that in the last of the five *pesukim* we discussed, the king's name is written אֲחַשְׁרֵשׁ, missing both letters ו. According to the *Malbim* whom we mentioned above, this makes sense, for by this time in the Megillah, Achashveirosh had totally proven himself to be useless, and Mordechai was in fact running the kingdom. The Torah thus also took away another letter ו, to emphasize this point.

Three's Company

We find the number three to be a recurring number in the Megillah. In (3:8), Haman gave three reasons to Achashveirosh to justify why the Jews should be killed. They are, that this nation is "מְפֻזָּר וּמְפֹרָד בֵּין הָעַמִּים בְּכֹל מְדִינוֹת מַלְכוּתֶךָ — scattered and separate among the peoples throughout all the provinces of your kingdom," "וְדָתֵיהֶם שֹׁנוֹת מִכָּל עָם — and their laws differ from those of every people," and finally, "וְאֶת דָּתֵי הַמֶּלֶךְ אֵינָם עֹשִׂים — and they do not keep the king's laws." Perhaps this is why Haman (in 3:13) also chose the threefold formula of "לְהַשְׁמִיד לַהֲרֹג וּלְאַבֵּד — annihilate, kill, and destroy," to describe what he wanted to do to the Jews.

In an effort to combat these three reasons to kill us mentioned by Haman, we find that Mordechai did three things (4:1). These are: "וַיִּקְרַע מָרְדֳּכַי אֶת בְּגָדָיו — Mordechai tore his clothes," "וַיִּלְבַּשׁ שַׂק וָאֵפֶר — he donned sackcloth and ashes," and finally, "וַיֵּצֵא בְּתוֹךְ הָעִיר וַיִּזְעַק זְעָקָה גְדֹלָה וּמָרָה — he went out into the midst of the city and cried a loud and bitter cry."

In 4:3, the Jews also tried to combat this *gezeirah* in three ways, by "צוֹם וּבְכִי וּמִסְפֵּד — fasting and weeping and lamenting."

Esther had a threefold approach as well (4:16): "לֵךְ כְּנוֹס אֶת כָּל הַיְּהוּדִים הַנִּמְצְאִים בְּשׁוּשָׁן וְצוּמוּ עָלַי וְאַל תֹּאכְלוּ וְאַל תִּשְׁתּוּ שְׁלֹשֶׁת יָמִים לַיְלָה וָיוֹם — go, assemble all the Jews who are present in Shushan and fast on my behalf, and neither eat nor drink for three days, day and night"; "גַּם אֲנִי וְנַעֲרֹתַי אָצוּם כֵּן — also I and my maidens will likewise fast"; and "וּבְכֵן אָבוֹא אֶל הַמֶּלֶךְ אֲשֶׁר לֹא כַדָּת — then I will go to the king contrary to the law."

Finally, Haman also suggested three things that should be done to honor the person whom the king wishes to honor (6:8). These are: "יָבִיאוּ לְבוּשׁ מַלְכוּת אֲשֶׁר לָבַשׁ בּוֹ הַמֶּלֶךְ — let them bring the royal garment that the king wore"; "וְסוּס אֲשֶׁר רָכַב עָלָיו הַמֶּלֶךְ — and the horse that the king rode upon"; and "אֲשֶׁר נִתַּן כֶּתֶר מַלְכוּת בְּרֹאשׁוֹ — and the royal crown should be placed on his head." Although the king refused to give someone else his crown, he too told Haman to do three things to Mordechai to show him honor (*pasuk* 9). They were wearing the king's royal garment, riding the king's horses, and "וְקָרְאוּ לְפָנָיו כָּכָה יֵעָשֶׂה לָאִישׁ אֲשֶׁר הַמֶּלֶךְ חָפֵץ בִּיקָרוֹ — and announce before him, 'So shall be done to the man whom the king wishes to honor!'"

> לֵךְ כְּנוֹס אֶת כָּל הַיְּהוּדִים הַנִּמְצְאִים בְּשׁוּשָׁן וְצוּמוּ עָלַי וְאַל תֹּאכְלוּ וְאַל תִּשְׁתּוּ שְׁלֹשֶׁת יָמִים לַיְלָה וָיוֹם גַּם אֲנִי וְנַעֲרֹתַי אָצוּם כֵּן וּבְכֵן אָבוֹא אֶל הַמֶּלֶךְ אֲשֶׁר לֹא כַדָּת וְכַאֲשֶׁר אָבַדְתִּי אָבָדְתִּי:
>
> GO, ASSEMBLE ALL THE JEWS WHO ARE PRESENT IN SHUSHAN AND FAST ON MY BEHALF, AND NEITHER EAT NOR DRINK FOR THREE DAYS, DAY AND NIGHT; ALSO I AND MY MAIDENS WILL FAST IN A LIKE MANNER; THEN I WILL GO TO THE KING CONTRARY TO THE LAW, AND IF I PERISH, I PERISH. (ESTHER 4:16)

Why does Esther tell Mordechai to inform the Jews of Shushan to "fast on her behalf," *and* "neither eat nor drink for three days, day and night"? Isn't this redundant?

Haman drew his lottery on the thirteenth day of Nissan, two days before Pesach. Esther's three day fast thus included the first day of Yom Tov, part of which is Seder night. Esther was asking Mordechai to tell this to all the Jews, that they should both fast on her behalf from not eating regular food for three days, as well as a special "אַל תֹּאכְלוּ — do not eat" matzah, and "וְאַל תִּשְׁתּוּ — and do not drink" wine at the Seder, although these during regular years are an integral part of the *mitzvos hayom*.

> וְהַמֶּלֶךְ קָם בַּחֲמָתוֹ מִמִּשְׁתֵּה הַיַּיִן אֶל גִּנַּת הַבִּיתָן וְהָמָן עָמַד לְבַקֵּשׁ עַל נַפְשׁוֹ מֵאֶסְתֵּר הַמַּלְכָּה כִּי רָאָה כִּי כָלְתָה אֵלָיו הָרָעָה מֵאֵת הַמֶּלֶךְ: וְהַמֶּלֶךְ שָׁב מִגִּנַּת הַבִּיתָן אֶל בֵּית מִשְׁתֵּה הַיַּיִן וְהָמָן נֹפֵל עַל הַמִּטָּה אֲשֶׁר אֶסְתֵּר עָלֶיהָ וַיֹּאמֶר הַמֶּלֶךְ הֲגַם לִכְבּוֹשׁ אֶת הַמַּלְכָּה עִמִּי בַּבָּיִת הַדָּבָר יָצָא מִפִּי הַמֶּלֶךְ וּפְנֵי הָמָן חָפוּ:

> THEN THE KING RETURNED FROM THE ORCHARD GARDEN TO THE HOUSE OF THE WINE FEAST, AND HAMAN WAS FALLING ON THE COUCH UPON WHICH ESTHER WAS, AND THE KING SAID, "WILL YOU EVEN FORCE THE QUEEN WITH ME IN THE HOUSE?" THE WORD CAME OUT OF THE KING'S MOUTH, AND THEY COVERED HAMAN'S FACE. THEN SAID CHARVONAH, ONE OF THE CHAMBERLAINS BEFORE THE KING, "ALSO, BEHOLD THE GALLOWS THAT HAMAN MADE FOR MORDECHAI, WHO SPOKE WELL FOR THE KING, STANDING IN HAMAN'S HOUSE, FIFTY CUBITS HIGH!" AND THE KING SAID, "HANG HIM ON IT!"
> (ESTHER 7:7–8)

Angered by what he had heard from Esther that Haman is the one who wanted to kill her nation, Achashveirosh got up from the feast, and went outside to cool off. He then returns, lucid and ready to hear the case. It appears as if Achashveirosh had learned his lesson from making hasty decisions while he is drunk, like he had done at the beginning of the Megillah, when he decided Vashti's fate while drunk.

Pesach
פֶּסַח

הָשַׁתָּא הָכָא, לְשָׁנָה הַבָּאָה בְּאַרְעָא דְיִשְׂרָאֵל.
Now we are here, next year let us be in Eretz Yisrael.

We generally say לְשָׁנָה הַבָּאָה בִּירוּשָׁלַיִם at the end of special occasions, including at the end of the Haggadah on Pesach night. Why, then, do we also say this now at the beginning of the Seder?

The *Sar Shalom* of Belz explains that when Mashiach comes, the borders of Eretz Yisrael will extend to the entire world. We may thus understand that "הָשַׁתָּא הָכָא, לְשָׁנָה הַבָּאָה בְּאַרְעָא דְיִשְׂרָאֵל — now we are here, next year let us be in Eretz Yisrael," does not only mean that we want to travel to Yerushalayim by next Pesach. It can also mean that right now we are here in *galus*. Next year, this same ground that we are standing on, in what is now *Chutz La'Aretz*, should be Eretz Yisrael.

עֲבָדִים הָיִינוּ לְפַרְעֹה בְּמִצְרַיִם, וַיּוֹצִיאֵנוּ ה' אֱלֹקֵינוּ מִשָּׁם בְּיָד חֲזָקָה וּבִזְרוֹעַ נְטוּיָה. וְאִלּוּ לֹא הוֹצִיא הַקָּדוֹשׁ בָּרוּךְ הוּא אֶת אֲבוֹתֵינוּ מִמִּצְרַיִם, הֲרֵי אָנוּ וּבָנֵינוּ וּבְנֵי בָנֵינוּ מְשֻׁעְבָּדִים הָיִינוּ לְפַרְעֹה בְּמִצְרָיִם. וַאֲפִילוּ כֻּלָּנוּ חֲכָמִים, כֻּלָּנוּ נְבוֹנִים, כֻּלָּנוּ זְקֵנִים, כֻּלָּנוּ יוֹדְעִים אֶת הַתּוֹרָה, מִצְוָה עָלֵינוּ לְסַפֵּר בִּיצִיאַת מִצְרָיִם. וְכָל הַמַּרְבֶּה לְסַפֵּר בִּיצִיאַת מִצְרַיִם הֲרֵי זֶה מְשֻׁבָּח.

WE WERE SLAVES TO PHARAOH IN MITZRAYIM, AND HASHEM, OUR GOD, TOOK US OUT FROM THERE WITH A STRONG HAND AND WITH AN OUTSTRETCHED ARM. IF THE HOLY ONE, BLESSED BE HE, HAD NOT TAKEN OUR FOREFATHERS OUT OF MITZRAYIM, THEN WE, OUR CHILDREN, AND OUR CHILDREN'S CHILDREN, WOULD HAVE REMAINED ENSLAVED TO PHARAOH IN MITZRAYIM. EVEN IF ALL OF US WERE WISE, ALL OF US UNDERSTANDING, ALL OF US KNOWING THE TORAH, WE WOULD STILL BE OBLIGATED TO DISCUSS THE EXODUS FROM MITZRAYIM; AND EVERYONE WHO DISCUSSES THE EXODUS FROM MITZRAYIM AT LENGTH IS PRAISEWORTHY.

Why does this paragraph begin with "עֲבָדִים הָיִינוּ לְפַרְעֹה בְּמִצְרַיִם — *we were slaves to Pharaoh in Mitzrayim*," and continue "וְאִלּוּ לֹא הוֹצִיא הַקָּדוֹשׁ בָּרוּךְ הוּא אֶת אֲבוֹתֵינוּ מִמִּצְרַיִם — *if the Holy One, blessed be He, had not taken* our forefathers *out of Mitzrayim*," instead of "*... had not taken* us *out of Mitzrayim*"?

We of course were not actually in Mitzrayim, which is an event that the B'nei Yisrael experienced over thirty-three hundred years ago. Yet, at the same time, it is important to frame ourselves in the mindset that the Exodus is as important to us today as it was for the people who actually left; for it is only because of this event that we are a Jewish people today. We therefore begin the Seder by including ourselves within the Pesach story, as if to say that our lives, as well, are dependent on the fact that the Jews were once slaves, and were freed. Once this recognition and appreciation is set into place, we then explain how this is so in the practical sense, that "וְאִלּוּ לֹא הוֹצִיא הַקָּדוֹשׁ בָּרוּךְ הוּא אֶת אֲבוֹתֵינוּ מִמִּצְרַיִם, הֲרֵי אָנוּ וּבָנֵינוּ וּבְנֵי בָנֵינוּ מְשֻׁעְבָּדִים הָיִינוּ לְפַרְעֹה בְּמִצְרָיִם — If the Holy One, blessed be He, had not taken our forefathers out of Mitzrayim, then we, our children, and our children's children, would have remained enslaved to Pharaoh in Mitzrayim."

> וָאֶקַּח אֶת אֲבִיכֶם אֶת אַבְרָהָם מֵעֵבֶר הַנָּהָר וָאוֹלֵךְ אוֹתוֹ בְּכָל אֶרֶץ כְּנָעַן, וָאַרְבֶּה אֶת זַרְעוֹ וָאֶתֶּן לוֹ אֶת יִצְחָק, וָאֶתֵּן לְיִצְחָק אֶת יַעֲקֹב וְאֶת עֵשָׂו. וָאֶתֵּן לְעֵשָׂו אֶת הַר שֵׂעִיר לָרֶשֶׁת אֹתוֹ, וְיַעֲקֹב וּבָנָיו יָרְדוּ מִצְרָיִם.

> AND I TOOK YOUR FATHER AVRAHAM FROM BEYOND THE RIVER, AND I LED HIM THROUGHOUT THE WHOLE LAND OF CANAAN. I INCREASED HIS OFFSPRING AND GAVE HIM YITZCHAK, AND TO YITZCHAK I GAVE YAACOV AND ESAV. TO ESAV I GAVE MOUNT SEIR TO POSSESS IT, AND YAACOV AND HIS SONS WENT DOWN TO MITZRAYIM.

The Baal Haggadah says "to Yitzchak I gave Yaacov and Esav," and then describes Esav's inheritance before discussing Yaacov. Also, we are told of Esav's inheritance, yet only told of the beginning of Yaacov's *galus*. Why?

Yaacov and Esav both received *berachos* from their father Yitzchak. Esav's *berachah* was simple: a good place in *Olam Hazeh*. Yaacov's was much more complicated, and needed a few hundred years in Mitzrayim to become the nation that would be ready to accept the Torah and become Hashem's own. So first we speak about Esav, and get the quick and easy story, which isn't even our focus tonight, out of the way. Then we turn to Yaacov. And indeed, Yaacov's story only begins when he goes down to Mitzrayim.

וְלָבָן בִּקֵּשׁ לַעֲקוֹר אֶת הַכֹּל.

AND LAVAN WANTED TO UPROOT EVERYTHING.

Where do we find that Lavan wanted to uproot the entire Jewish people?

As we explained in *Parashas Balak* (page 252), *Chazal* (Gemara *Sanhedrin* 105a, and *Targum Yonason*) tell us that Lavan and Bilaam were in fact the same person. This being so, Bilaam was hired by King Balak to curse — and thereby uproot — Klal Yisrael.

וַיָּגָר שָׁם — מְלַמֵּד שֶׁלֹּא יָרַד יַעֲקֹב אָבִינוּ לְהִשְׁתַּקֵּעַ בְּמִצְרַיִם אֶלָּא לָגוּר שָׁם, שֶׁנֶּאֱמַר: וַיֹּאמְרוּ אֶל פַּרְעֹה, לָגוּר בָּאָרֶץ בָּאנוּ, כִּי אֵין מִרְעֶה לַצֹּאן אֲשֶׁר לַעֲבָדֶיךָ, כִּי כָבֵד הָרָעָב בְּאֶרֶץ כְּנָעַן. וְעַתָּה יֵשְׁבוּ נָא עֲבָדֶיךָ בְּאֶרֶץ גֹּשֶׁן.

"AND HE SOJOURNED THERE"; THIS TEACHES THAT OUR FATHER YAACOV DID NOT GO DOWN TO MITZRAYIM TO SETTLE THERE PERMANENTLY, BUT ONLY TO LIVE THERE TEMPORARILY. THUS IT IS SAID, "THEY SAID TO PHARAOH, WE HAVE COME TO SOJOURN IN THE LAND, FOR THERE IS NO PASTURE FOR YOUR SERVANTS' FLOCKS BECAUSE THE HUNGER IS SEVERE IN THE LAND OF CANAAN; AND NOW, PLEASE, LET YOUR SERVANTS DWELL IN THE LAND OF GOSHEN."

The *B'nei Yaacov* told Pharaoh that the reason they want to "dwell" in Mitzrayim was "כִּי אֵין מִרְעֶה לַצֹּאן אֲשֶׁר לַעֲבָדֶיךָ — for there is no pasture for your servants' flocks." What about the fact that there wasn't any food for them either? Why didn't they mention to Pharaoh that the people also need food?

I once saw in a *sefer* that since all the food had run out in Canaan, the people resorted to eating grass, which would normally only be eaten by animals. However, in Mitzrayim, where there was food, the grass was still available exclusively for animals to eat. This is why the *B'nei Yaacov* told this reason to Pharaoh.

Another reason why the *Shevatim* focused on their flocks was because they wanted to convey to Pharaoh their sole reason for relocating to Mitzrayim was so that they could feed their animals. Once they can return to being self-sufficient, they would be on their way. This reinforces what the *Haggadah* says, "שֶׁלֹּא יָרַד יַעֲקֹב אָבִינוּ לְהִשְׁתַּקֵּעַ בְּמִצְרַיִם — our father Yaacov did not go down to Mitzrayim to settle there permanently." Yaacov never had any intention of remaining in Mitzrayim long term. Thus, the *Shevatim* told Pharaoh their main reason for coming.

A third approach into why the brothers stressed their flocks is because they were following Yosef's instruction. We know that Yosef coached his brothers before taking them to Pharaoh. Yosef knew that if he told them to say that they needed fertile land for their animals, Pharaoh would send them straight to Goshen, where they could live among themselves undisturbed. So they did not mention their own food shortage, because Yosef knew that this would not make the effect on Pharaoh that he wished.

בְּיָד חֲזָקָה — זוֹ הַדֶּבֶר, כְּמָה שֶׁנֶּאֱמַר: הִנֵּה יַד ה' הוֹיָה בְּמִקְנְךָ אֲשֶׁר בַּשָּׂדֶה, בַּסּוּסִים, בַּחֲמֹרִים, בַּגְּמַלִּים, בַּבָּקָר וּבַצֹּאן, דֶּבֶר כָּבֵד מְאֹד.

"WITH A STRONG HAND," THIS REFERS TO THE DEVER (PESTILENCE) AS THE TORAH SAYS (SHEMOS 9:3): "BEHOLD, HASHEM'S HAND WILL BE

UPON YOUR LIVESTOCK IN THE FIELD, UPON THE
HORSES, THE DONKEYS, THE CAMELS, THE HERDS
AND THE FLOCKS, A VERY SEVERE PESTILENCE."

How does "בְּיָד חֲזָקָה — with a strong hand," refer to the *Makah* of *Dever*, where the animals died? Shouldn't a *makah* that didn't affect the people's bodies be treated as a somewhat weaker *makah*, not a strong one?

If we count the *makos* using our fingers, we will notice that *Dever* is the fifth *makah*. *Dever* is the *makah* that completes the first set of *Makos* into a hand. Perhaps this is why it is termed "יָד חֲזָקָה — a strong hand."

Another possibility is that Hashem's killing the Mitzrim's horses, camels, and donkeys severely crippled their ability to run after B'nei Yisrael. This is why, despite the fact *Dever* only affected the animals, it was truly a strong blow to the Mitzrim, and can be considered coming from a יָד חֲזָקָה, a strong and crippling hand.

Lastly, we know the Mitzrim worshipped sheep as their god. By inflicting a *makah* against a group that included the sheep, Hashem shows that His strong Hand will not be held back by anyone who gets in His way, or who prevents the Jews from leaving Mitzrayim. This also explains, even though *Dever* did not directly affect the Mitzrim, how fierce Hashem's Hand, His יָד הַחֲזָקָה, can be.

> בְּמִצְרַיִם מָה הוּא אוֹמֵר? וַיֹּאמְרוּ הַחַרְטֻמִּים אֶל
> פַּרְעֹה: אֶצְבַּע אֱלֹקִים הוּא.
> וְעַל הַיָּם מָה הוּא אוֹמֵר? וַיַּרְא יִשְׂרָאֵל אֶת הַיָּד
> הַגְּדֹלָה אֲשֶׁר עָשָׂה ה' בְּמִצְרָיִם.

WHAT WAS SAID IN MITZRAYIM? "THE EGYPTIAN
MAGICIANS SAID TO PHARAOH, 'THIS WAS THE
FINGER OF HASHEM.'"
AND WHAT WAS SAID AT THE SEA? "YISRAEL SAW
THE GREAT HAND THAT HASHEM DID AGAINST
MITZRAYIM."

During the *Makah* of *Kinim*, the Egyptian magicians admitted "אֶצְבַּע אֱלֹקִים הִוא — this was the Finger of Hashem." And, after *Krias Yam Suf*, the B'nei Yisrael appreciated "Hashem's Hand"; "וַיַּרְא יִשְׂרָאֵל אֶת הַיָּד הַגְּדֹלָה אֲשֶׁר עָשָׂה ה' בְּמִצְרַיִם — Yisrael saw the great hand that Hashem did against Mitzrayim." What is the difference in perception between a finger and a hand?

The hand turns the five individual fingers into a group. When the *Chartumim* reacted to *Makas Kinim* by admitting that it was Hashem's work, they looked at it only as a "finger." When faced with the fact that they couldn't imitate this *makah*, they agreed that *this* must have been Hashem's doing. But, that doesn't mean anything about the other *mofsim* and *makos*, like Aharon's staff swallowing the other staffs, and the *makos* of *Dam* and *Tzefardeya*, which we have seen until now!

A Jew, on the other hand, understands that everything is from Hashem. We are able to piece together the small events — the small "miracles" that happen to us now and then during our lives — and use them to appreciate the bigger picture, that also includes the parts that that we do not see. A non-Jew will analyze what is happening, and a Jew will appreciate them. When the B'nei Yisrael experienced the *makos* at the Yam Suf, they understood that they were part of a wider *Yad Hashem*.

Shavuos
שָׁבוּעוֹת

Why do we read *Megillas Rus* on Shavuos?

One of the reasons given in answer of this question is that Rus was of course a convert, who accepted the Torah out of choice. This makes for a very sensible reading on Shavuos, the day of the Jewish people's *kabbalas haTorah*.

Those of us who are born *frum* Jews can take a very important lesson from a convert. A convert accepted the Torah on the day of his or her conversion. This day was not a special date on the calendar. It was an ordinary day, which could have happened during any part of the month, of the week, and even any time of day. And this regular day became *kabbalas haTorah*! The same is true with us, when we celebrate Shavuos. Shavuos is indeed a red letter date on the calendar. But it's like an anniversary, which is something that reminds us once a year of a special and essential part of our life, that we really could and should be celebrating every day. Seeing a convert like Rus reminds us of this truth, that we can turn any and every day into a potential *kabbalas haTorah*.

וַיְהִי בִּימֵי שְׁפֹט הַשֹּׁפְטִים וַיְהִי רָעָב בָּאָרֶץ וַיֵּלֶךְ אִישׁ מִבֵּית לֶחֶם יְהוּדָה לָגוּר בִּשְׂדֵי מוֹאָב הוּא וְאִשְׁתּוֹ וּשְׁנֵי בָנָיו: וְשֵׁם הָאִישׁ אֱלִימֶלֶךְ וְשֵׁם אִשְׁתּוֹ נָעֳמִי וְשֵׁם שְׁנֵי בָנָיו מַחְלוֹן וְכִלְיוֹן אֶפְרָתִים מִבֵּית לֶחֶם יְהוּדָה וַיָּבֹאוּ שְׂדֵי מוֹאָב וַיִּהְיוּ שָׁם:

NOW IT CAME TO PASS IN THE DAYS WHEN THE JUDGES JUDGED, THAT THERE WAS A FAMINE IN THE LAND, AND A MAN WENT FROM BEIS LECHEM YEHUDAH TO SOJOURN IN THE FIELDS OF MOAV, HE AND HIS WIFE AND HIS TWO SONS. AND THE MAN'S NAME WAS ELIMELECH, AND HIS WIFE'S NAME WAS NAOMI, AND HIS TWO SONS' NAMES WERE MACHLON AND CHILYON, IMPORTANT PEOPLE, FROM BEIS LECHEM YEHUDAH, AND THEY CAME TO THE FIELDS OF MOAV AND REMAINED THERE. (RUS 1:1–2)

Pasuk 1 tells us that a family went from Beis Lechem Yehudah to Moav, but does not mention any of the people's names. Why aren't the names mentioned until *pasuk* 2? Also, why does *pasuk* 2 repeat the fact that Elimelech and his family were from Beis Lechem Yehudah, which was already said in *pasuk* 1?

The *pesukim* are contrasting who and what Elimelech was before he left home, and who he was in Moav. In his hometown of Beis Lechem Yehudah he was an "אִישׁ," an important person. But a person leaves much of his reputation behind when he leaves a place where he is well known. He must start anew, and rebuild. In Moav, the *pasuk* is telling us, he was no longer an "אִישׁ." He was now just a regular person, Elimelech, with an ordinary family of Naomi, Machlon and Chilyon.

וַיָּמָת אֱלִימֶלֶךְ אִישׁ נָעֳמִי וַתִּשָּׁאֵר הִיא וּשְׁנֵי בָנֶיהָ:

NOW ELIMELECH, NAOMI'S HUSBAND, DIED, AND SHE WAS LEFT, WITH HER TWO SONS. (RUS 1:3)

Everyone with a family who passes away leaves their wife and children behind. What special point is the Megillah telling us that after Elimelech died, Naomi was left, with her two sons?

A person may die and leave a widow and orphans. But, when these people live around other Jews, they will never be "alone." Naomi and her children, on the other hand, went to Moav to follow their husband and father. They had nothing in Moav other than Elimelech. Then when Elimelech died, his family was truly left alone.

וַיָּמֻתוּ גַם שְׁנֵיהֶם מַחְלוֹן וְכִלְיוֹן וַתִּשָּׁאֵר הָאִשָּׁה מִשְּׁנֵי יְלָדֶיהָ וּמֵאִישָׁהּ:

AND BOTH MACHLON AND CHILYON ALSO DIED, AND THE WOMAN WAS LEFT BEREFT OF HER TWO CHILDREN AND OF HER HUSBAND. (RUS 1:5)

The Megillah tells us that "וַיָּמֻתוּ גַם שְׁנֵיהֶם — both Machlon and Chilyon *also* (גַם) died." Why does the *pasuk* use the ostensibly extra word "גַם — also"?

We know that children are not punished for the parents' sins unless they too continue doing that *aveirah*. Now, we know that Elimelech was punished for leaving Eretz Yisrael in time of famine, instead of remaining with the Jewish community there. After Elimelech's death, his children Machlon and Chilyon were now able to return to Eretz Yisrael. Since they did not, they *too* were guilty of their father's *aveirah*, and as a result were punished by death, like their father.

> וַתֵּצֵא מִן הַמָּקוֹם אֲשֶׁר הָיְתָה שָׁמָּה וּשְׁתֵּי כַלֹּתֶיהָ
> עִמָּהּ וַתֵּלַכְנָה בַדֶּרֶךְ לָשׁוּב אֶל אֶרֶץ יְהוּדָה:
>
> THEN SHE LEFT THE PLACE WHERE SHE HAD BEEN,
> AND HER TWO DAUGHTERS-IN-LAW WITH HER,
> AND THEY WENT ON THE ROAD TO RETURN TO
> THE LAND OF YEHUDAH. (RUS 1:7)

Why does the *pasuk* say the apparently repetitive "וַתֵּלַכְנָה בַדֶּרֶךְ — they went on the road," after already having said "וַתֵּצֵא מִן הַמָּקוֹם אֲשֶׁר הָיְתָה שָׁמָּה — then she left the place where she had been"? Going — journeying — on the road is the way that she left Moav!

The Megillah is telling us that both of these steps were meaningful unto themselves; Naomi had a reason to leave Moav, as well as a reason to return home to the land of Yehudah.[43] Naomi had no reason to remain in Moav any longer. Her husband had lost his money and died there, and her two children died there, as well. Certainly, she had no fond memories binding her to the place. So she decided to leave; "וַתֵּצֵא מִן הַמָּקוֹם אֲשֶׁר הָיְתָה שָׁמָּה — then she left the place where she had been." At the same time, she heard that the famine in Eretz Yisrael was over, and had every reason to return to the place where she had once lived. The Megillah thus also tells us "וַתֵּלַכְנָה בַדֶּרֶךְ — they went on the road," to return home.

> וַיִּקַּח בֹּעַז אֶת רוּת וַתְּהִי לוֹ לְאִשָּׁה וַיָּבֹא אֵלֶיהָ וַיִּתֵּן
> ה' לָהּ הֵרָיוֹן וַתֵּלֶד בֵּן:
>
> AND BOAZ TOOK RUS, AND SHE BECAME HIS
> WIFE, AND HE CAME TO HER, AND HASHEM
> ALLOWED HER TO CONCEIVE, AND SHE BORE A
> SON. (RUS 4:13)

---

43 This approach is patterned on the Steipler's explanation of Yaacov Avinu's "וַיֵּצֵא — he left" and "וַיֵּלֶךְ — he went," in the *Birchas Peretz* to *Parashas Vayeitzei*. See page 74.

Why does the Megillah use the unusual terminology of "וַיִּתֵּן ה' לָהּ הֵרָיוֹן — Hashem allowed her to conceive," instead of the expression of "וַתַּהַר — she conceived" that is usually used by the Torah?

Rus had been married to Machlon for ten years, and never had children during that time. Her childlessness is what prompted Boaz to marry her in an act of *yibum*. If Rus would have had children before this time, she would have never married Boaz, and never began the Davidic line that we read at the end of the Megillah.

Hashem had thus taken away Rus's ability to conceive throughout the entire time she was married to Machlon. And now, when she married Boaz and was finally in the position to bear a child that would fulfill her task of being David HaMelech's great-grandmother, Hashem finally allowed her to bear a child: "וַיִּתֵּן ה' לָהּ הֵרָיוֹן — Hashem allowed her to conceive."

Tisha B'av
תִּשְׁעָה בְּאָב

We know that the first night of Pesach, the Seder night, always occurs on the same night of the week as Tisha B'av. These two special times are also unique in other ways, which we do not find in regard to other *Moadim* or times of the Jewish Year.

The Ramban (in his *Sefer Toras Ha'Adam*) tells us that "כָּל הַמִּתְאַבֵּל עַל יְרוּשָׁלַיִם הֲרֵי זֶה מְשֻׁבָּח — anyone who mourns over Yerushalayim is praised." This of course reminds us of "וְכָל הַמַּרְבֶּה לְסַפֵּר בִּיצִיאַת מִצְרַיִם הֲרֵי זֶה מְשֻׁבָּח — anyone who extensively discusses *Yetzias Mitzrayim* is praised."

Another important factor that Pesach and Tisha B'av share is that each one has a buildup beforehand. The *aveilus* of Tisha B'av is preceded by steps: the Three Weeks, the Nine Days, *Shevu'a Shechal Bo*, until we are finally hit by the sheer *aveilus* of Tisha B'av itself. These steps serve to prepare us, and bring us into a mood that we actually feel the *Churban*.

Pesach, too, involves much preparation. We begin learning its *halachos* thirty days before. The women start cleaning. We stop saying *tachanun* from *Rosh Chodesh Nissan*; this is the month of the *Geulah*! *Erev Pesach* is a Yom Tov. Then, when the night finally arrives, the *Seder* includes many steps. Like Tisha B'av, all of this is to bring us to the proper mindset of actually making ourselves feel like we left Mitzrayim, as best as we possibly can.